LOVE AND HATE

LOVE AND HATE
The Natural History of
Behavior Patterns

IRENÄUS EIBL-EIBESFELDT

Translated by Geoffrey Strachan

ALDINE DE GRUYTER
New York

Originally published as *Liebe und Haß. Zur Naturgeschichte elementarer Verhaltensweisen*, © R. Piper & Co. Verlag, Munich, 1970

ALDINE DE GRUYTER
A division of Walter de Gruyter, Inc.
200 Saw Mill River Road
Hawthorne, New York 10532

This publication is printed on acid free paper ⊚

Library of Congress Cataloging-in-Publication Data
Eibl-Eibesfeldt, Irenäus.
   [Liebe und Hass. English]
   Love and hate : the natural history of behavior patterns / Irenäus Eibl-Eibesfeldt ; translated by Geoffrey Strachan. — 1st Aldine pbk. ed.
      p.   cm. — (Foundations of human behavior)
   Originally published: London : Methuen, 1971.
   Includes bibliographical references and indexes.
   ISBN 0-202-02038-X (alk. paper)
   1. Aggressiveness (Psychology) 2. Social interaction.
3. Comparative psychology. I. Title. II. Series.
BF575.A3E3313   1996
155.2—dc20
                                            95-37462
                                             CIP

Manufactured in the United States of America

10 9 8 7 6 5 4 3 2 1

TO MY CHILDREN, ROSWITHA AND BERNOLF

Contents

Preface to the
Aldine Paperback Edition

There are turning points in evolution. Structures and behavioral patterns that evolved in the service of discrete functions sometimes allow for unforeseen new developments as a side effect. In retrospect, they have proven to be preadaptations, by serving as raw material for natural selection to work upon.

The origin of maternal nurturing was one such turning point in the evolution of vertebrate behavior—one of those celestial moments that Stefan Zweig would call a *Sternstunde*. My book, *Love and Hate*, now restored to the English-reading public, discusses this event. When it was first published in 1970, it was intended to complement Konrad Lorenz's book, *On Aggression*, by pointing out our motivations to provide nurturing, and thus to counteract and correct the widespread but one-sided opinion that biologists always present nature as red in tooth and claw, and by presenting intraspecific aggression as the prime mover of evolution. This simplistic image, regrettably, is nonetheless still with us, all the more regrettably because it hampers discussion across scholarly disciplines. Thus I am even happier that the new edition will be available to a broader public with an interest in human affairs.

In this book, I discuss the phylogenetic origin of our behavior and motivations, which provide the basis for our cultural evolution and thus for our humanitarian hopes. My goal is that the book might contribute to overcoming the barriers that still exist between representatives of the natural sciences and those of the humanities and the social sciences, who continue to perceive biologists who remind us of our biological heritage as presenting a fatalistic view of man-as-unchangeable beast.*

*Here and elsewhere in this context, "man" refers to the human species. A more exact rendering of *Mensch*, less awkward here than paraphrase, it should be construed (like the German word) as gender free and inclusive—ed.

Love and Hate came out in German in 1970. The British edition followed in 1971; the American, in 1972. Thus far the book has been translated into thirteen languages, and with the fall of the Iron Curtain, further translations are under way. The German edition continues to sell consistently, and passed the 100,000-copy mark a couple of years ago. The book traces the origin of prosocial, altruistic behavior, with the evolution of maternal (or parental) nurture as its starting point. With nurturing came the motivation to take care of another individual, as well as the rich repertory of caretaking patterns such as feeding, grooming, and protection. In the young, the motivation to seek protection and care as well as the signals to trigger such responses evolved in turn. These characteristics proved to be preadaptations useful for the evolution of adult bonding.

Comparative analyses reveal that bonding rituals such as courtship, patterns of behavior that reinforce existing bonds between group members, and many behavioral patterns showing appeasement can be derived from parental nurturing behavior and from infantile appeals.

With the evolution of individualized brood care, love, defined as an individualized bond, also originated in the context of parental nurturing, wherein the upbringing of the young takes a lot of investment in time and effort. It is important that the adults invest in their own (rather than others') offspring, and for the young it is important not to lose the parents by mistakenly seeking contact with other adults. The vulnerable youngsters would risk being attacked and even killed. Thus individual bonding must be characterized by a certain exclusivity.

With individualized bonding and exclusivity, the mother-child bond emerged as the first manifestation of "us against them." Many mammals have the capacity to establish individualized bonds to conspecifics, and thereby form small groups in which each group member knows the others. They form a sort of extended family, held together by the familial disposition evolved in the parent-child context. Also, in humans, this familial disposition is at the roots of in-group versus out-group behavior. The familial disposition allows humans today to live in groups numbering millions, bonded by symbols and ideology. If we look at the basic mechanisms employed to bond members who are not close kin, we find that they tap into the existing phylogenetic adaptations of familial origin mentioned above. At the level of the kin-based society, one common means of bonding is through wider extension of kinship principles, terminology, and accompanying behavior beyond the circle of close kin to more distant kin, and in some cases to non-kin.

This is done by the creation of segmentary lineage systems and other systems of descent: Groups trace themselves to a common ancestor and are held together by both kinship and reciprocity.

In societies based on segmentary kinship, ideology thus calls on the metaphor of kinship to create fictive descent from mutual ancestors or creators, thus bonding all as quasi-blood relatives. Indeed, terms to address persons who are not blood relatives are often derived from terms that characterize familial relations. And regardless of group size, we tend to demarcate ourselves according to the familial pattern of "ourselves and others." We greet the resulting cultural plurality as an enrichment, and value it also as a means to secure and to elaborate human existence in the stream of life. At the same time, we deplore the competiveness and fear that lead to intergroup aggression and warfare. Are we thus trapped in a positive feedback cycle promoting aggression and war?

I view our nurturing dispositions as the all-important antagonists of our violent ones. Since the mid-1960s, I have been engaged in the cross-cultural documentation of human social behavior, and in watching people through the camera, I have observed and documented predominantly friendly interactions—even in cultures whose members engage in frequent acts of violence and war. But humans are first and foremost familial, and within the family nurturing predominates, and so, too, in the individualized group in which everyone is familiar with the other, and whose members are thus as a result bonded quasi-familially. Leaders in such individualized groups are chosen for their prosocial abilities. Those who comfort group members in distress, who are able to intervene in quarrels and to protect group members who are attacked, who share, who in brief show abilities to nurture, are chosen by the others as leaders, rather than those who use their abilities in competitive ways. Of course, group leaders may need, beyond their prosocial competence, to be gifted as orators, war leaders, or healers.

Manifestations of repressive dominance are tabooed within the group, but not so between members of different groups, as the long history of intergroup aggression attests. But humans also have the capacity to become familiar with non-group members, and in the course of history, societies of millions of members have grown, and finally even the idea of a "family of man" has emerged. Our prosocial motivations seem stronger than our motivations for aggression, which, after all, can be sublimated in many ways. We must be aware, however, that in order to achieve world peace, the problems that were traditionally at one time solved by war and aggression now need to be solved by peaceful means. These problems are well known. Different populations on our planet seek to survive, and to keep their resources and their identities. But both are threatened by the global pressure of population increase that is about to ruin not only the ecological conditions necessary for survival, but also the social environment necessary for peace.

The text of the new edition of *Love and Hate* remains unchanged, since further investigations have confirmed the basic theses. I could have added a number of new examples, but then the book would have become bulky. In the original text of the book, I occasionally referred to now outdated ideas, e.g., *Arterhaltung* ('preservation of species'). We know today that selection does not operate at the level of species, but instead at the individual and group level. For those who are particularly interested in the subject, my treatise, *Human Ethology* (New York, Aldine de Gruyter, 1989) is available. As for war and peace, I refer my readers to a later book than the present one, *The Biology of Peace and War* (New York, Viking Press, 1979), in which I traced the cultural origin of war, its functions, and our potential for peace.

The key experience that led to this book struck me in 1954 on the Galapagos Islands. I was at that time a member of a diving expedition led by Hans Hass. I was fascinated by the large aggregation of marine iguanas covering the rocks on shore. They were evidently gregarious, since in some parts they basked tightly packed, side by side, yet they did not interact in the usual ways of birds and gregarious mammals, who show a rich repertory of prosocial behaviors, such as mutual feeding, grooming, and the like. The marine iguanas interacted only by display and submissive behavior. Even their courtship consisted of dominance displays by the males, and if a female was ready to copulate, she invited the male with a submissive posture, by lying flat on her belly. Later I found that in reptiles social behavior is generally based on dominance and submission, and so the question of how friendliness and love came into the world began to fascinate me. The result was this book.

I. E.-E.

Acknowledgments

For the help they have given me during the course of my work I am indebted to a great many people, not all of whom can be thanked individually. I have received hospitality from countless mission stations in various countries and also received assistance through their local authorities, as well as from the consulates of Austria and the Federal Republic of Germany. My particular thanks are due to Professor Konrad Lorenz, who assisted my work in every possible way, and to Dr. Hans Hass, with whom I have made a number of expeditions. In the course of these, many of the lines of argument presented here were evolved both in conversation and in the observations we made together. I must also thank Dr. Inga Steinvorth de Goetz and her daughter, Frau Elke Fuhrmeister de Goetz, who made possible my journey to the Upper Orinoco. I should also mention with especial gratitude the collaboration of Herr Hermann Kacher, who drew all the illustrations for this book. In conclusion I must thank the Max Planck Institute, the Thyssen Foundation, and the A. V. Gwinner Foundation for the financial support they gave to my research.

I. E.-E.

1

The "Human Beast"— a Modern Caricature of Man

In the history of mankind one bloody chapter follows another almost without interruption; and the picture has remained unchanged right up to the present day. The only difference is that now we possess atomic weapons, and in the event of war we run the risk of destroying ourselves. We have subdued the forces of nature, we have conquered epidemics and wiped out the beasts of prey that once threatened us. Now we are our own greatest enemy, unless we succeed in taming our aggressive urges.

Is there the slightest prospect of our doing this? Are we not ruled by an innate aggressive drive, by a lust for killing which at best can be repressed but never eliminated? In recent times this has been repeatedly asserted.

"Cain rules the world. If anyone doubts it, let him read the history of the world," wrote Leopold Szondi in 1969 (*201*).* In his view a murderous inclination is inherent in all men and he speaks of a "Cain-tendency," a drive factor with which we are born. Robert Ardrey has sketched a similar portrait of mankind (*8*).

The same thesis has been put forward in the weekly and daily press. Thus, *Time* magazine (*204*) says that man is "one of the world's most aggressive beasts who fundamentally enjoys torturing and killing other animals, including his fellow man. . . . His hormones urge him to copulate with his sisters and

* The italic figures in parentheses in the text refer to the list of sources at the end of the book.

daughters just as well as other animals do generally. But his cortex tells him to barter his females to strangers for political advantage. . . . He would like to murder his father, but his natural impulse is cunningly suppressed: one day he will be the old man."

So the argument runs thus: man is by nature inclined to kill, but understanding and reason enable him to curb these impulses. One could speak of a concept of the tamed beast. The good * in man is, in this view, a cultural achievement, while the evil is a consequence of dark impulses, over which he has no control.

This thesis of man's antisocial, "killer" nature is not new. It had already been advanced by the English philosopher Thomas Hobbes (1588–1679), when he recognized in man only the drive for self-preservation and the lust for power. According to Hobbes, the struggle of all against all, which is the logical outcome of this drive, can be prevented only by an absolute sovereign forcing men against their will to unite.

But equally old is the contrary thesis of Jean-Jacques Rousseau (1712–1778) that man in his original state is peaceful and friendly and is corrupted and made aggressive only by civilization. The argument about the "true" nature of man continues to the present day and there has been no shortage of advocates for the two extreme viewpoints.

The Hobbesian thesis has reappeared in various guises in the course of time. In this sense Thomas Huxley (1888) (*101*) interpreted Darwin's "struggle for existence" as a ruthless contest in which only "the strongest, the swiftest and the most cunning" remain alive. He compares the animal world with a gladiators' show: the participants are well treated and the next day they are sent out to fight. The only difference is that the spectator has no need to give the "thumbs down," for no quarter is given. Peter Kropotkin (1903) (*122*), on the contrary, holds that mu-

---

* We generally refer to aggression as "evil," and to love and friendship and everything that brings individuals together as "good." This is correct insofar as aggression, despite its contribution to the preservation of the species (and therefore in this sense a "good"), does carry with it a tendency toward pathological degeneration and thereby endangers our existence. We are often too aggressive, rarely too friendly.

tual aid is as much a natural law as mutual struggle. He points out that this view can also be found in Darwin but that people have paid more attention to Darwin's catch phrases than to his principal ideas.

The modern champions of the "human beast" theory refer both to the findings of behavioral research (or ethology) and to those of psychoanalysis. Both schools of thought have established that man has an innate aggressive drive, but these champions interpret this fact in a one-sided way. Some use it to justify and excuse aggressive behavior; others, while rejecting this extreme, conservative attitude, do not (curiously enough) protest against the misuse of behavioral research but reserve their fury for the science of ethology itself, as if it were responsible. Thus Arno Plack (*163*) accuses the ethologist of adhering to the doctrine that "all is struggle," of claiming that the aggressive drive is the basic drive in all living things, and of using this doctrine of the antisocial nature of man to justify a culture based on violence. Many of the criticisms mustered in Ashley Montagu's book *Man and Aggression* (*154*), are aimed in the same direction. One must therefore assume that these two men seriously believe ethology teaches that human nature is unchangeable and sees an innate aggressive drive as the dominant motive in human conduct.* It is the concern of this book to refute such views.

My basic premise here is that if a certain behavior pattern or disposition is inherited, this by no means implies that it is not amenable to conditioning, nor must it be regarded as natural in the sense that it is still adaptive (i.e., conducive to survival). A behavior pattern developed in the course of the history of the species can lose its original function. Thus, a strong aggressive

---

* Wolfgang Hädecke (*79*) has pointed out the danger of an ideological misuse of ethology: "The nature of ethological research, which is undogmatic and anti-ideological on principle, does not exclude the possibility of its being misused in a specific direction and furnishing arguments for such misuse. If ethologists do not guard against it, their findings may be placed at the service of one of the oldest doctrines in the world: that of the immutability of human society, and in particular the age-old principle of dominance and submission which is all too readily invoked. A science which investigates principally (though by no means exclusively) the inherited, and presumably unchanging, elements in our behavior lends itself to inappropriate use in this sense: indeed one must call it *misuse*. . . ."

drive may once have stimulated man's intellectual development and brought about the distribution of man over the whole earth, through the severe competition among different human groups. But an excess of aggressiveness today can lead us to total self-annihilation. One should not therefore accept aggression without reservation simply because it is innate, but strive to control it. After all, man is by his very nature a cultural being. Cultural control patterns do regulate his inborn impulses, as explained in more detail on page 31. This allows for a greater adaptability in our species, since cultural control patterns can change rapidly when circumstances demand it. Indeed we are now searching for new ways, since the traditional ones seem to a certain degree outdated. And it is here that ethological research can help us find the adequate measures by providing insight into man's nature. Ethology, as a biological science, seeks to investigate the functioning of those physiological mechanisms that influence a behavior pattern so that, by understanding the function structures we may be able to eliminate disturbances. In this process of investigation it may well become clear that some of the phylogenetic adaptations (those acquired in the course of the history of the species) are now retained like so much historical ballast, which is as useless—or even dangerous—to the organism as the caecum or "appendix." Behavior, too, has its "appendixes."

The basis for Plack's reproach that ethologists have recently been tracing everything back to the aggressive drive is not very clear, for Konrad Lorenz (*141*), whom Plack cites specifically in this connection, speaks insistently of a "parliament of instincts," making it quite plain that an animal is motivated by different systems of drives which often conflict. The aggressive drive is only one drive among many. But as the reproaches have nevertheless been made, it must be admitted that in previous discussions of aggression too little emphasis has hitherto been given to the social potential of men and animals.* It is in these tend-

---

* In my own *Ethology: the Biology of Behavior* (*Grundriss der vergleichenden Verhaltensforschung*) I have described in great detail the mechanisms that lead to the formation and cohesion of social groups. Hans Hass (*83*) also gives some striking observations about bonds, regarded from a general functional viewpoint, in his valuable book *Energon,* in which organic and economic structures are analyzed and compared.

encies toward sociability that the key to overcoming the problem of aggression will be found. I therefore propose to speak in some detail about the mechanisms for establishing bonds, those natural opponents of aggression, on which we can base our hope for a less bellicose future. Among the higher vertebrates, social repulsion (aggression) and social attraction form a functional entity, and I propose to present them as such here.

My thesis in this book is that both aggressive and altruistic behavior are preprogrammed by phylogenetic adaptations and that there are therefore preordained norms for our ethical behavior. In my opinion, man's aggressive impulses are counterbalanced by his equally deep-rooted social tendencies.* It is not only conditioning that programs us to be good—we are good by inclination. If we can demonstrate this, then my opening thesis—that goodness is merely a secondary cultural superstructure—is disproved. We will argue that the disposition to cooperation and mutual aid is innate, as are many specific behavior patterns of friendly contact. Why all these tendencies have not so far sufficed to restrain our aggressive feelings in all situations will also be discussed.

My starting point is the fact that as human beings, despite all our aggressiveness, we live in groups. I pose the question of just how we manage this. By what means do we maintain and form bonds with our fellow-men, in spite of the "aggression barrier"? Are there innate bonding drives that hold the aggressive drive in check? What part is played in this by the sexual drive? How do sociability and love develop both phylogenetically (in the course of evolution) and ontogenetically (during the lifetime of the individual)? And how does hate evolve?

The methodological approach I have used in this investigation is that of comparative biology, which proceeds from the understanding of our evolutionary history. As there are some misconceptions in lay circles about the value of comparisons between animals and man—and there are even some specialists in the humanities who speak in this connection of "inadmissible arguments by analogy" (171)—I intend before beginning the discussion to consider the basic concepts of ethology and the

---

* These friendly dispositions can themselves be misused of course: one has only to think of the dangers of excessive loyalty to a leader.

methodology of comparison, and to show how one can interpret similarities between species. To the reader untrained in biology it is not immediately apparent that we can learn things from the behavior of some bird or mammal that are significant for the understanding of our own species. At this point there is a discussion of the mechanisms of phylogenetic development and of such frequently used concepts as "adaptation," "ritualization," and "selection." I will then discuss aggression and bond-forming behavior patterns in both animals and man. I will show that the capacity to establish a personal bond has evolved phylogenetically, along with care for the young, and that to a certain extent this is repeated in the ontogenetic development of the individual. The human child first acquires the capacity to love another through love for its mother. The child would find it difficult, if not impossible, to identify with a group without first passing through this phase.

Man was originally created for a life in individualized groups. The transition to life in the anonymous community produces problems of identification. On the one hand the urge clearly exists to form a bond with strangers as well. On the other hand we can observe the inclination to cut oneself off in groups from others. We are inclined to cast members of an alien group in the role of enemies, giving rise to the question of whether we are adopting certain attitudes of mind involuntarily. For those engaged in peace research the illumination of these processes is of great importance. Man usually has less fellow feeling for strangers, and by the same token his aggressiveness toward them is less inhibited. This is one of the reasons why conflicts between different groups tend to be aggravated. The awakening of a new sense of social unity is therefore of vital concern. I shall discuss the prospects for this at the very end of my work.

In this book I make quite frequent use of the term "love." By this I mean not only sexual love but more generally the emotional, personal bond between one man and another, or the bond arising from identification with a particular group. The counterpart of love is hate, both hate as an individualized emotional rejection and the group hatred that arises from it. Strictly speaking we can only use the terms "love" and "hate" in this sense in the case of man. In animals all we can do is to note purely descriptively either the individualized striving for contact and a bond or their aggression. Statements about the emotions that go with such behavior are fundamentally impossible for epistemological reasons. By analogy we can only conjecture that, at least in higher vertebrates, the relevant behavior patterns are also accompanied by corresponding emotions. Certainly the describable behavior patterns of making contact and rejection are often similar in animals and man. Such similarities often justify us in tracing them to the same roots. If, therefore, I speak on occasion of love, without expressly differentiating between animals and man, I am using this as a shorthand description for the sake of clarity, just as the physiologist will speak of "hunger" and "thirst" in animals.

Most of the drawings in this book are drawings based on film stills and still photographs. The details of the sources will be found in the captions. So that the reader can form an impression of the quality of the reproductions, some of the photographic originals are reproduced on pages 230–231. Other photographs that served as originals may be found by the interested reader in my own *Ethology: the Biology of Behavior*.

2
Preprogramming in Human and Animal Behavior

INNATE APTITUDE

Human beings are generally convinced that they act of their own free will. We think we have the ability to decide freely either to do this and to refrain from doing that. But when our anger is roused does it not sometimes cloud our clear judgment? And then do we not involuntarily say many things that would not be said in a different mood? Moreover are there not certain situations in which we react absolutely automatically and in what is in principle the same way, without reflecting in advance?

When speaking to babies we give a friendly smile and raise the pitch of our voices. We nod our heads encouragingly in conversation generally. When perplexed, we scratch our heads. In many respects we behave like programmed computers. The comparison is by no means far-fetched, for we do indeed react predictably—if this were not true, there could be no science of behavior. But this, in turn, means that at some stage in our development we must have been "programmed," and the question of how this process of equipping us with behavior programs has taken place elicits varying opinions.

Basically several methods are conceivable. Since animals and men have the ability to learn, they could acquire their behavior programs in the course of their ontogenetic development (i.e., their development as young individuals), as much through self-conditioning as from the example of their parents. But there is the alternative possibility that organisms come into the world already equipped with behavior programs. This would mean that they have been programmed in the course of their phylogeny (the evolution of the species)* and that their behavior patterns are innate, just like the physical structures with which they are born.

The "environmental theory" puts forward the view that, apart from a few reflexes, as human beings we learn our entire behavior programs in the course of our ontogenetic development. The newborn baby comes into the world a blank page, as it were. Only recently Ashley Montagu (*154*) said: "There is in fact not the slightest evidence or ground for assuming that the alleged 'phylogenetically adapted instinctive' behavior of other animals is in any way relevant to the discussion of the motive-forces of human behavior. The fact is that with the exception of the instinctoid reactions in infants to sudden withdrawals of support and to sudden loud noises, the human being is entirely instinctless." This belief in the exclusively cultural determination of human behavior is widespread. It is the underlying premise, too, for a number of political utopias. According to the environmental theory, not only physical motor sequences but also the human being's dispositions, such as, for example, the striving for dominance or aggressiveness, are the product of conditioning. Those who consider either tendency to be antisocial will speak of bad programming through education and advocate the rearing of children in such a way that the undesirable tendencies never develop.

In practice man has proved to be firmly resistant to attempts to educate him differently in quite specific areas. Perhaps there are after all elements of preprogramming in human behavior and, if so, in which areas?

It was initially in animals that biological behavioral research showed that specific motor patterns could be present as "adaptations" evolved by the species. Animals come into the world with an innate capacity for certain movements. As soon as it is hatched a chaffinch knows how to open its beak wide to beg for

* By means of mutation and selection. See p. 33.

food, a chicken how to peck for corn and a duckling how to dabble in the mud for food. And a duckling will do this even if it has been hatched by a hen; it will not, for instance, follow the foster-parent's example and peck for grains of corn. The duckling has inherited this coordination of movements for filtering mud from its parents as an "inherited coordination" or fixed action pattern. To be precise, it is not, of course, the motor pattern that is inherited, but only the set of instructions encoded in the genes on the basis of which those nervous structures and connections develop that underlie the behavior pattern. Inherited motor patterns are not necessarily always fully matured at the moment of birth or hatching. Many behavior patterns mature only gradually, as experiments have shown. Thus F. Sauer (*177*) by rearing whitethroats individually and insulated from sound, has established that they developed their species-specific calls and song without any example to copy. It is true that certain environmental conditions have to be fulfilled for this development to take place; what is striking is that the bird develops the species typical song pattern without being exposed to the patterned information of the song. We can therefore assume that the information about the song pattern is all contained in the genome and is decoded during the ontogenetic process of self-differentiation.

When carrying out a deprivation experiment, ethologists are concerned with how the observed adaptedness of a behavior pattern comes about. If two birds sing the same song, if two mammals exhibit the same expressive movements or otherwise show their behavior to be molded to fit certain environmental features, in all such cases we are forced to assume that a common pool of information has been tapped. That means that information about the environmental feature which the behavior in question copies or was shaped to fit must have at some time been fed into the organism. This acquisition of information can take place during ontogeny by learning or during phylogeny. By withholding patterned information we can check whether the adaptedness in question is a result of individual learning or of phylogenetic processes.

Inherited motor patterns have also been demonstrated in

mammals. The Central European red squirrel hides nuts in autumn as a provision for winter. In so doing it follows a uniform pattern: with the nut in its mouth it climbs down to the ground and looks about until it finds the base of a tree trunk, scrapes out a hole with its forepaws, lays down the nut, presses it in firmly with its nose, and finally scrapes back the loose earth over the nut with its forepaws. This behavior pattern is not seen at all in baby squirrels, for they are born in nests, blind and naked. But I have reared several squirrels in such a way . that they had no examples to copy and no opportunity to learn how to hide nuts by trial and error. Nevertheless, these animals were able to carry out the species-specific hiding technique. When I gave nuts to the grown squirrels for the first time, they began by eating them. When they had eaten enough, they started to hide the nuts. Each squirrel would run round the room with the nut in its mouth until it finally began scrabbling away in a corner; after that it laid down the nut, pressed it down with its nose, and finally made the raking over and pressing down movements with its front paws—although it had not dug up any soil. This shows clearly that what we have here is the blind unfolding of a hereditarily programmed behavioral sequence (*45*).

Observing inexperienced squirrels teaches us something else besides. In their efforts to hide the nuts the squirrels show a marked interest in vertical obstacles. It is most frequently beside table legs, chair legs, or in corners of the room that they begin their digging movements. This innate preference for vertical objects stems from the fact that squirrels most frequently bury things at the bases of tree trunks or rocks, which facilitates finding them again later. Thus these animals not only inherit the mechanisms for hiding food, but also, in broad terms, a knowledge of the most suitable hiding places.

But what about human beings? Are we also equipped with innate motor patterns? Certainly a baby does not need to learn how to suck; it can also smile, cry, cling, and much else besides. But many human behavior patterns develop only gradually in the course of growing up, and it is hard to establish which of these have simply matured and were therefore programmed in advance. Human beings cannot be reared so that they are deprived of experience. Nevertheless, children are occasionally born blind, or even blind and deaf, and the study of such children is particularly informative in relation to the question under discussion. Blind and deaf children grow up in permanent darkness and silence. They never see their mother's smile nor hear the sound of a human voice. If the most extreme tenets of the environmental theory were true we should expect such children to differ greatly in their behavior from healthy people who have grown up normally. But in observing children born deaf and blind I have established that this is not so. At many crucial points they behave almost exactly like us. For example, they smile and laugh as we do when they are happy and emit the correct sounds when they do so. In addition, they weep as we do, stamp their feet, clench their fists, and frown when something annoys them (Fig. 1).

The possible objection that the children might have learned,

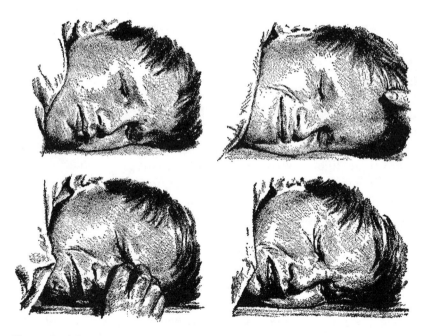

Fig. 1. Facial expressions of a nine-year-old girl born deaf and blind. Above, left: relaxed mood; right: smiling; below: crying (from film stills by the author).

say, to smile because they had constantly been rewarded with friendly encouragement whenever they "happened" to show a behavior pattern similar to smiling, can easily be overcome. Even severely mentally handicapped children smile, laugh, and weep—though it is impossible, even with great effort, to teach them to eat with a spoon. It is unthinkable that they could have learned complicated motor patterns while failing over tasks that are much simpler to learn. Anyone still insisting on the hypothesis of learned behavior would have to postulate, as a supplementary hypothesis, a particular innate disposition to learn. Nor will the argument hold water that the children could have explored with their fingers the faces of their parents or those who look after them and thus read the expression and copied it. I know a boy who was born blind and who, probably as a consequence of thalidomide damage, possesses only little stumps of hands with which he cannot feel anything. His facial expressions are essentially normal; he laughs, for example, as we do when one plays with him.

One final argument that can be marshaled against the learning theory is that such children also develop a whole range of "naughtiness"—for example, typical human angry behavior. Certainly no one has taught them this, nor can they have had the opportunity to feel adults who were stamping their feet, clenching their fists, and looking angry—and so assemble data about the expressions and gestures of anger. Ultimately such behavior patterns evolve directly without the educative pressure of the environment. The same is true of certain basic social attitudes. Normal children are afraid of strangers. This same shyness of strangers is also shown in blind and deaf children, who can distinguish familiar people from strangers by smell. They reject strangers at first, even though they have never been treated badly by strangers. Quite the reverse: everyone makes an effort to be nice to these children.

There is nevertheless a limit to the data we can obtain from blind and deaf children, since many of the most complicated human behavior patterns—say greeting and flirting—are elicited via the eye and the ear. These gates of perception are closed in deaf and blind people so there is no possibility of experimenting with them. But more is innate than is commonly supposed; this I have observed in a ten-year-old girl, born blind but with perfectly good hearing. She played the piano for me and I paid her a compliment. She immediately blushed and turned her face briefly toward me and then looked down, just as any sighted girl does when she is bashful.

If we wish to know how much in the complicated behavior patterns of mankind is innate, then we must generally rely on comparisons between different cultures. One may take as a starting point man's tendency to vary culturally whatever can be modified. In New Guinea alone several hundred dialects are spoken. This is part of the tendency of human beings to isolate themselves into small groups, especially by means of customs— a phenomenon known as "club-formation" when it occurs within an ethnic group. But if one finds that, in certain situations, such as a greeting, or the behavior of a mother toward her child, the same behavior patterns recur repeatedly even among the most differing peoples, then it is highly probable that these are innate behavior patterns. Charles Darwin in his day worked on this assumption and in so doing laid the foundations for the comparative study of the expression of emotions in man and animals. But he lacked the means for objective documentation of behavior. In his day film was not yet available. This situation has long since changed and today man is certainly the most filmed being on earth. One might therefore suppose that it would be no problem to verify this question about innate elements in human behavior. One would have only to take films from one of the larger film archives of psychologists or anthropologists and examine, say, the greeting behavior of different peoples for common invariables, taking great care that these represent unposed natural documents of human behavior (for man alters his behavior considerably if he notices that he is being filmed).

But anyone who sets out to make use of film archives in this way will rarely come across such documents. There are certainly a great many films showing cultural activities such as mat-weaving, tool-making, or set dances. But how people greet one another, how they flirt, or cuddle a child has never been systematically documented.

During the past few years, in collaboration with my friend

Hans Hass, I have directed my efforts toward the collection of this kind of data. Using cameras with "mirror lens" attachments, containing prisms that permit filming to the side, we have filmed people in the most varied parts of the world without their knowledge. With each film document we made a written record of what the person did before and after being filmed and in what social context the behavior pattern in question took place, for it is only in this way that one can avoid an oversubjective interpretation—a great source of error. The comparison of such documents has revealed similarities extending to the details of the motor sequence. Thus, among the most differing

Fig. 2. In greeting with the eyes the eyebrows are jerked upward for about one sixth of a second. The series of people shown in Figures 2 and 3 shows in each case the facial expression at the moment of visual contact and on greeting with the eyes. They are drawn from film stills. Above: Balinese; below: Papuan (Woitapmin); (photographed by the author).

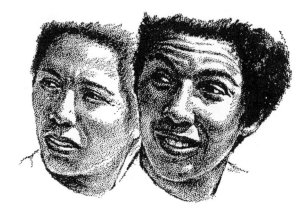

*Fig. 3. Greeting
with the eyes.
Above: French-
woman (photo-
graphed by
H. Hass); below:
Waika Indian
(photographed by
the author).*

peoples in the world a rapid raising and lowering of the eyebrows, accompanied by a smile, often also by a nod, serves for
a particularly friendly greeting at a distance (Figs. 2, 3, see also
p. 173).

Many of our innate motor patterns stem from an ancient
evolutionary inheritance, illustrated by the fact that we have
them in common with the anthropoid apes most closely related
to us. When threatening we may rotate our arms inward and
raise our shoulders. At the same time the small muscles that
make the hairs on our arms, back, and shoulders stand erect are
tensed, which gives us the sensation of a mild thrill. In the

chimpanzee we find threatening behavior that follows a similar pattern. The difference is that when the chimpanzee threatens, its fur bristles and this strikingly alters its appearance. In man the posture has remained, although most of the covering hair has been lost. The fur of our ancestors during the process of threatening most probably stood on end. When the upright position was developed, some peculiarities in the fur pattern evolved. Leyhausen (*135*) has pointed out that the hairs on the human body—unlike those on anthropoid apes—grow upward on the shoulders and upper arms, so that the hair forms veritable tufts on the shoulders of very hairy people. If this was true of our forefathers, who were probably much more thickly covered with hair, then when their hair bristled the region of their shoulders would be particularly emphasized. Even today the human male tends to emphasize his shoulders by means of clothing and ornament (Figs. 4 and 5). In this he may well be guided by an innate preference.

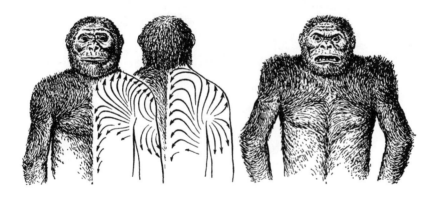

Fig. 4. *The direction of the hair in modern man is such that when our hair bristles the most marked effect would be to magnify the outline of our shoulders, if we were still covered by hair. This was almost certainly the case with our ancestors, as a reconstruction copied from P. Leyhausen shows. In this drawing the direction of the hair in modern man on front and back is transferred to a hypothetical ancestor: his probable appearance when the hair stands on end is shown. Even today men with a lot of body hair have tufts of hair on their shoulders. Even after the loss of covering hair, the human male has retained the tendency to emphasize his shoulders.*

Fig. 5. In the most varied cultures the human male has a tendency to emphasize his shoulders in his dress. Above: Waika Indian; center: Kabuki (Japan) (both photographs by the author); below: Alexander II of Russia (from a contemporary portrait).

Other threatening movements that we share with the anthropoid apes are stamping of the feet when annoyed and baring canine teeth in a rage. The baring of the teeth is especially interesting. Baboons, which are equipped with particularly long upper canines, pull their lower lips down at the corners when threatening, so that the canines are exposed to their full extent. We do just the same, although we do not possess long upper canines. Thus the motor pattern has outlived the reduction in size of the organ originally displayed (Fig. 6).

In the chapters that follow I shall be describing further innate motor patterns in man. At this point it is enough to state

Fig. 6. When threatening, the mandrill draws down the corners of its mouth, so that the full extent of the upper canine tooth is visible. Human beings do the same, although our upper canines are now nothing like as long. Above, left: mandrill; right: Kabuki actor portraying rage (both from photographs by the author); left: small girl in a rage (from a photograph in E. von Eckstedt, Forschung am Menschen, Stuttgart, 1963).

that there are phylogenetic adaptations in human movement, many of them clearly very old.

INNATE RECOGNITION

A frog, which only a short time ago swam around a pond as a tadpole, snaps at small moving insects immediately after its metamorphosis, without first having to learn how to do so. Insects that stay still, on the other hand, are not recognized as prey. And if one investigates by means of various "dummies," or stimulus objects, exactly what it is that releases the motions of catching prey, one will see that the frog snaps at any small moving object, even at small leaves or pebbles. Thus the drive to snap at such moving things is innate to it and, provided there are no ethologists at work, such behavior does indeed lead the frog to its goal, for in its natural habitat the principal moving objects are insects.

The ability to react to certain "key stimuli" with prey-catching actions calls for special apparatus for receiving and processing stimuli. These "stimulus filters" are, as it were, adjusted to specific stimuli or combinations of stimuli. We call them "innate releasing mechanisms" (I.R.M.). It is via such releasing mechanisms that a great many of the social behavior patterns like courtship and fighting are also activated. In these cases there has not only been an adaptation on the receiving end to the signals transmitted by the fellow species member: the latter has for its part also developed specific transmission devices that act as "releasers." These can be physical structures (combs or manes), characteristic coloring, scents, sounds, or even expressive movements. In the spiny lizard the blue lateral stripes of the male elicit fighting behavior in conspecifics of the same sex. Females that have had blue stripes artificially painted onto their gray sides are attacked just like rival males. European robins recognize their rivals by the patch of red on their breasts and will even attack a tuft of red feathers mounted on a branch in their territory (*128*). Turkey hens recognize their young only by their calls and kill chicks that are dumb, but will foster a stuffed polecat containing a built-in microphone that emits the calls of a turkey poult (*181*). Rhesus monkeys isolated from birth prefer pictures of their own species which are projected on the wall of their cage to other pictures. They emit contact sounds, invite them to play, and when the projection is switched off they quickly learn how to project these pictures for themselves by pressing a lever. At the age of two months, these socially inexperienced rhesus monkeys also recognize the expressions of their conspecifics. The picture of a threatening monkey then makes them shrink back and emit sounds of fear, while their rate of approach falls off rapidly. This understanding of expressions must be attributed to an innate releasing mechanism, for the monkeys have never seen their own kind (*176*).

The fact that we ourselves react blindly to the simplest dummies or decoy devices suggests that human beings too are equipped with innate releasing mechanisms.* For example, certain attributes of the human infant make us regard it as "cuddly"; the word itself is already expressive of the inclination we feel to pick the child up and cuddle it. The hallmarks "of cuddliness" are chubby cheeks, a forehead which is high and protruding in relation to the small face, relatively large eyes, a small mouth for sucking, a head that is large in proportion to the body, chubby body shapes and more besides (*137*). It is noteworthy that in experiments with dummies these traits, even when presented individually, have an extremely powerful effect. I recently saw some simply made cat-figures, the most striking feature of which was two great chubby cheeks. This childish feature by itself suffices to give the object a friendly "appeal"

---

* Recent experiments by Ball and Tronick (*Science*, 1971, **171**, 818), which were published after this book was in production, prove the existence of innate releasing mechanisms that allow humans to react adaptively to stimulus situations, independent of prior exposure. Babies, only two weeks old, responded to symmetrically expanding shadows, which optically specify an approaching object, with an integrated avoidance response. This response did not occur for asymmetrically expanding or contracting shadows, which specify an object on a miss path or a receding object. Other experiments demonstrated that in reaction to a visual cliff, babies freeze and display avoidance responses and that some characteristics of Gestalt perception can be found in them, e.g., the capacity to recognize one object as the same thing when presented at different distances. These findings are of great theoretical importance, since they are proof of the existence of innate data processing mechanisms in man.

Fig. 7. The "infant schema": the attributes of a small child (big head in relation to body, high prominent forehead, chubby cheeks, short rounded limbs, small mouth for sucking, etc.) are often greatly exaggerated in the dolls produced by the toy industry, which increases the protectiveness-releasing effect of these "cute" little objects. In commercial art the childish attributes of women are frequently exaggerated as well as the sexual attributes (see also p. 137).

and so to make it salable. The infant's chubby cheeks are structures differentiated specifically as "releasers," that is, for the purpose of transmitting signals. They have not been shown to have any mechanical function in sucking. Other attributes of the small child can also be represented in isolation with success. Indeed, if exaggerated they can even have the effect on occasion of a "super-normal object," that is, one that produces a superstimulus. Another feature of the small child is the head–body proportion: a large head on a relatively small body. Walt Disney, in his own way a master manipulator of stimulus-objects, for example, created a little dog that walks through his cartoons with an overlarge head and tiny body. The effect is distinctly appealing. Equally "cute" is Disney's Bambi, the deer with the exaggeratedly high forehead. Disney also makes use of the childish attribute of clumsiness (lack of coordination). It can furthermore be pointed out that the lapdogs kept by elderly spinsters in compensation for frustrated parental drives also display childlike attributes. One has only to think of Pekingese or pugs (Fig. 7). And if one observes the relationship between the two, one will notice that the owners fondle their dogs and talk to them, just as if they were small children.

In a similar way there must be innate releasing mechanisms that govern our understanding of facial expressions; for in this field, too, we are susceptible to the simplest "dummy" effects. For this reason an eagle, for example, looks noble to us because with its hooded eyes, narrow slit of a mouth, and corners of the mouth turned down "disdainfully" at the base of the beak, its expression resembles that of a bold man with his eyes fixed on a distant goal. Such a man wrinkles his brow, as if shading his eyes to gaze into the distance, and presses his lips resolutely together, so that the corners of his mouth are turned down.

An arrogant man lifts his head so that his nose is held high in relation to his eye; at the same time he lowers his eyelids and often breathes out, too, as if he were rejecting all the sensory stimuli coming from the despised enemy in an almost ritualized form. The whole behavior pattern can be interpreted as a ritualized movement of withdrawal. In the camel the angle of the head, due to the particular position of the internal ear cavities, makes it look as if its nose were permanently raised in scorn. Although we know perfectly well that this does not in any way reflect a particular temperament on the part of the animal, we find it unattractive. Similarly, certain animals look friendly to us if, thanks to some kind of structure or marking, they appear to have the corners of their mouths turned upward (*137*).

Sexual signals operate in a comparable manner. It should be mentioned that apart from characteristics we perceive with our sense of sight (such as a man's broad shoulders, a woman's breasts), olfactory signals also play a part. J. LeMagnen (*134*) has established that women are aware of certain musk substances that men cannot smell. Only if men are injected with the female hormone, estrogen, can they smell them too. And the olfactory threshold of women themselves shows variations with the ovulation cycle. Then with the arrival of the menopause the ability to smell these odorous materials disappears. It may be supposed that men give off smells of a similar type without themselves being aware of it. Here it is noteworthy that there are some Mediterranean dances in which the men wave little kerchiefs in front of the girls of their choice. Before the dance the kerchiefs are often worn under their armpits and thus impregnated with their smell.

When people perceive something that arouses their interest their pupils dilate. If normal male subjects are shown photographs of naked girls in a sequence of slides their pupils become dilated. Homosexuals, on the other hand, respond with a strong pupil reaction to pictures of men. According to E. H. Hess (*87*) this automatic reaction operates like a lie detector and is therefore suited to testing decoy devices. R. G. Coss (*32*) has tested the effectiveness of artificial eyespots by this method and established that two eyespots painted side by side arouse more attention than three or a single one. Furthermore they have a stronger effect displayed horizontally than obliquely or vertically. We shall discuss further the great significance of eyes in human social contact. Serrated shapes also evoke a stronger emotional response (measured by the enlargement of the pupils) than rounded ones. This could be an innate response to the tooth pattern of a predator's teeth. The attention-arousing effect of such signals is used in advertising as an eye catcher; thus in the word OMO, the name of an English soap powder, for instance, both eyespots and teeth pattern are enlisted to attract attention.* In our speech rhythms certain cues are given in the intonation and sentence structure, to which we respond in a stereotyped manner. There are some features of speech intonation which are similar over a wide range of cultures. Political

* Staring eyes have a threatening effect and spellbinding eyespots are therefore widely used as protective devices on uniforms, ships, houses, and the like [Koenig (*111*)].

speakers know how to provoke their listeners to "spontaneous" applause, not only through the repetition of the same slogans but also through the rhythm and cadence of their delivery. By activating collective aggressive feelings in this way they can reinforce the cohesion of the group.

Without the aid of biological knowledge, both demagogues and professional advertisers have succeeded in similar ways in influencing the free will of individual people and groups of people through the correct presentation of the appropriate keystimuli. It is well known that these processes of persuasion do not always unconditionally serve the general good. But if man wishes to defend himself against this exploitation of his drive mechanisms, then the first essential is a precise understanding of these mechanisms and of the stimuli that set them in motion.

DRIVES

Animals do not generally wait passively for things to happen. They tend to be active by nature. Particular inner drives determine a searching behavior, and if one offers the animal different things experimentally one can discover what kind of mood it is in. If it is hungry, then it will be on the lookout only for food and will not take any notice of other things. If it is thirsty it will look for water; if it is in an aggressive mood it will look for a rival; if it is sexually aroused it will search for a sexual partner. The physiological mechanisms that produce such specific propensities have been thoroughly investigated. Very many innate behavior patterns are linked to spontaneously activated groups of motor cells in the central nervous system, which constantly produce impulses impelling the organism toward a motor discharge. The centrally produced excitation can accumulate. This causes restlessness in the animal looking for releasing stimulus situations that would allow it to work off the built-up impulses in specific movements. If it can find no opportunity to do this, then the behavior pattern can be directed at substitute objects through the inner drive accumulation, and in extreme cases even run off in a "vacuum." A well-fed starling that has no opportunity to catch insects will from time to time fly up spontaneously from its perch to snap at nothing, return to its perch, make a killing motion, and then an equally vain swallowing motion (*136*).

As human beings, we are also moved by inner drives. We become hungry and thirsty, while our sexual appetites are subject to variations that can be traced back to physiological processes within ourselves. Many of our drives have a disruptive effect in modern social life, for example the aggressive drive, which fulfills an important function in the higher vertebrates (see p. 69), but in modern human society has lost much of its original value. It has indeed become a major source of danger, for man's inner motivation impels him to work off this drive, while the adequate societal opportunities for him to do so are not always available. Without understanding the biological processes, man projects his periodic attacks of anger "outward"—in his personal social life against the people nearest to him and, within the context of the larger group, against minorities and neighboring nations. As the preservation of world peace has now become a matter of life and death for humanity, the investigation of the structures underlying aggressive behavior is, as already emphasized in Chapter 1, of the utmost importance.

Man certainly does not possess fewer innate drives than other higher mammals; if anything, he possesses more. For example, he possesses a speech drive—even children born deaf begin to chatter. And many of his drives are more strongly developed than in animals; one has only to think of our curiosity drive, which motivates learning.

INNATE LEARNING DISPOSITIONS

In an environment that changed little it was possible for life forms with rigid preprogramming to survive. But changing circumstances called for an individual capacity to make adaptations in behavior. Animals have to make use of their experience, which means being able to learn—to learn what is correct at the appropriate time for the preservation of the species. In order to do this an animal must be so programmed that in every experience it recognizes both the reward and the punishment stimulus. What these are at any given moment varies from species to species. And not all stimuli are associated by an animal in the same way. If one provokes nausea in rats through drug injection, they will associate this with the food they have previously eaten and not with aural and visual stimuli received at the same time. They do, on the other hand, associate sensations of pain with such stimuli. This type of selective associating calls for particular phylogenetic adaptations (*65*).

Animals turn out to have special abilities for learning; for the thing to be learned, the point in time when it is learned, as well as the ability to retain it. Thus certain birds have to learn their songs, yet some of them recognize innately what they are "supposed to" imitate. If one plays them tape recordings of different songs they choose as a model the song of their own species. Learning often takes place only at a specific period of receptiveness, and once learned it is retained. For example, many birds learn the object of sexual activity in early youth, long before they have reached sexual maturity. Jackdaws and turkey-cocks originally reared by hand later make courtship displays at humans, even when they have subsequently been living with conspecifics (*178*).

Immelmann (*102*) had male zebra finches reared by "Bengalese finches" (striated finches). After three months he separated them from their foster parents and put them together with females of their own species, with whom they finally mated. Only after this did he conduct an experiment in which the male zebra finches were allowed to choose between females of their own species and Bengalese finches. Then it became clear that the lesson learned during the short period of their rearing was the stronger one, for the zebra finches from now on chose Bengalese finches as mates.

Man is similarly talented in his learning in quite special ways, the most striking being his ability for learning language. We also find that man is especially responsive to specific environmental influences at particular phases of his ontogenetic development. In man's development there are sensitive periods in which certain basic ethical and aesthetic attitudes become fixated as in imprinting, as for example "primitive trust" (*Urvertrauen*) (see p. 223). If such a period is allowed to pass unfulfilled, then this can lead to lasting damage (see p. 219). On the other hand man's readiness to become fixated on attitudes as in imprinting is also highly dangerous, and the quite proper question arises of whether it is right to fixate children politically and religiously by means of education.

"In order to be fair to children," writes Hans Hass (*82*) "up to their sixteenth year one ought to teach them only those ethical beliefs which are universally held. One should warn them of the danger of premature fixation and explain to them that the decision is theirs and theirs alone and must one day be made by themselves—even if they take a stand opposed to their own parents and society. For the moment, naturally, that is a utopian idea. But perhaps there are hints of such a development which can already be discerned in modern youth" [p. 206].

Many of man's dispositions to learn point to his ancient heritage. Chimpanzees threaten by banging noisy objects. In the wild they use their own "drumming trees"; in captivity they beat against metal doors developing individual skills in this. Jane van Lawick-Goodall (*132, 133*), who lived for many months in a chimpanzee area of East Africa, observed how one of the males in her relatively tame chimpanzee group managed to put on an impressive display with empty petrol cans. He struck them, pushed them along before him, and finally managed to use three empty cans at once. This enhanced his status enormously. Since each chimpanzee certainly learns his own particular drumming method, and since he will eventually learn it one way or another, whether he grows up in a zoo or wild, one may deduce an innate learning disposition, perhaps in the form of special innate releasing mechanisms which enable the animal to know when it does the "correct" thing from the point of view of preservation of the species. Percussive musical instruments are among the oldest used by men. We, too, readily use them for threatening and display (e.g., war drums); for this reason it is natural enough to suppose an innate learning disposition that we inherited from our primate ancestors.

Ancient primate behavior must quite often have been retained in man in the form of innate learning dispositions. Thus, guardian figures designed to ward off demons and showing a phallic display are widespread among the most varied cultures. For this reason these figures were often wrongly interpreted as fertility spirits, until their protective function was recognized (*56, 214*). What is interesting is that male genital presentation as a territorial threat and demonstration of dominance is a behavior pattern common among various primates. When a group of vervet monkeys is feeding, several males always sit and keep watch with their backs to the group and display their vividly colored genitals. If an unknown member of the species approaches, the "guards" have an erection. (In many primates in captivity one can see the same thing if one approaches the cage and so provokes a threat.) These "guards" presenting their genitals play the part of living frontier posts. Apart from their genitals, they also make a display of a threatening face. In its origin this behavior can very likely be explained as a ritualized threat to mount. In very many mammals, mounting by males is a demonstration of dominance, which is also shown on occasion by females toward lower-ranking conspecifics. This can also be established as a tendency in man. A. Festetics (in a verbal communication) has told me that Hungarian shepherd boys rape male strangers who enter their territory. Kosinski in a novel (*116*) writes the same thing of Polish shepherd boys. In July 1962, according to newspaper reports, the victorious Algerians humiliated the French Consul by assaulting him sexually. The initiation rites of French youth gangs include the leader having anal coitus with the aspirants (Roumajon cited by Wickler) (*217*). In this connection the initiation ceremonies at some American colleges are noteworthy. Aspirants to one fraternity at Cornell have to undress in a dark room and stand with their backs to the seniors. They are told to bend over in what amounts to a presentation of the backside. They come to this ceremony bringing a four-and-a-half-inch nail which they grease with petroleum jelly and then hand over to the seniors. When they bend over, they hold out their hands to receive the nails back again, but are given instead a can of beer. The light is then switched on and a drinking bout begins (*203*). In scuffles between young men one can sometimes observe mounting from behind, embracing and, on occasion, powerful thrusting with the loins. All this points to the fact that mounting is a gesture of dominance and threat for us. It is possible that self-exposure is derived from it, for investigations show that many pathological exhibitionists are in no way disturbed in their sexual behavior. This exhibitionism, normally suppressed in men, is manifest in many male fashions (*218*). Thus the original behavior pattern generally seems to underlie what is now a behavioral rudiment (see p. 33), but the tendency continues to be expressed in a number of ways, some of them cultural.

People in the most varied cultures carve figures that display a threatening face and an erect penis. These are set up as guardian figures at the entrances of houses, in the fields, in the interiors of houses. Such figures are known from both the Old and New Worlds, from Africa, Asia, and Polynesia, but they have mostly been wrongly interpreted. I collected them on Bali and discovered in the process that these so-called "fertility spirits" in reality served to protect the house and the fields. Recently I acquired some small amulets in Japan which might well be taken for fertility charms, especially since they can be bought at temples during fertility festivals. Many of these amulets display a threatening face, and if one opens a panel in the back one discovers a carved penis in a little shrine. Orderly as the Japanese are, they write on the back what the amulet offers protection against—for example, "against car accidents." The protective function once again. Even nowadays, it seems, all unpleasant occurrences are the fault of evil spirits (Fig. 8)!

Thus, ancient innate dispositions can even be discovered in cult objects. A lot more in our cultural manifestations may be similarly predetermined. We do not yet know about these matters—and an open field offers itself for comparative research.

For all the incompleteness of our knowledge one thing is already proven: the theory that man is shaped by his environment alone does not hold good. Man, especially in his social behavior, is preprogrammed to a decisive extent. A whole series of motor patterns are innate to him as inherited coordinations (fixed action patterns). He is equipped with drive mechanisms and with innate releasing mechanisms that permit him to recognize specific releasing stimulus situations before he has any experience of them, and to respond to them in a manner that contributes to the survival of the species. Nor can he be as easily influenced through just any kind of learning. Phylogenetic adaptations determine the direction and limits of

Fig. 8. The phallic threat in primates: left: Papuan with penis sheath; right: hamadryas baboon sitting on guard; below: guardian figures from Bali; bottom: phallic protective amulets from Japan (from specimens belonging to the author—see also I. Eibl-Eibesfeldt and W. Wickler, 1968, and I. Eibl-Eibesfeldt, 1970).

the adaptive modifiability of his behavior. Drives, learning dispositions, and innate releasing mechanisms can influence man's inclinations in a quite decisive way. How far this applies to his social behavior in particular is what I shall try to establish in the following chapters. Despite his phylogenetic adaptations, man is rightly described as a cultural being. For it is chiefly by means of cultural patterns that he exercises control over his innate drives. In animals the case is quite different. Their discharge controls too are generally subordinated innately to a system of drives. But in the course of man's genesis the innate discharge controls were clearly reduced to a secondary status, while the drives remained intact. The replacement of innate controls by cultural ones meant a gain in adaptability. An Eskimo needs different arrangements for the diversion of aggressive or sexual impulses from a Masai or a modern city-dweller. Man's freedom from rigid innate patterns enables him to make himself at home in different environments. And cultural controls can also be adapted more quickly to changes in the conditions of life. We ourselves live in an age in which we are searching for new formulas to govern our drives. The old ones are undoubtedly no longer suited to the situation of mass society, and this is shown by the disorders in human social behavior we observe today.

3
Phylogeny and Ritualization

MECHANISMS OF EVOLUTION

Every organism has a long "phylogeny," or evolutionary history, behind it and many of its characteristics can be explained and understood only if we know the course its evolution has taken. Today we are well informed about the development of animals' physical characters thanks to research in comparative anatomy and the interpretation of fossil finds. The fact of evolution is generally acknowledged. But we are still debating whether the principle of mutation and selection is in itself sufficient to explain rapid evolution, or if we ought not to assume other additional evolutionary factors. The question also arises of whether some kind of direction-giving factors lie behind phylogenetic development and furthermore whether, in the field of behavior, one can assume a continuous evolutionary process right up to man himself.

If we survey the course of evolution on the basis of the fossils, the first thing we discover is that out of all the animal species alive during the Paleozoic era only a small percentage have living descendants today. The majority have died out. Again and again the current of life has strayed up evolutionary dead ends, which certainly gives the impression of a blind process of trial and error. Comparative anatomy and physiology further teach us that all organisms carry their history around with them as "historical burdens." They are the product of countless restructurings. Land vertebrates that evolved from aquatic vertebrates reconstructed their blood circulation, but did not conceive it completely afresh. Technically better solutions could be imagined (*119*). Equipment which is no longer used wastes away into an often troublesome rudimentary organ.

Today we are very well informed about the mechanism of evolution. As long ago as Darwin it was established that parents transmit their characteristics to their descendants, but that in the process there is a certain amount of dispersion. Not all the offspring of a pair are identical. Some prove to be better adapted to specific demands of the environment than their siblings, and consequently will be more successful in competition with them and produce more offspring, while the less well-adapted ones are subject to a process of negative selection and leave fewer offspring. In this way the evolution of a species is propelled in the direction of better adaptation. Thus every genetic variation which carries with it an advantage in the selection process is *adaptive*. An adaptation *results* from this process; adaptation is not the product of a development directed toward a particular end.

The chemical bases of heredity are the deoxyribonucleic acids (DNA) of the cell nucleus, which consists of two long chains of components intertwined with one another. Each component is in its turn made up of a sugar molecule, a phosphate group, and one of the four bases: adenin (A), guanin (G), cytosin (C) and thymin (T). Both of the DNA chains are linked together via this base so that A and T and C and G always combine in complementary fashion. The linear sequence of these base pairs represents the text in which the organism's blueprint—or set of instructions for development—is set down. They control the protein synthesis of the cells, which in this way translates the text into characters. Each variation in the linear sequence of the bases means a variation in the genetic blueprint. Variations (or mutations) take place in the most different directions, but the rate of mutations is never very high so that the species remains relatively constant and holds onto what is already tried and tested. On the other hand, sufficient new genetic variations are "tried out" as individuals that carry the mutant hereditary tendencies enter into competition with the rest. The deviation of the mutant animal from the norm can be considerable. In fruit fly populations, wingless individuals crop up spontane-

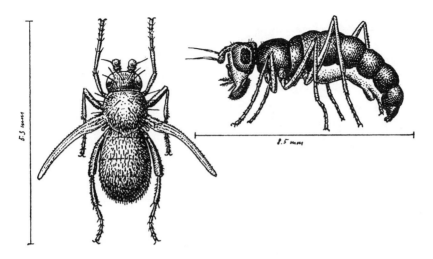

Fig. 9. Flies from Kerguolen incapable of flight. Left: Amalopteryx
maritima; *right:* Calycopteryx moseleyi (*from C. Chun,* Aus den Tie-
fen des Weltmeeres, *Jena, 1903*).

ously again and again. Mutants of this type are generally not
competitively viable. But on occasion even sports like this may
have a chance. On the windswept Kerguelen Islands are flies
and butterflies incapable of flight. No insects capable of flight
live there—they would be far too easily blown away by the wind
(Fig. 9). In these quite exceptional conditions those insects incapable of flight prove to be the better "adapted." Thus all the
mutations which led to winglessness were of positive selective
value. In the course of generations the mutants in this direction
have prevailed. We can see similar processes at work elsewhere.
The peppered moth settles on the trunks of birch trees with
outspread wings, blending into them remarkably well because
of its light coloration. Darker colored individuals sometimes
occur, but on the light stems they stand out and are therefore
quickly caught by birds. In areas of England, the Industrial
Revolution brought changes to the environment. The sooty
tree trunks are dark and here it is the light-colored moths that
stand out. The darker ones, on the other hand, now escape the
predator and survive. In some districts today dark peppered
moths are predominant (Fig. 10). It is in this way that selection

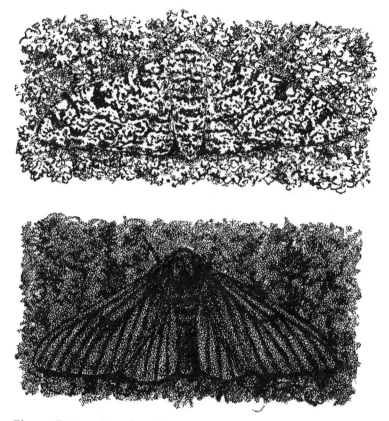

Fig. 10. Peppered moths. Above: normal form on birch bark; below: the dark variety that survives in sooty industrial areas.

determines what is adaptive in a given situation. Selection determines the course taken by evolution, while mutations, though they follow their own inner laws, occur quite haphazardly in relation to external circumstances.

Every environment offers possibilities of existence to a whole range of living organisms. In the gardens of Central Europe, for example, insectivorous robins live side by side with blackbirds that eat fruit and pull up worms not accessible to the robins. Then there are lesser spotted woodpeckers that peck insects, which no other birds can get at, out of the bark of trees. Through this specialization they avoid competition with other insect-eaters. In the same garden there would also be room for a seed-eating chaffinch and finally a hawfinch that cracks hard-shelled seeds and nuts which again no other bird can do. Each of the species listed here will be represented in a garden only in limited numbers, for the food supply is limited. Nevertheless specialization in feeding habits enables very many more birds to exist side by side than if all had the same diet. There are to some extent a fixed number of "vacancies" or ecological "niches" than an animal can fill by cultivating the appropriate forms of adaptation, competition being the decisive factor. A good example of this is provided by the Darwin (or Galápagos) finches of the Galápagos Islands (*47, 129*). They are descended from a common ancestral form that migrated there before there were any other passerine birds as competitors. The original form spread over the Islands and under the stimulating influence of geographic isolation developed into seed-eaters, insect-eaters, plant-eaters—and even a woodpecker finch that grubs insects out of branches just like a lesser spotted woodpecker. It has a straight beak like a woodpecker. All it lacks is the long tongue with which woodpeckers extract their food out of the insects' bore-holes or "galleries." It compensates for this lack by using a tool. When it has opened an insect's gallery it flies to the nearest cactus, breaks off a spine, holds it lengthwise in its beak, and pokes out the insect.* The various species of Darwin finch still resemble one another closely, which makes their close relationship clear. The only marked difference lies in the shape of their beaks, which reflects their various feeding specializations (Figs. 11 and 12).

All such processes of speciation (or variation within a species) are due to a genetic variability that ultimately takes place through random mutation. Some biologists find it hard to accept that phylogenetic development, which has created so many wonderful adaptive forms, is nothing more than the blind workings of the principle of mutation and selection. But so far we know of no other way. It is conceivable that adaptations achieved by individuals may also have had an effect on the heredity of a species and thus have brought about rapid adap-

* I have published a detailed account of the Darwin finches and a photographic documentation of the use of the tool in my book *Galápagos*.

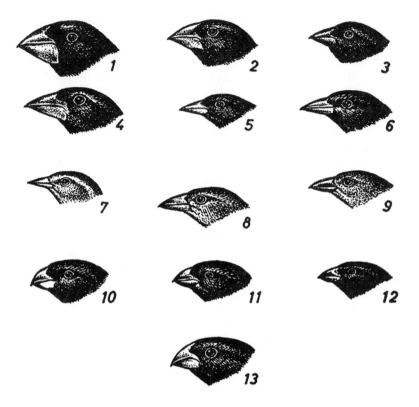

Fig. 11. The beak shapes of the Darwin finches of the Galápagos Islands reflect their different feeding habits. The large, medium, and small ground-finches (1, 2 and 3), for example, feed on seeds of various sizes. Like the European hawfinch the large ground-finch can also crack seeds with hard shells, which none of the others can tackle. The following list gives a survey of the various specializations: Omnivorous with preference for vegetable food: *1. Large ground-finch* (Geospiza magnirostris); *2. Medium ground-finch* (G. fortis); *3. Small ground-finch* (G. fulginosa); *4. Large cactus ground-finch* (G. conirostris); *5. Sharp-beaked ground-finch* (G. difficilis); *6. Cactus ground-finch* (G. scandens). Insectivorous: *7. Warbler-finch* (Certhidea olivacea); *8. Woodpecker-finch* (Catospiza pallida); *9. Mangrove-finch* (Cactospiza heliobates). Omnivorous with preference for insects: *10. Large insectivorous tree-finch* (Camarhynchus psittacula); *11. Medium insectivorous tree-finch* (C. pauper); *12. Small insectivorous tree-finch* (C. parvulus). Herbivorous: *13. Vegetarian tree-finch* (Platyspiza crassirostris) *(from I. Eibl-Eibesfeldt).*

tation by the species to particular environmental circumstances. For this process, however, postulated by the Frenchman Lamarck, we have, as yet, no proof. Indeed it is highly questionable whether in the last analysis such a mechanism would be of advantage to the species. For such a facility for adaptation might well cause species to get caught in evolutionary blind alleys even more easily than they do without it. Ultimately every species has to cope with unpredictable changes in the environment. And it is only because it continues to produce sport by means of its mutation mechanism—including flies that are blind or unable to fly—that all the possibilities are explored. These sports, normally selected out, but which continue to be born free from generation to generation, are to some extent the life insurance of the species. Through them the course of life will flow on, if through drastic environmental changes animals that have hitherto been the best-adapted ever become maladapted. A conscious direction is something we always read into evolution retrospectively; strictly speaking it cannot be proved.

The fact that we are nevertheless drawn toward Lamarckian lines of thought is due to our everyday experience. We know that exercise strengthens our muscles, that the soles of our feet are hardened by running barefoot, and that generally we will learn quickly to adapt to a new situation. We accept these things naïvely as given facts, without realizing that these abili-

Fig. 12. Woodpecker-finch with a cactus spine, probing an insect grub out of its gallery (from photographs by the author).

ties presuppose specific mechanisms which control our adaptability in such a way that it does not occur chaotically in all directions, but that adaptation is the consequence. These mechanisms are themselves a product of phylogenetic development. And it is here that Lamarckism in fact presupposes what it seeks to explain.

"The rationalization" of evolution—in the true sense of the word—is reached in man only with the development of speech and writing. Both give us a certain degree of independence from the laborious mechanism of mutation and selection. Man can first investigate the various possibilities intellectually and then transmit the solutions arrived at orally or in writing. This is decisive progress vis-à-vis the animals, which can also transmit skills but must always rely on showing the other creature the skills to be passed on. Macaques (see p. 59) have learned to wash potatoes by imitation. Man can pass things on independently of objects. He can transmit his instructions in words: he does not even need to speak them himself. He can set them down in writing for all to read. Our accumulative culture, the most essential character of man, is based on these abilities.

But rapid evolution that is culturally directed conceals a danger. Cultures are quickly formed and cut themselves off on the basis of their own particular cultural patterns. These different cultures behave like separate biological species, which is why Erikson (58) has even described them as "pseudo-species." In New Guinea, several hundred dialects are spoken, and in the Alps, where I come from, every fair-sized valley has its own dress and customs and its own "local pride" by means of which the community sets itself apart from the others. This differentiation is, of course, of positive value and certainly no one would want to forgo the cultural variety of mankind. But there is danger in this tendency of groups to fence themselves off, for it is often done in a spirit of hostility. This is even true of the setting up of groups within ethnic groups. The tendency toward "cultural speciation" (sometimes known as "club-formation") mitigates against a wider social cohesion. What must be done through education for tolerance is to eliminate the element of hostility from man's habit of fencing himself off.

INTERPRETING SIMILARITIES

In order to establish criteria for the comparison of behavior patterns and thereby for the reconstruction of phylogenetic courses of development, we must first make an excursion into morphology. The evolutionary genesis of physical traits can primarily be reconstructed in the light of sequences of fossil finds. In this way it has been shown that the forefoot of the horse, with its single hoof, is derived from a limb with five digits. By comparing species living today we can establish even more remote similarities. All vertebrates, for example, despite otherwise quite varied modes of life, reveal fundamentally the same structure in their axial skeletons, internal organs, and central nervous systems. And within this group of animals one can in turn group together fishes, amphibians, reptiles, birds, and mammals as each forming natural classes on the basis of characteristics they have in common. These five classes of vertebrate each have their own relationships with one another. By many characteristics, birds are more closely related to reptiles than to mammals. Even if we had not found the missing link, the archaeopteryx, in the limestone of Solnhofen, Bavaria, we could have assumed a relationship between the two classes and trace the birds back to reptilian ancestors.

According to the degree of similarity it is possible to deduce a closer or more distant relationship between animals. By classifying types of animals according to the characteristics they have in common, we can obtain a kind of family tree, if at the same time we adopt the hypothesis that the greater the number of species that have a character in common the older it is. And the hypothesis that the commonest characters are also the oldest is confirmed by fossil discoveries.

As every schoolboy knows, Charles Darwin first became convinced of the fact of speciation—variation within a species—through the comparison of animal species living today. On the Galápagos Islands he saw the finches now named after him and interpreted their striking similarity as a sign of a natural relationship.

But not every similarity indicates a genetic relationship.

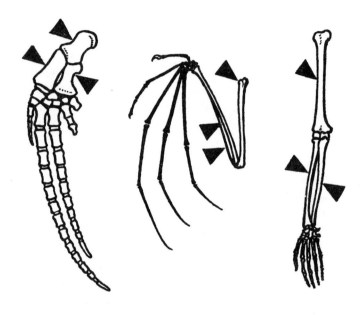

Fig. 13. The relationship between the forelimbs of the whale, bat, and man which are outwardly extremely dissimilar is revealed in the bone formation. Upper arm bone, ulna, and radius can be demonstrated to be homologous elements in each case.

There are also parallels that are explained only by a similarity of function. An animal that has to move through the water develops a body shape that offers the water as little resistance as possible. Fishes, penguins, ichthyosauri, and whales developed their outward similarity parallel yet independently of one another, for they were subject to the same selective pressures. Similarities of this kind are known as analogies, to distinguish them from homologies, which are based on a common genetic link (Figs. 13 and 14).

The situation is often complicated by the fact that adaptations with a common genetic basis may develop independently, as for example the flippers of ichthyosauri, penguins, sea turtles, and whales. Viewed as flippers these characters are analogous, but from the viewpoint of their original structure as land vertebrates' limbs they are also homologous.

How does one differentiate in practice between homologies and analogies? The similarity of the particular form will indicate only a relationship if the structure is complicated and if it occurs within a related group of animals, even in species with quite different ways of life. In such cases analogous development is less likely, though even then it is not ruled out. The criterion of outward similarity will suffice only in the rarest cases to prove that two species are related. One must generally look for further "criteria of homology." Thus the skull bones of many vertebrates are often quite differently shaped. The nasal bone can be long and narrow or short and broad, but from their particular positions in relation to the other bones of the skull one can always identify nasal bones, temporal bones, intermaxillary bones, etc., in different species and recognize them as homologous. A homology is ultimately proved by the existence of intermediate forms as exist, for example, in the sequence of fossil horses.

From such criteria one is in a position to identify physical characteristics as homologous, so that the statement that a characteristic is homologous to that of another animal also signifies a genetic relationship between the two animals and inheritance from a common ancestor.

But if one now turns to the behavior of closely related animal species one becomes equally aware of similarities. For example,

Fig. 14. The mole and the mole-cricket have evolved their digging legs independently of one another as adaptations to life in the earth. (Figs. 13 and 14 from K. Lorenz, Darwin hat doch recht gesehen, *Pfullingen, 1965.)*

almost all male ducks show as a courtship movement the behavior patterns described as the "grunt-whistle" and "head-up–tail-up," while the females show "inciting" behavior. The movements are so typical that one recognizes them every time, although there are slight variations from species to species. They always fall into groups that are as characteristic of particular classification systems as physical characters. And this is not particularly surprising, for ultimately physical structures are at the basis of behavior patterns, which can be traced back to the physiological functioning of the structures. Being patterns in time, behavior patterns show a greater degree of freedom than physical characteristics. They occur with different forms of intensity and are superposed, or overlaid, in different combinations. Thus various innate expressive movements can be superposed on one another in differing degrees of intensity, which produces a great wealth of expression, as Lorenz (*139*) has shown with the facial expressions of dogs (Fig. 15). The investigation of innate behavior patterns is made more difficult by the fact that they are not always observable. Nevertheless, by means of film and tape recording they can be converted into material that is available at any time. In order to interpret similarities one uses the morphologists' criteria for identifying the homology already described: (1) the similarity of the particular form (or in this case of the motor pattern); (2) the similarity of position of the pattern within the whole (in this case within the whole behavioral sequence); and (3) the criterion of linkage by intermediate forms.* With the help of this last criterion one can identify as homologous behavior patterns which are in themselves dissimilar.

Thus a comparison of courtship behavior in the pheasant family shows that the peacock's courtship is homologous to the food-enticing behavior of the domestic cock, and has evolved from the food-enticing of a common ancestor (*179*). A domestic cock attracts hens to himself like a hen attracting her chicks. He scratches the ground a few times, then steps backward and pecks at the ground while emitting sounds to attract the females. If he

---

* But here one is generally limited to the comparison of living species, since fossil traces of behavior patterns are only rarely available to us.

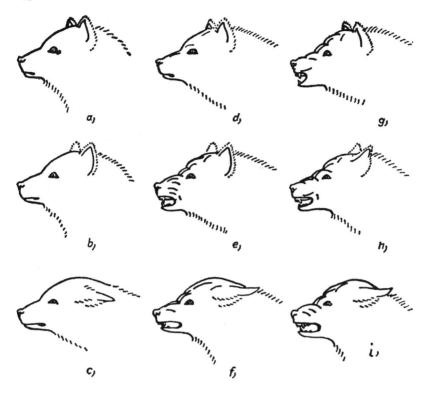

Fig. 15. Different facial expressions of the dog resulting from the superposition of differing intensities of fighting and flight intention. From (a) to (c) vertically: increasing readiness to flee; from (a) to (g) horizontally: increasing aggression; the other drawings show the corresponding combinations (from K. Lorenz, 1952).

finds a crumb of food he picks it up and lets it fall again. Often he only pretends to have found food and shows the hen pebbles instead, but even this symbolic enticement with food leads to success. The hen hurries up and searches in front of the cock. The courting ring-necked pheasant attracts his hens in a similar manner and so does the impeyan pheasant, which bows deeply before the hen and pecks hard at the ground. If the hen is attracted and searches in front of him, he spreads his wings and tail feathers, keeps his head down, and remains still. Only his fanned-out tail bows slowly and rhythmically up and down.

The peacock pheasant scratches on the ground like a food-enticing domestic cock and bows before the hen. If she draws closer to him, he moves his head rapidly backward and forward in her direction. If he is given food, he offers it to the hen, which one can interpret as ritualized feeding. Normally he does not feed her; nevertheless, the hen still pecks on the ground in front of him. The peacock, finally, simply spreads his tail feathers, shakes them, and takes a few steps backward. He then bows his fanned-out tail forward and holds his neck upstretched with the beak pointing downward. The hen comes running up to search on the ground at the focal point of the "concave mirror" formed by his tail-fan. When they spread their tails, young peacocks still entice by scratching and pecking—a piece of evidence for the interpretation of the peacock's courtship as ritualized food enticement. If one knew neither the linking intermediate forms nor the less ritualized youthful stages of the peacock's courtship, then one would scarcely deduce a derivation from food enticement (Fig. 16).

Behavioral similarities can result from some particular function. Most birds drink by dipping their beaks into water, filling them, and then raising their heads to swallow the water. But independently of one another a number of birds from dry regions have evolved a way of drinking by sucking. Zebra finches, sandgrouse, and others keep their beaks immersed and suck up the water, with their esophagus acting as a pump. Here we are dealing with genuine analogies in behavior (*214*). Behavior patterns that occur in care of the young are time and again ritualized by different birds and mammals quite independently of one another into gestures of appeasement, which are used by the adult animals in courtship and greeting. It is noteworthy that, again quite independently of this, even in social insects (bees and ants) the feeding of the young has become a bond-forming gesture. Once the feeding of the young is evolved within a group of animals then it is to some extent on the cards that this cherishing behavior pattern will be generally adopted as a friendly gesture. In most cases receptive arrangements are developed in the young animal that enable it to recognize the brood-care behavior of the parent animal as friendly behavior (p. 21).

Fig. 16. The derivation of the peacock's courtship from enticement with food. Above left: food-enticing domestic cock; below left: food-enticing ring-necked pheasant; above right: courting impeyan pheasant (left) and peacock pheasant (right); below: courting peacock. The hen, attracted, searches for food on the ground in front of him (from R. Schenkel, 1956).

THE ORIGIN OF RELEASING RITES

Using the example of the courtship of pheasants, we have discussed how behavior patterns of enticement with food gradually became transformed into a purely symbolic action—a signal in the service of courtship. This process is described as "ritualization." Every behavior pattern that accompanies a state of excitation in an animal regularly enough to be characteristic can become the point of departure for such a development. It can then serve to identify an emotional state to another animal. If a girl blushes we know she feels embarrassed, and if someone strikes a table with his clenched fist we know something has annoyed him. Now if it is of advantage to the transmitter of the expression of emotion for another animal to understand him, then this expression will progressively become transformed into a signal through the process of natural selection.

Many mammals twitch their tails in excitement. In the porcupine this gesture has been ritualized into a threatening movement. When threatening it shakes its tail very quickly and all the spines on its tail rattle against one another. The effect is heightened by the fact that, with the differentiation of the movement as a threatening gesture, the spines on the tail have been adapted into hollow rattling-organs. We can trace a similar development in snakes. Here, too, twitching the tail is a widespread expression of excitement. Out of this the rattlesnake has developed both a threatening movement and, in its rattle, an additional organ which emphasizes the movement.

Apart from such accompanying manifestations of excitement, there are also behavior patterns fulfilling a particular function, which are adapted into expressive movements. The evolution of the peacock's courtship from food-enticement, already mentioned, is an example of this. The black woodpecker possesses two expressive movements that are derived from chiseling into wood. As a territorial demarcation signal it drums rapidly on rotten branches, producing a sound that carries a long way. Translated into our language this would mean something like "Men at work here," and rivals thus are warned off. Females, on the other hand, are attracted by it. The second expressive movement is the "signing-off" knock. When a bird has had enough of chiseling it will sit outside the nest-hole entrance and peck slowly and emphatically against the edge of the hole until relieved by its mate (*189*).

A further example we have mentioned is the showing of teeth in monkeys and man as a ritualized threat. Then there are numerous cases of flight and avoidance movements being ritualized as expressive movements. A sand lizard which is submitting to another lies flat on the ground and paddles with its legs. It is,

Fig. 17. Flirting Turkana woman: contact made with the eyes; smile; lowering of the head with eyelids closed as a ritualized form of avoidance ("flight") (from film stills by H. Hass).

Fig. 18. Flirting Samburu girl. She makes contact with the eyes, lowers her eyelids, then looks away. The ritualized flight is confined to the eye movements. It is no more than hinted at in the head movements (from film stills by the author).

as it were, fleeing on the spot and thus expressing its readiness to flee. In the mating foreplay of many mammals the flight of the female is ritualized. This "coy behavior" is an invitation to pursuit. It is also encountered in an especially highly differentiated form in human coquetry. Turning toward a person and then turning away are typical elements of human flirting behavior, in this case most frequently expressed in the language of the eyes. Once a girl has made contact with her eyes, she frequently bows her head and lowers her eyelids. This is often combined with looking away. But then she generally resumes quick contact with her eyes again (Figs. 17 and 18).

When slightly embarrassed, people all over the world hide their faces either partly or completely. This is certainly a ritualized hiding movement (Figs. 19–21). It can also be observed in flirting girls. I have even observed a small boy who had been born blind hiding his face with his hands in embarrassment.

Fig. 19. Three-year-old German girl bashfully hiding behind her hands (coquetry) (from film stills by the author).

In the process of their differentiation into signals, behavior patterns undergo a number of typical modifications (50). They are generally simplified, but at the same time they become exaggerated in the manner of mime. Often the movement is rhythmically repeated, as for example with the drumming of the woodpecker. Expressive movements furthermore frequently occur at a typical degree of intensity, which makes them unmistakable signals. The fact that variable behavioral sequences can be compressed into new rigid motor patterns is shown by the

Fig. 20. Hiding the face in shame. Above: Samoan woman: she was looking at the photo of a young man. Reaction to the remark: "You seem to be very interested in him." Below: Balinese woman: reaction to a compliment (from film stills by the author).

Fig. 21. Move to cover the lower part of the face as a sign of embarrassment. Above: Turkana warrior, after a compliment on his headdress (from film stills by H. Hass); below: Waika warrior: he was flirting with my female companion (by showing his tongue, see p. 143), whereupon his companions teased him (from film stills by the author).

dance of the cleaner fish. The cleaner-wrasse, a native of tropical coral reefs, lives by cleaning other fish; when approaching its hosts it see-saws up and down as it swims. In the course of the fish's phylogeny this behavior pattern has arisen from the conflict between the impulse to swim right up to the host fish and the impulse to escape to the safety of the coral reef (46).

As expressive movements are developed, morphological structures emphasizing the movements develop accordingly. Where the hair bristles in fright, manes often develop; where feathers stand up, ornamental feathers often grow. With ritualization behavior patterns take on a new function, and hand in hand with this goes a change of motivation. Male mounting, which has become a greeting gesture of baboons, is as little sexually motivated as the male genital presentation already mentioned.

Alongside the phylogenetic process there are two further processes of ritualization at work: ontogenetic ritualization, in the course of the development of the young individual; and traditional ritualization, which is transmitted from generation to generation. These two play a particularly significant role in human beings. The formal sequence of ritualization in movements acquired through such learning processes is similar to that of phylogenetic ritualization. For these movements are also exaggerated in pantomime and accentuated through additional equipment. Simplification and rhythmical repetition can also be observed here and there. We should not be surprised at such similarities, for the requirements of the receiver of a signal are constant, whether it is a question of phylogenetic, traditional, or ontogenetic ritualization. For the way a signal evolves is dictated by the receiver. The receiver is the one who recognizes the meaning of a particular behavior pattern in his partner and in so doing elevates it to the status of a signal.

We can find examples of ontogenetic ritualization in the begging movements of zoo animals. If a movement is repeatedly rewarded with feeding by the spectators then the animal learns to approach visitors with such movements. Generally it is a question of intention movements: seizing, scrapping, snapping, or licking, which are then repeated especially emphatically and rhythmically. Sometimes, however, animals invent more out-of-the-way movements. In the bear pit at Berne I have seen a bear that always turned round lengthways on the spot when it wanted something. Another sat on the ground, with hindlegs outstretched and its forepaws hooked onto its toes, rocking back and forth with its mouth open.

In the case of human beings traditional rites play an important social role. It is true that our repertoire of facial expressions is essentially innate. We do not need to learn how to laugh and cry. But much is also passed on to us culturally. Thus the Ceylonese indicate that they are ready to do something by a slight sideways swaying of the head. A European has to learn this particular form of affirmation.* In Greece one says "no" by tossing one's head upward and back with the eyes almost closed. For an emphatic negative either one or both hands are raised with the palms toward the interlocutor, just as Central Europeans do for an angry refusal. Probably this particular form of negation is derived from a general human gesture of social refusal. Central Europeans, along with many other peo-

ples, have ritualized the sideways head shake of refusal into
"No." Most things in our gestures are shaped by tradition, but
often an innate basis can be proved. Similarities between expressive movements and other signals can also be produced by
innate preferences in the receiver of the signal (cf. the example
of the emphasizing of shoulders, p. 18).

It is, for example, universally comprehensible that a man's
intentions are friendly if he emphatically lays down his weapons
or at least "presents" them so that they offer no threat to the
other person. When an armed man gives a greeting he will
therefore be doing the same thing in principle everywhere in
the world. But the form the sequence takes can of course be
different. For a military salute a European presents arms. A
Masai, greeting another, thrusts his spear into the ground in
front of him. A Waika Indian with friendly intentions holds
bow and arrow in the same hand; the medieval knight would
put aside his weapons before approaching a strange castle; and
even today a soldier will lay down his weapons when he enters
a house as a guest. The rites of gift-giving to establish and confirm friendly relations are numerous (see p. 142).

As with innate dispositions, which determine the form taken
by cultural rites, parallels can also be seen in the display dances
of men in different cultures. These are always demonstrations
of strength and follow a pattern that is essentially the same: the
dancer stamps on the ground, leaps high in the air and often
also brandishes weapons. A Tyrolean dancer, a Scotsman doing
the Highland fling, a Cossack dancer, and a Turkana warrior
are fundamentally showing off in the same way. Gardner's sensations photos (*71, 72*) of Papuans at war show that the warriors in the front line indulge in similar displays of strength
(Fig. 22).

The formation of traditional rites follows the same pattern
as that of phylogenetic rites. Behavior patterns are simplified

* Affirmation on a matter of fact is conveyed among the Ceylonese, as
among ourselves, by nodding the head. For example, if one asks: "Do you
drink coffee?" a nod of the head indicates a positive answer. But if one
asks: "Shall we have a drink of coffee?" (or "come and have some coffee")
then assent is given by a swaying of the head. A negative answer is given
by shaking the head, as with us.

to become mere symbols. The knight's removal of his helmet as a greeting gesture becomes the momentary raising of the hat, the lifting up of the visor becomes the hand on the cap brim in the military salute. Movements are once again exaggerated theatrically; one has only to think of the ritualized forms of walking in the military march (intended as a show of strength), or in the measured tread of the presidents of colleges on solemn occasions (intended as a demonstration of dignity). In the ritualized washings of Indians in the Ganges quite specific components of the act of washing are carried out repeatedly in a simplified and at the same time exaggerated form. In the process one observes the compression of movements into new units. The same is also true of ritualization in speech. Only the initiated will recognize in the *"Hawidjere"* of the Viennese the old greeting formula: *"Habe die Ehre"* ("I have the honor") and

Fig. 22. *Threatening in human and its cultural ritualization in the dance. Left: Papuan threatening in front of his enemies (Dugum Dani), from a photograph by M. C. Rockefeller, in R. Garner and K. G. Heidner. Right: Cossack dancer (from a front-page picture for* Bunte Illustrierte *magazine* 49, 1965*).*

in *"Gschamster Diener," "Ihr gehorsamster Diener"* ("your most obedient servant"), or in the English "good-bye," the original phrase "God be with you."

Among many peoples one comes across the use of spitting as a magic charm, even among Central Europeans. We spit into our hands before beginning a task. This is not, surely, so as to get a better grip but in order to bring us luck in our endeavors. All that generally remains is the gesture.

Like expressive movements in animals, human rituals are also basically signals. They signal power, submission, friendship, and the like. A very important function of rituals is group cohesion. Human groups evolve customs with the help of which they distinguish themselves from others. We shall discuss this complex in greater detail later on.

We can therefore summarize: behavior patterns can be compared with one another, just like morphological structures, and if one takes as a basis the criteria used by morphology to identify homologies one can reconstruct their phylogenetic evolution. Many similarities of behavior, however, are explained by similar environmental demands. These analogous behavior patterns are similar in different species because they fulfill similar functions and are not necessarily a sign of common genetic origin. In the process of ritualization, behavior patterns are turned into signals (expressive movements), often accompanied by the development of special physical structures. The original behavior patterns thereby undergo modifications designed to make the signal striking and unmistakable. This is also true of signals that arise in the process of cultural ritualization.

4

The Advantages of Sociability

Some animals live in groups, some are out-and-out loners, but often an animal species is both sociable and aggressive at the same time. As both tendencies have evolved phylogenetically, it makes sense to inquire into the advantages of each in the selection process.

The advantages an animal derives from social combination vary considerably. The Mexican *Leiobunum cactorum* (a species of harvester) cluster together in the dry season in bundles of thousands. In this way they protect themselves against drying out. Animals that become separated from their fellows will quickly seek to rejoin the group. Particular scents attract them to their own kind (*210*). The emperor penguins of the Antarctic survive the severe winter storms by huddling close together to reduce their heat loss. In this way they withstand gales of over 60 mph and temperatures of −76° F. (*165*).

Most fish in the upper ocean live in shoals. Their urge to be with their conspecifics is patently very strong, for individuals that have lost the shoal dart this way and that in a panic in their efforts to rejoin it. Particular signals, for example black markings on the dorsal or caudal fins, ensure that they keep together. These groups are open, and any member of the species can join. They are, moreover, anonymous: the members of a shoal of fish do not generally know one another individually. First and foremost the shoal of fish is a defensive grouping against predators. This may come as a surprise, for at first sight it might seem as if the concentration of so many fish in one place would make it easier for a predatory fish to capture its prey. But this is not the case. Before making its catch, a predatory fish must come right up to its prey and be able to focus on it. Before it can focus on one particular fish in a shoal, however, the latter has generally plunged back among the others and the predator must switch its attention to another. This constant alteration of targets confuses it, and this confusion in turn protects the prey. In the Indian Ocean and off the Galápagos Islands I have observed predatory fish employing special tactics in an attempt to cut off individual fish from the shoal. Once they succeeded in this the predators had no further difficulty in taking the isolated fish out of the clear water (*44, 46*).

Birds flock for similar reasons; in addition, they will help one another in danger by banding together to mob a bird of prey. Associations of higher vertebrates and insects are also generally defense communities. Jackdaws will attack a dog with a jackdaw in its mouth. Rhesus monkeys and baboons attack anything that seizes a young one. Its cry of help is a signal that releases an attack as a simple reflex action. My marmosets, which are completely tame, attack and threaten me if their young emit a cry of fear. As the little monkeys are very curious to explore me and cry out when they have frightened themselves with their own curiosity, I am the quite innocent target of such attacks. Defense against enemies is an important factor leading to the development of groups of animals. Protection and defense of the young certainly came before true parental care (i.e., feeding and cleansing of the young). In almost all fish and all reptiles which nurture their young, this care is limited to defense against enemies. In the simplest cases one of the adults remains with the offspring; indeed, often both parents remain together for the joint defense of the young—even in the case of fish. This is one of the roots of lasting pair formation, which in extreme cases can be maintained for life. There can, however, be partnerships without brood tending. Butterfly fish, for example, remain together for life, perhaps because in the case of rare fish in the vast spaces of a reef, the chances of finding one another again are too small (*217*).

A further advantage of social combination is that it makes possible the division of labor. The male can take over the defense of the young and the female the tasks of feeding, cleaning, and keeping them warm. Wolves that live in packs hunt together, some of them overtaking and cutting off the prey while the rest of the pack pursue and seize the prey. The division of labor attains its most sophisticated form in insect states. In these, different castes arise, each with different tasks. Among the leaf-cutting ants of tropical South America, for example, we find three different worker castes: the largest workers defend the nest as soldiers, the medium-sized workers cut and transport the pieces of leaf, and the minima workers, the smallest, process these leaves into compost for the fungi from which these agricultural ants live. In addition, the minima workers accompany the medium-sized workers and protect them at their work from the attacks of the parasitic flies that try to lay eggs on their necks. When the cut leaves are being transported, the minima themselves ride on the piece of leaf to defend the carrier (*53*). Such division of labor permits extreme specialization and thereby increased efficiency. The same is also true of human society.

Life in the group also makes possible the creation of traditions. In various apes and monkeys an individual's inventions are imitated by others and retained for generations by means of tradition. When the macaques of Koshima Island (Japan) were fed with sweet potatoes one female discovered that it was possible to wash off the earth sticking to them. The others imitated her and now this habit is a group-specific character (*104, 107, 108*). The monkeys of this region were also fed on corn which was scattered on the shore. In the beginning, they picked up the grains individually until the female that had discovered how to wash potatoes also found out how to scoop up the mixture of sand and grain and wash it in the water. This discovery too was taken over in the course of time by other members of the group. In Kyoto a female learned to warm herself by the open fire, as the guards did. After a short time all the members of the group were doing it. Even among chimpanzees living in the wild there are group-specific habits passed on by tradition. The members of a family or larger group will often help one another to the point of self-sacrifice; short of that they will often do many things not directly in their individual interest. This raises the question of the evolution of altruistic behavior. Can it be explained by the principle of selection?

The answer must be yes. For in the case of social animals we should not so much think of the individual animal as of the group, in which the hereditary tendencies of the individual animal are in any case contained. A group in which individuals will sacrifice themselves, and their lives if need be, for the defense of the group or of their young will transmit its inheritance more successfully than a group that produces no individuals ready to defend it. For the same reason, although individuals that, for example, snatch food away from the others or fight without restraint will have certain immediate advantages within their group, they will weaken the group as a whole and will put it at a disadvantage in competition with other groups. Brutal, antisocial variants may at first prevail within a group, but their genome is less successful. For example, should a mutant occur in a bird population which causes a young bird to push all its siblings out of the nest, then this individual alone will survive and most probably produce offspring. The pushers among the offspring will, in turn, not only push nonpushers out of the nest, but each other as well. Thus, on the average, only one or two birds will survive, a number too low for the species to survive predation and accidents. For this reason these mutants will never prevail within the population (*215*).

Groupings of animals can be classified into two major categories according to whether they are open or closed. Open groups are those in which the members will permit others, not previously belonging to the group, to join. The members of an open group do not generally know one another; they are also interchangeable at any time. An example of an open group we have cited is the shoal of fish.

A closed group, on the other hand, is an intolerant entity. Strange conspecifics are not automatically admitted to the group; if they attempt to join they are repulsed. This means that the members of the group recognize one another either individually or by means of a distinguishing mark specific to all members of the group. On occasion an intolerant group is simulated, as in the case of the blind *Typhlogobius californiensis,* a species of Goby, in which two fish of different sexes defend a common territory. The male fights every other male of the species and the female equally fights all other females. These fish have nothing against other fish of the opposite sex, however, and one partner can be substituted for another without much ado. The situation is quite different in the case of the authentically conjugal teleost fish, for example the anemone fish (*Amphiprion xanthurus*), where male and female are aggressive toward every conspecific and tolerate only the sexual partner known to them individually (*216*).

In many fish, birds, and mammals that live in pairs the young are looked after by both parents. When they become independent they can leave the group. The pair-bond is sometimes broken at the same time, but often the pair remain together as a nuclear family. If the young remain with their parents, extended family groups are created, the members of which frequently know one another individually.

Family groups sometimes grow into lineages in which several generations are combined. Such extended families can still remain individualized groups up to a certain size and in this case will show complicated social hierarchies (see p. 85). But if the group grows beyond a certain size, it generally exceeds the capacity of the individual animal to recognize group members as individuals. In such cases members recognize one another by a common sign. Rats mark one another with urine and thus create a common group scent. If one removes a rat from a group and puts it back again three days later, it will be attacked because it has lost the group scent in the meantime. Conversely a strange rat will be accepted if one smears it with the urine of different members of the group to which it is a stranger. In this case we are dealing with anonymous closed groups. Up to a certain point human beings live both in individualized and in anonymous groups of varying degrees of exclusivity (see p. 225) (*50*).

A brief survey shows that combination into groups brings various advantages. The evolution of altruistic behavior makes complete sense on Darwinian principles. Even mutual aid to the point of self-sacrifice of the individual is of species-preserving value. Among vertebrates the development of altruistic behavior must be of relatively recent date in the history of the earth. It is true that such behavior can be observed in fish, but only among the group of teleost fish, itself very young in the history of the earth. In amphibians and reptiles altruistic behavior patterns seem to be limited to a few rare cases of defense and carrying of the young. Adults never help one another. There are certainly a few "gregarious" reptiles, but if one observes these animals more closely one sees no friendly interaction of any kind. The marine iguanas of the Galápagos Islands, for example, often lie in hundreds beside and on top of one another on the rocks, but the only social contact they make with their fellows is limited to an occasional threat: even their courtship consists of modified threatening behavior. They neither groom one another, feed one another, nor help one another in time of danger; there is no individualized bond. In most birds and mammals there is a fundamental difference. They help one another and will look after one another with a whole range of affectionate behavior patterns. With their capacity for cooperation and for altruism the social vertebrates—and by a parallel development the social insects—have achieved a higher degree of organization. It is this step forward that has formed the basis for our own human society. We now turn to the question of precisely what it was that gave the impetus for this development.

5
The Ethologist's
View of Aggression

ADVANTAGES OF INTOLERANCE

Animals of very many species fight their own kind, and man is
no exception to this. On the contrary, his whole history is,
among other things, a history of acts of violence, and this aggressive trait characterizes our own time. Even if we were to make
a case for the view put forward in the first chapter of the social,
friendly nature of man, we must not overlook his inclination
toward antisocial behavior and intolerance; it is a fact we must
come to grips with. We shall be solely concerned here with
intraspecific aggression, that is, the remarkable fact that animals
of a given species do fight their conspecifics. There is also aggression between species—predators attack their prey—but this
we will leave aside for the moment. We shall confine ourselves
to emphasizing implicitly that the two forms must be clearly
distinguished. Intra- and interspecific often employ quite different motor sequences: a cat attacking a mouse behaves quite
differently from when it is attacking a rival. These two basically
different behavior patterns can be activated through electric
stimulation of quite different parts of the brain.

We emphasize the need to make this distinction because intra-
and interspecific aggression are sometimes uncritically treated
as the same, as for example in the discussion of Y. Z. Kuo (*127*),
who succeeded in bringing up cats and mice to live peaceably
together and who concludes from this that a harmonious communal life among men is possible. R. Dart (*34*) has attempted
to explain the aggressiveness of modern man through the preda-

tory way of life of his australopithecine ancestors. These ape-
men, who lived about 1.7 million years ago, killed their prey
with antelope bones: it is this "aggressiveness" which is said to
be the root of man's aggressiveness. Robert Ardrey (*8*) follows
Dart's arguments. What both of them overlook is the fact that
herbivores are by no means more peaceable than predators.
Bulls attack other bulls. Cocks have even become symbols of
aggressiveness.* A predatory way of life has thus by no means
been the prerequisite for the development of intraspecific aggression. This raises the question of the possible selective advantages of aggressive behavior. Given its wide distribution it is
by definition extremely unlikely that aggression is only a useless by-product of other vital functions.

In his classic work *Territory in Bird Life*, Eliot Howard (*98*)
has already given a clear reply. He showed that through their
aggressive behavior passerine birds stake out particular areas as
their territories, which they maintain against other members of
the species. Generally a pair defend a territory together. As a
result of this intolerance, neighbors do not nest too close to one
another, and this is important. Among other things, members
of the same species have the same food requirements and in this
respect are one another's strongest competitors. If European
robins were not such bad neighbors several pairs might well
nest very close together. Since these birds do not have a very
great radius of action, they might very quickly exhaust their
food supplies in bad weather and none of the pairs would rear
its young successfully. Aggression causes animals to keep their
distance and hence promotes the distribution of animals of one
species over a wider area. Furthermore, an animal that has acquired no territory cannot breed. Thus territorial behavior is
also an important mechanism of population control. In this way
overpopulation to the point where the essentials of life are exhausted is avoided (*223*). Pressure from neighbors also leads to
less favorable areas being populated by a species. This aids the
preservation of the species since such areas can supply reserves
for the resettlement of favored areas if the normal population

* In the Tyrol men wear cock's feathers, known as *"Schneidfeder"* ("spunk-
feathers").

has been killed off by epidemics or other catastrophes. The distribution effect of territorial aggression also applies in the case of animals that live in closed groups (see p. 60). In such cases it is the groups that exercise pressure on one another to ensure that each keeps its distance.

A further advantage of aggressive behavior occurs in fights between rivals. A great many vertebrate males fight with their own kind in the mating season. The stronger and healthier ones are in this way selected for reproduction, and this is particularly important in cases where the males are responsible for the defense of the young. On the Galápagos Islands the bull sea lions swim tirelessly up and down the coastline chasing back into shallow waters those young ones from their own harem who venture too far out to sea. They are protecting them from sharks *(43)*. It stands to reason that the strongest ones are the best at performing this task.

TOURNAMENTS

Aggressive behavior does not offer only advantages to a species. In a fight there is always the danger that a member of the species will be injured or killed; and this does nothing to promote the preservation of that species. If cichlid fish, for example, regularly killed their rivals in battle then the species in question would be robbing itself of its reserve of young males, which is needed to compensate for losses caused by predators, accidents, and the like. To spare the life of the species member is thus as important as on occasion to fight him. In animals that can cause physical damage to an opponent a conflict is produced by two opposing selective pressures. How is it resolved?

The simplest way would certainly be for aggression to be counterselected in cases where, equipped with dangerous weapons, one conspecific could easily kill another. Interestingly, however, this is not the case. What we observe, rather, is that fighting animals have often developed very complicated rules of combat that make it possible for them to fight without shedding blood. I have had striking experience of this on the Galápagos Islands, where the seaweed-eating marine iguanas live in hundreds on the volcanic rocks. For most of the year these reptiles are thoroughly tolerant but in the mating season the males each stake out a few square yards of rock as their territories. There they will tolerate a few females, but they attack males approaching the area. In doing so they do not bite one another, and this is important, because they possess very sharp three-cuspidated teeth with which they could easily inflict injuries. The bloodless tournament begins with a threat display: the occupant of the territory erects the crest on his neck and back and shows himself to his opponent broadside on. At the same time he raises his body off the ground and runs on fully outstretched legs, which makes him appear larger. He opens his mouth, threatening to bite, and nods his head. If the rival does not retreat the occupant of the territory rushes at him. When I saw this for the first time I believed the animals would both bite each other. But nothing of the kind occurred. Before the iguanas met they lowered their heads and butted against each other, skull to skull. A fight now developed, in the course of which each strove to push the other from the spot. Horn-like scales on the top of the head prevented the combatants from losing their grip. The fight ended when one had been pushed from the spot. But it could also have been ended if one of them realized that he was no match for his opponent. The animal in question lay flat on his belly in a submissive posture in front of the victor, who at once stopped fighting and waited in a threatening posture for the loser to leave the field (Fig. 23) (47).

Tournaments are widespread in the animal kingdom. Rattlesnakes never bite one another, and rivals fight according to strict rules. They raise the front third of their bodies, swing back and then strike their heads together until one of them collapses and gives up. Many birds, fishes and mammals also fight in a ritualized manner. But not all fighting animals follow this pattern. Dogs and wolves after preliminary threats will fight to wound one another. In the course of the exchange of bites one of them finally realizes that he is beaten. He will then seek safety in flight or break off the fight by means of submissive behavior. To do this the loser rolls onto his back and urinates a little. This behavior is formally similar to that of a cub offering itself to its mother to be cleaned, and can be interpreted

Fig. 23. Rival fight between marine iguanas. Above: two males fighting by butting their heads together; below: the loser (right) lies flat in a submissive posture before the victor (from photographs by the author).

as an infant appeal. Indeed one often sees the assailant turn to parental-care behavior and lick the loser dry (**Fig. 24**) (*141, 180*). In any case he stops fighting, his aggression inhibited. While the marine iguana can switch off the aggression-eliciting stimuli with his submissive posture and thereby appease his rival, a dog may actually use puppyish behavior to arouse a friendly mood in his opponent.

A number of vertebrates do not have any aggression-inhibiting mechanisms at their disposal. These are in the first place animals that do not possess any dangerous weapons and secondly species in which the capacity for flight is so highly developed that after a short fight they can outdistance their opponents. After a short exchange of bites a hamster can escape out of range of his opponent with a few leaps. For this reason the evolving of special means of inhibiting aggression was unnecessary.

*Fig. 24. Appeasement behavior in the wolf. Behind: submissive pos-
ture, lying on the back; in front: begging for food. Through this
infantile behavior, a friendly mood is aroused in the opponent (from
R. Schenkel, 1967).*

Countless investigations have shown that fighting behavior
in animals is preprogrammed through a whole series of phylogenetic adaptations (see p. 8). There are innate and therefore
species-specific motor patterns for fighting. To give only a few
examples, cichlids, even when they have been reared in isolation, pit themselves against a rival by beating him with their
tails and pushing or pulling at one another with their mouths.
Marine iguanas reared in isolation fight by butting their heads
together. Lava lizards, on the other hand, lash one another with
their tails. Fighting cocks reared in isolation kick at one another with their spurs, and handreared roe buck attack with
their antlers.

The behavior patterns of fighting are generally activated by particular signals from the conspecific. We have already mentioned how the blue lateral stripes of the spiny lizard provoke rival fights and how European robins react aggressively to another's red breast. Male sticklebacks acquire a red belly in the breeding season, and this character releases aggressive behavior in conspecifics of the same sex. Even a simple beeswax dummy without fins will be attacked provided it has a red underside; and sticklebacks reared in isolation react in the same way (*33, 205*). Rats that have been made aggressive by an electric shock will ignore a dummy whether it is moved or not. But they will attack a living or a dead rat—though the latter only if it is moved (*208*).

In all these cases, social experience is not a necessary prerequisite for the development of the behavior pattern. This has been established by American investigators as well: doves that have grown up socially isolated will attack another dove if their accustomed food reward is suddenly suspended during training (*9*).

The varying aggressiveness of different strains of mice is determined genetically. If one gives the offspring of aggressive mice to mothers from peaceable strains to rear, they still grow up aggressive. And correspondingly the young of peaceable mothers remain peaceable even if reared by aggressive foster mothers (*130, 141*).

THE AGGRESSIVE DRIVE

A noteworthy feature of intraspecific aggression is its spontaneity. Aggressive behavior is by no means simply released by specific key stimuli; what we observe, rather, is that animals that have been unable to fight for a long time will grow steadily more ready to fight, clearly on the basis of drive mechanisms peculiar to them. These pugnaciously disposed animals will then actively seek out a releasing stimulus situation which will permit them to work off the fighting drive evidently building up within them.

A. Rasa (*167*) has investigated the build-up and discharge of aggressive impulses in the cichlid *Etroplus maculatus*. If one keeps males of this species of fish in isolation for some time, they cannot be mated right away because they will make violent attacks on every female put with them. But if one puts another male into the aquarium, then the resident male will hurl himself upon the rival and once his aggressive impulses find an adequate outlet in this whipping boy, he can also court the female. One can also set up the experiment in such a way that the tank is divided into two compartments by a pane of glass and place a pair of cichlids in each. The two rivals will fight through the glass and will each mate with the female supplied to him. But if one pair is removed then the remaining male, for want of a rival, will attack his own female and end by killing her.

The physiological processes underlying this kind of build-up of excitation have not yet been investigated precisely. By means of electrical brain stimulation it is possible to release not only physical fighting behavior but also true "appetitive behavior" for fighting (i.e., a fighting mood). By applying electrodes to the brains of otherwise free-ranging chickens in a particular way, von Holst and von Saint-Paul caused them to wander about restlessly (*96*). It seemed as though the chickens were looking for something specific, and the investigators checked this by offering it different objects. If the chicken was made thirsty by the brain stimulus, then it searched for water, taking no notice of rivals or sexual partners offered at the same time. If, on the other hand, it had been sexually stimulated, then it reacted only to sexual partners; and finally, if it was aggressively aroused, it went on searching until it was offered a rival, which it at once attacked. In many vertebrates aggressive readiness fluctuates with the level of the male sex hormones in the yearly cycle. Tame male squirrels regularly become aggressive in the spring and will even attack their keepers. After the breeding season aggressive behavior declines. One can also activate extremely premature aggressive behavior through artificial hormone dosing. After a dose of testosterone, young turkeys fight one another, which is not their normal practice. In addition, there are indications that Catecholamine metabolism in the central nervous system plays a certain role in the build-up of readiness for aggressive action, but the details are not known. The systems of drives underlying aggression must be innate in animals. Kruijt (*123*) reared fighting cocks in isolation. The grown animals fought their own kind with the species-typical behavior patterns. If given no opportunity to fight, they would attack their own tails or strike at their own shadows with their spurs, clearly demonstrating their appetitive behavior for fighting. Some current experiments of my own show that if one places hamsters and house mice, reared in social isolation, into a T-shaped maze, they will generally choose the end chamber that is baited with a freely accessible conspecific of the same sex, which they can fight. The conspecific located at the end of the other arm is in a little wire cage so that it cannot be attacked, and this is noticeably less attractive. Thus, even socially inexperienced mammals show an appetitive behavior for fighting.*

We can confirm, therefore, that phylogenetic adaptations determine the aggressive behavior of a great many vertebrates. Many animals are preprogrammed in such a way that they react to particular signals with aggressive behavior patterns. The basic patterns of motor sequences thus activated are inherited as fixed action patterns. Fighting behavior, furthermore, is not always purely reactive. The spontaneity and appetitive behavior for fighting which are demonstrable even in socially inexperienced animals lead one to suppose the existence of innate drive mechanisms.

Hypotheses claiming that aggression in animals is something exclusively learned are consequently no longer tenable. Of course this does not mean that learning plays no part in the development of aggressive bel avior. Scott's experiments, to mention just one example (*186*), have shown very plainly that one can make a mouse very aggressive through a series of vic-

---

* The behavior of the socially inexperienced hamsters and mice does, however, alter very quickly. Once they have discovered where the conspecific available for fighting is, they will several times in succession run purposefully down there and have a fight. If the partner defends itself and they are bitten for their pains, they will avoid conflict in the future and choose the arm of the maze in which the caged conspecific is located. Even more noteworthy is the fact that even those subjects that never get bitten finally give up fighting. After repeated runs that led to fights they showed themselves to be increasingly aggression-inhibited. I presume that they become acquainted with their opponents and that this inhibits further aggression.

torious fights. Repeated defeats, on the other hand, subdue aggressiveness.

AGGRESSION IN MAN

There is wide disagreement about the nature of aggression in man—even whether it is universal or not. Helmuth (*85*) disputes the view that aggression is a world-wide phenomenon. He cites the Eskimos, Zuñi Indians and Bushmen, in whom he alleges an absence of aggressive acts. In making this claim he was evidently thinking of group aggression, acts of war and not of aggression generally, for otherwise it would not have escaped him that male Eskimos have singing duels and beat their wives, or that the Zuñis have extremely cruel initiation rites, and that acts of aggression are thus wholly a part of the daily life of these peoples, whom he describes as peaceable. Rasmussen (*168*) has described a brawl between man and wife among the Polar Eskimos. The man beat his wife because she would not grind a knife. But he soon left her, stoned his dogs, and finished by breaking the knife that had been the cause of the quarrel. An hour later Rasmussen heard the two of them joking together contentedly. Noteworthy is the evident need to work off the aggressiveness once it is activated. According to Rasmussen an Eskimo might even kill a man, if he is in his way, and if he is strong there will be no social retribution. But the idea of warfare, village against village or tribe against tribe, is alien to them.

Writing about the Zuñis, H. Helmuth (*85*) says: "From no sentence of R. Benedict's account of the life of the Zuñis (*13*) can any possible aggressive behavior be concluded to be present in them" (p. 269). Yet P. Weidkuhn (*220*), who then read through Ruth Benedict's book *Patterns of Culture*, found that she had described how women attack their rivals and beat them, how people suspected of witchcraft are hung up by their thumbs until they confess, and how punitive masked gods beat the children with yucca whips at initiation rites.

During the summer 1970 and spring 1971 I lived with a !Ko Bushmen band near Takatswane (Kalahari). I was surprised to observe many acts of aggression (hitting, kicking, biting, etc.)

among them, in particular among playing groups of children (52). Older reports even describe territorial defense. Nonetheless the Bushmen are often used to illustrate the fact that hunters and gatherers are of a peaceful nature. Much of the confusion seems to stem from a different use of the term "aggression." Anthropologists often use "aggressive" as a synonym for "belligerent" and consider only warfare as an aggressive act, whereas ethologists deal with the observed behavior patterns and label as aggressive every act that leads to a spacing or subordination, even a display.

The Arapesh of New Guinea are frequently cited as another example of culturally determined peaceability. But even these people, who allegedly never strike one another, are not without their aggressive feelings. Margaret Mead (*146, 147*) writes that their children are instructed not to vent their rage on other children but on objects. If two children at play get into a fight an adult at once intervenes and separates them. The aggressor is taken away and held fast. He is allowed to stamp his feet in rage, scream, roll in the dirt, and throw stones or firewood at the ground, but he is not allowed to touch another child!

"The habit of venting his anger at other people on the objects of his immediate environment is retained throughout his life. An angry man will spend an hour at a time striking his gong or chopping at his own palm trees" [Margaret Mead (*147*), p. 50] (retranslation from the German).

The Hopi Indians suppress physical forms of aggression and find fighting competitions tasteless. They learn to smile even at enemies and always to speak in a friendly manner with a quiet voice. They learn sharing and cooperation, but one form of aggression remains open to them. With a tongue as sharp as a poison dart, writes Eggan (*40*), they practice constant guerrilla warfare against their conspecifics.

Cultural differences certainly exist in human aggression. But convincing proof that a human group is wholly lacking in aggressive behavior has so far never been produced. It could indeed exist only in well-protected, out-of-the-way places or in a tolerated minority within a larger body of people that afforded protection. But in fact aggressiveness—the disposition to aggression—seems to be distributed throughout the world. And primitive and culturally advanced peoples do not seem to differ fundamentally in their aggressive disposition. The Indians of the South American rainforest, Papuans, or African tribes are generally no less aggressive than members of civilized nations, for fundamentally aggression finds the same expression throughout the world. Threat display by means of ornament, weapons, and male bearing shows the same basic feature in the most varied cultures. By means of feathers, bearskin hats, and the like men make themselves look taller, emphasize their muscles and wrists, and often exaggerate the width of their shoulders. Men put on an air of calm and adopt haughty expressions for effect. The facial expressions of threatening and rage are, so far as has been established, the same in all cultures. People from widely different cultural areas stamp their feet in anger—probably a ritualized intention to attack—and clench their fists in annoyance.

Widespread throughout the world, too, is the glorification of aggression, whether in heroic sagas, in the form of symbolic animals (eagle, lion, bear, cock, etc.), or coats of arms. Scars acquired in fighting are displayed with pride. The Waikas (rainforest Indians of the Upper Orinoco) carefully shave the hair on their heads so that one can see the scars they have acquired in club fights (see p. 78), and in Austria, Germany, and Switzerland it used to be regarded as manly to have oneself scarred, for ornament, with a duelling sword. National holidays celebrate aggressive historical events. Courage is everywhere accepted as a virtue, even by pacifists. Today's world-wide tendency to put a taboo on aggression represents a quite new and hopeful development. It derives from a growing humanitarian consciousness and has certainly gained impetus in the face of the threat of self-annihilation, through modern weapons technology.

Among men as well as animals, aggression leads to the territorial "fencing-off" of groups and within groups to the formation of social hierarchies, or ranking orders. Territorial aggression promoted the spread of human beings over the earth and has even resulted in the settlement of barren areas, insofar as the more aggressive peoples, or those with more sophisticated weapons technology, have driven others into enclaves. And this has remained true right into modern times: one has only to think of the settlement of North America or Australia by Europeans. By the moral standards of today such facts are painful to contemplate, but the facts cannot be argued away—one need look no further than the Old Testament.

Nevertheless, in order to make clear that I intend no justification of aggression, let me emphasize once again that not everything that was once adaptive will retain this species-preserving function necessarily forever. Thanks to environmental changes, it is not all that uncommon for an adaptation to reverse itself, for it to be retained as a historical vestige, while it has become in effect a selective hindrance.

Many features of human territorial behavior point to our ancient primate heritage. We have mentioned the phallic statues used as boundary markers and to ward off evil spirits, which recall the male genital presentation of monkeys standing guard as living frontier posts. Human beings defend both individual territories (including personal property) and group territories. In addition, every individual shows the unmistakable tendency to keep his distance from strangers, except in special circumstances (buses, mass meetings). He thus follows the pattern of many other social animals which maintain an individual distance. R. Sommer (*191*) has conducted experiments in libraries: if a person sat down at a table already occupied while others were still free, the original occupant would move away. If there was no possibility of moving away, then those people who felt subjectively hemmed in would erect symbolic barriers between themselves and their neighbors, for instance, by laying down a ruler as a demarcation line. Once a certain distance was crossed they would leave their seats, even when, objectively speaking, they still had enough room. There are many situations in daily life in which these territorial inclinations of man become clear. Somebody already seated in a train compartment has the right to stare at a newcomer without this being interpreted as rudeness. The fact that the newcomer also recognizes the territorial right of the original occupant emerges from the fact that he will ask politely if there are any seats free, indeed he may often ask formally whether he "may" come in.

The person who got there first clearly has certain rights that we grant him. Interestingly, this is already pronounced in the higher primates. If a chimpanzee has captured a gazelle or a young baboon, this prey belongs to him. Even when the successful hunter is of low rank a higher-ranking chimpanzee will only rarely dispute his possession of it (*133*). If a female is put with a captive male hamadryas baboon and shortly afterward another male arrives, the newcomer will not pay any attention to the female. He will indeed tend to look away conspicuously. He respects the fact that the other baboon got the female before him. The possessor's own behavior is also striking: smacking his lips he presents his rump and appeases the newcomer, rather as we soften unpleasant news for a fellow human being with a friendly remark. Translated into our language, the baboon is saying: "I'm sorry but she's mine" (H. Kummer, verbal communication).

We regard certain areas of space either temporarily or permanently as our own and are inclined to react angrily to infringements by others. This is particularly noticeable in young children and in mentally ill people, who will, for example, defend their seats at table or their beds with great bitterness [Staehelin (*197*)].

A family regards its house and garden as its domain, as does a village community its village and fields. Even a community that is brought together only temporarily, for example in a railway compartment, will establish itself in time as a group with exclusive tendencies, and appeasement rites will be necessary for anyone who wishes to join it. Specific to man is the expression of aggression in intellectual fields. We defend our intellectual property and strive aggressively to promote ideas, even humanitarian ideals.

Pleasure as a motive for aggression is universal. It need not always express itself as a delight in brawling, although picking quarrels in pubs is not a habit confined to the Tyrol. There are very many forms of combative games, extending from contests on the lines of Bavarian finger-wrestling to chess or football. Underlying these aggressive exercises in rivalry is a pleasure principle. Clearly by these means aggressive impulses are discharged. Conversely the build-up of aggression is experienced as disagreeable tension. The phenomenon of aggression build-up and of relief of tension when it is worked off is not merely something we experience subjectively. It is possible to create a build-up of aggression experimentally, to measure it and similarly record the discharge of dammed-up aggression.

Students were invited to take part in experiments in the course of which they were intentionally annoyed. Their annoyance could be read from the increase in their blood pressure. After the angry ones were divided into two groups, they were told that the experimenter would now solve certain problems himself. At the same time the subjects were invited to communicate with the experimenter by pressing a button when he made a mistake. One group was given to understand that they would be giving the experimenter a punitive electric shock, while the others would only activate a blue signal light. The blood pressure of those who believed they were giving shocks to the experimenter fell quickly; for they were discharging their dammed-up feelings of aggression. But those who could only flash their lights remained angry, there being no reduction to speak of in their blood pressure (92).

In some further series of experiments (91) on a similar pattern, it was discovered that there are a great variety of ways of working off aggression. People can be annoyed by insulting notes. If they are permitted to reply in the same vein their blood pressure falls once more. One can also work off aggressiveness by watching a film with aggressive content; clearly one identifies with the story. The frequent showing of movie and television films with aggressive content shows that there is a demand, a market for them, and people like to work off their aggressive impulses in this way. The films are mostly so constructed that initially the spectator's aggressive feelings are aroused and then worked off again, probably on the "bad guy." * In daily life we often work off aggressive feelings, once aroused, on substitute objects, by slamming doors or even smashing things. I have observed a girl born deaf and blind who bit her hand when she was angry. Many people have evolved "safety valve" habits that enable them to work off their aggressive feelings in a "peaceful manner"—for instance "sing-

---

* Watching aggressive films activates aggressive feelings, yet once the feelings are aroused in the spectator, film plots do not always allow them to be worked off. The great quantity of violence, brutality, and sadism that is shown on the mass media therefore gives cause for considerable concern.

ing duels" or sporting contests, and also to regulate disputes without bloodshed.

The highly aggressive Waika Indians in the jungle on the Upper Orinoco are familiar with varying degrees of aggressive contest. At their festivals they often hold ritualized battles between hosts and guests. These generally take the form of a kind of boxing match in which the opponents take turns in striking one another's chest muscles with their fists. In another form of tournament the opponents strike one another hard on the sides with the flat of the hand. More serious disputes are fought out by the Waikas in the form of duels with staves: the opponents strike one another on the head so hard that ugly wounds are caused. The Waikas are later as proud of the scars from these wounds as members of German student associations used to be of theirs (*30*). By means of ritualized battle among these Indians, serious conflict between friendly villages is avoided, and this is important, for there are in any case quite enough serious battles between hostile villages.

A similar custom is known among the Central Australian aborigines. If two women have quarreled, each of them takes a hardwood cudgel; they take up positions facing each other and one of them holds out her head to her opponent to receive the first blow. After that she is entitled to strike back, whereupon the battle generally ends, unless the spectators take sides and begin their own free-for-all. The blows with the hardwood stick are delivered with full force. The thickness of the aborigines' skulls, which is considerable by European standards, prevents these duels from ending fatally. The men also fight in a ritualized fashion by thrusting their spears at their opponents' upper thighs. Grounds for such combats are adultery, social contacts across the lines of caste, and also the violation of certain rites (*19*).

The Eskimos, too, regulate most conflicts in a bloodless, ritualized manner. Among tribes of Siberia, Alaska, Baffinland, and Northwest Greenland opponents wrestle with each other. On occasion this can lead to death. The central Eskimo tribes living in the Arctic Circle from Hudson's Bay to the Bering Strait cuff one another's ears. In Western and Eastern Greenland, on the Aleutian Islands, and the west coast of Alaska there are singing duels at which, in Greenland, opponents also butt one another with their heads. The style of the songs performed follows a traditional pattern, but the texts are individually composed for each occasion. The audience is judge and applauds the better singer—even when he is actually in the wrong (*89*). All grounds for dispute, murder generally excepted, are settled in this way. But an East Greenland Eskimo can himself demand satisfaction for the murder of one of his relatives in this manner, especially if he is too weak for physical battle and is so confident of his singing ability that his victory will be assured [Holm (*93*)]. Let me describe an example that E. A. Hoebel (*89*) quotes from K. Rasmussen's 1908 findings. A certain E. had married the divorced wife of an old man, K. Now K. wanted his wife back again. E. would not give her up and so it came to a song-duel accompanied by gesture and dance.

K. sings:

> *Now I shall split off words—little, sharp words*
> *Like the wooden splinters which I hack off with my ax.*
> *A song from ancient times—a breath of the ancestors*
> *A song of longing—for my wife.*
> *An impudent, black-skinned oaf has stolen her,*
> *He has tried to belittle her.*
> *A miserable wretch who loves Human flesh—*
> *A cannibal from famine days.*

E. replies in his own defense:

> *Insolence that takes the breath away*
> *Such laughable arrogance and effrontery.*
> *What a satirical song! supposed to place blame on me.*
> *You would drive fear into my heart!*
> *I who care not about death.*
> *Hi! You sing about my woman who was your wench.*
> *You weren't so loving then—she was much alone.*
> *You forgot to prize her in song, in stout, contest songs.*
> *Now she is mine.*
> *And never shall she visit singing, false lovers.*
> *Betrayer of women in strange households.*

The opponents sang in this way an alternating sequence of stanzas. P. Bohannan (23) has described a similarly ritualized dispute among the Tiu of Nigeria.

In the Bavarian-Austrian area song-duels are still common today. A typical, somewhat coarser musical exchange runs:

Jetz hot oana gsunga
is eams Rotz owagrunna
Wann er no amoi singt
dan sohneuz ma eam
    gschwind!

(Now one man has sung
And his snot ran over
When he sings again
We'll wipe his nose quickly!

—*Und's Rotz-owarinna*
des geht di nix o,
leich mir dei Tüachl,
nocha putz i mir's scho!

The snot running over
Is none of your business
Lend me your hanky
And I'll clean it myself!

–*Und's Tüachl-herleicha,*
des is net der Brauch,
du nimm dir an Hadern
und putz dir dein Schlauch!

Lending handkerchiefs
Is not the custom
Find yourself a rag
And wipe your snout with
    that!)

These songs obviously have a strong aggressive motivation, and if the singers do not actually fight, it is because they have found other outlets. It simply cannot be denied that discomforting states of tension do exist, that there does exist a desire to release tension, an objective for the drive, and an object of aggression. But these are the essential defining characteristics of a drive! Given the wide distribution of aggression among human beings in particular and vertebrates in general, it seems far more probable that this disposition is not just an acquired one.

What is so remarkable about contest singing among Eskimos is that we are dealing here with serious aggressive conflicts that achieve resolution but which are completely ritualized. They are closely comparable to the verbal battles of modern parliamentarians, which take place before an audience of voters whose approval determines victory or defeat.

There have always been applications of ritualization to human aggression—even in warfare. Specific fighting rules of fairness and chivalry have been evolved in different cultures. One element of ritualization is the recognition of defeat by sparing the vanquished. However, this presupposes a certain measure of mutual trust. The winner must be able to rely on the loser abiding by the provisions of a treaty and not, for example, beginning a guerrilla war; while the loser expects that he will not be terrorized and plundered. But since for obvious reasons mistrust exists between combatants, infringements by individuals will suffice to begin an escalation of mistrust, and with it the deritualization of conflicts, as the Second World War showed to a remarkable extent. Even today the mistrust generated at that time is still blocking the strong tendency for contact universally present in mankind. After so many treaties have been broken, people cease to have much regard for treaties.

If human beings have no means of working off their aggressive feelings they experience a build-up of aggression. The discharge can then take dangerous and violent forms, as in the case of "expedition choler" (*Polarkoller*). In our everyday life we experience periodic fluctuations of our inner aggressive readiness to act. That is to say, on occasions we are irritable and by the same token readily provoked to anger, without outside circumstances intervening. This points toward drive mechanisms that are probably similar to those which underlie aggression in animals. Further evidence of this is the dependence on the male sex hormones as found in animals. Finally we know of spontaneous neurological rage reactions. In some patients spontaneous firing of the cells in the temporal lobe and in the thalamus results in a feeling of rage and the execution of violent acts [Gibbs (*74*), Moyer (*157*), Treppert (*207*)]. Adler (*2*), Freud (*69*), and Lorenz (*141*) have all sought to explain the spontaneity of aggression by assuming an innate aggressive drive, and the hypothesis has, as we have said, much in its favor. It also explains our astonishing readiness for collective aggression. The less opportunity we have to work off this drive in our daily life, the readier we are to respond to aggression-releasing stimuli. A highly effective releasing stimulus is an actual or imaginary threat to one's own group. It releases strong emotions and throughout history demagogues have understood how to arouse this kind of enthusiasm and to harness it to their own ends. But aggression is also activated if the satisfaction of a need is frustrated. Starting from this fact, which is supported by many experiments, J. Dollard (*38*) and his collaborators developed the hypothesis that aggression in man arises primarily from his previous experiences of frustration. One can of course support this assertion if one stretches the concept far enough. But in reply to the supporters of the frustration hypothesis, Konrad Lorenz cited the notorious fact that extremely permissive upbringing produces extremely aggressive people. Plack's reply to this was that such people have in fact experienced their bitterest frustration when they were weaned. It has hitherto not been possible to formulate any conditions that will guarantee an upbringing without any frustration. One can always assume some kind of frustration, if need be weaning, or even an experience at birth, and thus explain every instance of aggression. But in the process the frustration hypothesis loses its scientific value.

Recently some of the American supporters of the frustration hypothesis expressed their views with a good deal more circumspection. L. Berkowitz (*16*) has pointed out that the connection between frustration and aggression cannot be exclusively learned, and that conditioning and innate determination can coexist in human beings. A similar opinion was expressed by Derek Freeman (*66, 67*).

The fact is that aggressive tendencies develop in the widest possible variety of educational circumstances. They can be developed to a greater or lesser extent while the social controls placed on them vary, but they are always demonstrable. It is certainly true that an upbringing that provides many experiences of deprivation fosters a person's aggressive disposition. But one can equally encourage aggressive feelings by indulging them—by allowing a child to act out its aggressive impulses freely or even rewarding it for doing so. The viewpoint that such children will work off all their aggressive feelings and then grow up to be peaceful citizens is based on a misunderstanding or the nature of drives, in that it assumes that each human being receives a specific quantity of aggression, which he can then work off.

What are the consequences for human social life if we assume an innate aggressive drive? Certainly all human governments must once and for all reckon with the fact that there is a permanent readiness for aggression in people, which develops of itself in spite of all educative efforts. To discipline it out of existence would be no more feasible than to eliminate from man's environment all stimuli which could conceivably elicit acts of aggression. But what does this mean for human society?

Berkowitz (*14*) believes that the existence of an innate aggressive drive opens up a frightening prospect: "An innate aggressive drive," he writes, "cannot be abolished by social reforms or the alleviation of frustrations. Neither complete parental permissiveness nor the fulfillment of every desire will eliminate interpersonal conflict entirely, according to this view. Its lessons for social policy are obvious: civilization and moral order must be based upon force, not on love and charity" (p. 4).

Sigmund Freud, on the other hand, takes the view that aggression cannot be eliminated but that it could be neutralized by activating all those forces which establish emotional bonds between people. He writes: "If willingness for war is a consequence of the destructive drive, then the answer is to call upon love (Eros), the opponent of this drive. Everything that creates emotional bonds between men must 'be pitted against war. These bonds can be of two kinds. Firstly: relationships as to a love object, though without any sexual purpose. Psychoanalysis does not need to be ashamed to speak of love in this context, for religion says the same: love thy neighbour as thyself. That is easily asked, of course, but hard to fulfill.

"The second kind of emotional bonds are those through identification. Everything that establishes significant points in common between people arouses such fellow feelings, such identifications. On these, to a great extent, rests the structure of human society" [Sigmund Freud (*69*), vol. 16].

Two fundamentally different theses are thus presented. Berkowitz pessimistically states that if the existence of an aggressive drive is assumed, only force and repression can bring about civilization and moral order. Freud, on the other hand, sees love as the natural opponent of aggression. Which of them is right?

Berkowitz takes a one-sided view of the dynamic aspect of the aggressive drive, which is ever ready—and which can therefore, in his opinion, be mastered only by repression. To a certain extent this is true. Just as one can educate people to increase aggression by rewarding aggressive acts, so one can also suppress aggressive feelings by punishment. Pacification of this kind, however, will at the same time strike at the spirit of initiative, which is positively correlated with aggression. We "attack" tasks, "worry" problems, and "master" them. Our ordinary speech expresses the fact that even culturally creative achievements are nourished by aggression. This is indeed one of the reasons why people have recently been subjecting the "achieving society" to critical scrutiny. It is rejected by champions of a peaceable society as leading to increased aggression. All the same I do not think we are obliged to accept the extreme view of Berkowitz. In any case repressive measures against aggression are only partly effective: it is widely accepted that the repression of a drive can have degenerative effects on the physiological machinery of aggression; nevertheless a certain aggressive readiness remains and the longer it goes without outlet, the readier it is to prevail when opportunity offers. It is possible to reduce aggression but certainly not to eliminate it completely. It is therefore, as Freud says, an "educational sin" not to prepare a person for the aggression with which he will sooner or later have to come to grips. All attempts to belittle aggression by referring to the alleged fact that it is learned—in the face of the available evidence to the contrary—are in the highest degree irresponsible.

We know that it is by no means necessary for the venting of pent-up aggressive feelings to result in human strife. Even the fulfillment of a common task uses up aggressive feelings. It is also possible to cultivate a wide variety of "safety-valve" habits that divert aggression; for example, types of competitive sports. Aggression can certainly be controlled in this way but only if the natural opponents of aggression are also brought into full play. Without activating the forces of the "libido," as Freud calls them, the control of aggression will not be possible.

SOCIAL HIERARCHY IN HUMANS
AND ANIMALS

If chickens from different sources are put together they will begin to fight, but in the course of a few days the battles will lose their vehemence and finally the group lives peacefully together. If one observes more closely, one can establish that in the course of the fighting a social hierarchy, or pecking order, is being established. The chickens fight one another in succession and grade themselves according to victory and defeat. One hen, *a*, which has beaten hens *b*, *c*, and *d*, is in the future superior to them. It takes precedence in feeding and in going to the preferred sleeping place, and it may peck a subordinate hen if the latter disputes its precedence at the feeding place. If hen *b*, for its part, has beaten hens *c* and *d*, then it is superior to these hens: thus linear ranking orders can be formed. But there are also more complicated relationships. Hen *d*, which is subordinate to hens *b* and *c*, may have happened to win a decisive victory over *a*. It will then remain subordinate to *b* and *c* but dominant over *a*.

By means of a pecking order like this, lasting aggressive conflicts within the group are avoided; for it is a means of controlling aggression. Among the higher vertebrates, however, high-ranking animals* also take over specific tasks in the service of the group. Among Chacma baboons the high-ranking males act as "scouts" in case of danger and look for escape routes. They decide when the troop moves on and the direction to be taken, and choose the sleeping places. They protect young and lower-ranking baboons from attacks by other troops and settle quarrels. Low-ranking baboons seek the protection of the high-ranking animals.

The manifold tasks of the high-ranking animals call for a

---

* In the higher primates the simple ranking-order terminology (alpha animal, beta animal, etc.) is no longer sufficient to describe the social relationships of the animals. Here the social position is best defined through a description of the role (brother, aunt, peripheral male, etc.). The role is determined by the frequency with which the specific behavior pattern is fulfilled. If it is altered, a new relationship "type" is adopted.

number of qualities. Among these, social qualities and experience count in the higher animals to an increasing extent,
alongside physical strength and aggressiveness. The dominant
status of a baboon or a macaque is by no means the product of
uninhibited aggression. It is not the especially aggressive animal that reaches the highest rungs on the ladder of rank, but
the especially friendly one that knows how to win the others'
sympathies. In baboons, rhesus monkeys, and Japanese macaques the ability of a male to make friendships with others is
a prerequisite for high-ranking status. A high-ranking male
must be tolerant toward young animals and allow them to play
round about it. It must furthermore be a good protector. Thus
positive social qualities determine status and not just the aggressiveness of an animal striving for dominance. Its status depends upon its recognition by the other members of the group,
and this will be withheld from a purely aggressive animal. This
is true, however, only for monkeys living under natural conditions. In the cramped conditions of zoo life, tyrants achieve
high positions in the pecking order (*175*).

It is true that a certain aggressiveness, which motivates a
striving for dominance, also goes with a high-ranking position.
But the trials of strength are to a great extent ritualized. We
have already mentioned Jane van Lawick-Goodall's chimpanzee, which improved its rank after discovering it was good at
making a noise with empty petrol cans.

Alongside social qualities the individual's experience is also
decisive for the establishment of dominance. With baboons this
counts for even more than physical strength, which is illustrated
by the fact that old males can lead a group even when their
physical strength is on the wane. Then generally two or three
old males will band together to form a central hierarchy group
(*39*). In their old age these monkeys acquire an impressive solemn garb of seniority, a long-haired silvery coat, which adds to
their stature and helps to compensate for their physical frail-
ties. Something akin to this can be observed in gorillas, chimpanzees and in man himself (*50*).

The formation of a ranking-order presupposes two dispositions that we miss in animal species which live on their own.

The animals must first of all show striving for dominance,* but they must also show a willingness to subordinate themselves if they cannot reach the top. Both are demonstrable in man. Vance Packard (*162*), in his excellent study *The Pyramid Climbers,* has shown how human beings strive for rank and announce each ledge achieved on the pyramid of status by means of corresponding symbols. The appeal to status is an effective factor in advertising, for people who have not yet achieved high status themselves show a willingness to mimic it by dressing like high-ranking people, by driving the same car, or wearing the same jewelry. Hence the advertising slogan: "Men of destiny wear . . ." Desmond Morris (*156*) has drawn attention to the interesting phenomenon of "dominance mimicry." People copy the clothes, jewelry and style of people of high social status, which causes the latter to evolve new fashions, in order once more to set themselves apart from their neighbors. O. Koenig cites various examples to show that the uniforms of victorious countries tend to be copied. The uniform of the Hungarian Hussars found imitators in Austria, Germany, Russia, and France. The Hungarians copied the notorious Turkish Guards regiment of the "Delis," who went first into battle, blind with rage after taking opium, and who formed the bodyguards of the highest dignitaries. The stronger person is willingly imitated. Morris had moreover drawn attention to the fact that frustrated pyramid-climbers create for themselves mountains with peaks they are able to conquer by taking up particular hobbies and striving to outstrip people with the same interests. Thus within his own group a pigeon fancier or a beer-mat collector can be king. These substitute pyramids provide a harmless way of satisfying the striving for dominance. They are instructive for us, because they show how strong this drive is within us. The fact that so far no one has been able to realize in practical terms the model of a society without a hierarchy—even the radical abolition of established hierarchies has

---

* Striving for dominance involves not only aggression against a conspecific, but also tolerance. Solitary animals cease their aggression only when a rival has retreated. In social animals a fight ends as soon as the lower-ranking animal acknowledges its subordinate position.

brought us no nearer to this ideal, for new systems of rank quickly develop—shows that we are probably dealing here with an innate disposition, one we carry around with us as a part of our primate heritage. In the individualized group, the status finally achieved is determined as much by human qualities, such as willingness to serve, altruism, and knowledge, as by simple aggressiveness. In the small individualized group, where everyone knows everyone else quite well, it is very difficult for one member of the group to convince the others that he possesses such qualities by mere pretense. In the anonymous community it is quite different (see p. 225).

Among human beings, too, age is equated with wisdom. Once upon a time this made sense, for old men really were in possession of a rich experience of life and accumulated knowledge. Thus the meeting of the elders—the senate—plays a great part in the life of both primitive and sophisticated peoples. Men of particularly high rank are always portrayed as dignified old men. But the increased life expectancy has led today to the situation of people occupying positions of power in their years of decline. J. D. Frank (*63*) has recently drawn attention to this. "Publicly acknowledged mental illness," he writes, "is rare in modern democracies, but creeping incapacity, under the pressure of old age and the burdens of office, is unfortunately far more widespread than we are led to believe. In this century alone at least six British prime ministers, and a very great number of cabinet ministers, have fallen ill during their tenure of office; in the U.S. both Presidents Wilson and Roosevelt, during their last months in office, were suffering from an advanced stage of arteriosclerosis . . . It is undoubtedly owing to Wilson's inability to carry out the business of government in a vigorous manner that America failed to join the League of Nations. At Yalta, Roosevelt, whose powers had already been seen to be failing in Quebec, was a dying man, incapable of briefing himself adequately for the conference . . ." (pp. 85–86). Similar examples could be adduced from the most recent German history. In politics, which apparently knows no pensionable age for its top jobs, this is particularly foolish and dangerous for society. In this matter respect for old age is clearly leading us up a blind alley.

The second disposition which is a prerequisite for the creation of a social hierarchy, namely, the disposition to subordination, is based on fear of the high-ranking individual (respect being a combination of honor and fear, as the German word *"Ehr-furcht"* shows). This disposition is alien to solitary animals. When I reared a badger I could never forbid it to do anything. If I scolded it when it opened a cupboard and pulled out my linen, the most it did was to stare at me, and if I gave it a smack on its nose it attacked me. It would not subordinate itself. A dog, on the other hand, quickly learns to obey.

Ranking order is a means of social organization and thereby of controlling aggression. So long as it is based on character and knowledge it is also acceptable to human society. But the authority which is founded on specialist knowledge will also have to be recognized. This has recently been pointed out by Herbert Marcuse (*144*): "What is probably biologically impossible," he writes, "is to manage without some kind of repression. It may be self-imposed, it may be imposed by others . . . For example, the authority of the pilot of an aeroplane is a rational authority. It is impossible to imagine a situation in which the passengers dictate to the pilot what he must do. The traffic policeman should also be a typical example of rational authority. These things are probably biological necessities; but political domination, domination that is based on exploitation and repression, is not" (p. 41).

Forms of hereditary title to leadership, and class or caste systems are to be rejected. Groups that cut themselves off from one another end up by being hostile to one another (see "pseudo-speciation," p. 40). All such kinds of barrier-building promote the danger of aggressive conflicts. If our goal is all-embracing human love, then we must overcome the division of mankind into classes. "The true love of humanity will surely come one day, but only after the abolition of classes in the world," writes Mao Tse-tung. In hereditary leadership the seeds of degeneracy are already to be found. When patience and submissiveness lead men into blind subjection they cease to be virtues. And this brings us to the problem of deciding the relative value of our behavioral norms, which we now turn to.

6
The Biological Basis for Ethical Norms

ON MAKING VALUE JUDGMENTS

How exactly do we know what is good and what is evil? Hitherto in our discussion we have avoided these concepts as far as possible, limiting ourselves to the consideration of what is advantageous in the process of natural selection. In the course of this it has emerged that certain behavior patterns, for example altruistic ones, are of advantage for the survival of the species, while others, such as the killing of a member of the same species, are to its disadvantage. If we wished to make a value judgment we could describe everything that is detrimental to the survival of the species as "evil"—what must be rejected. We are probably unconsciously following this criterion when we judge as "negative" all impulses that tend toward pathological degeneration and therefore threaten our social life, as is particularly the case with aggression. But how does the individual know what to do and what to shun? Does he learn the commandments or does he arrive at them rationally by posing the question: "Can I wish others to act as I would now like to?" Do we, in other words, act in accordance with Kant's fundamental moral law, so that the maxims which govern our will could at any time be elevated to form the basis of a general moral system, making a free and rational choice, independent of any kind of mechanisms of nature? Or do we, above and beyond this, have an a priori sense of what is good and what is evil? Are there in effect, in addition to those culturally determined norms, tested in practice and arrived at by reasoning, others that are innate and therefore biologically determined?

Christian theology holds that man is born with an awareness of the commandment to do good and shun evil. What is good and evil in individual cases is to be rationally deduced, the criterion being respect for the individual—love. This includes respect for the life of one's fellow-man. In short, according to this viewpoint, ethical norms are handed down in only the most general form and concrete rules of behavior are arrived at by paying heed to them. Some years ago, for example, a German survey on the question of artificial insemination with donors' sperm showed that it was unacceptable to the majority of married men. Christian theologians argued against artificial insemination on grounds of respect for the individual—in this case the husband. A more recent survey on the same question showed that the majority of married people of both sexes were now in agreement with the idea; nor were there any theological objections to this form of "adultery." Monogamy has also been justified by a similar argument.

But more than this, Christian theology attempts to infer a divine order in nature. The theological teaching of "natural law" assumes that the created world represents the realization of divine ideas. Since God's creatures lack reason the Creator directs them toward their goal by means of instinct. We, too, it is claimed, can take our bearings from this world and use it as a guide for our conscious behavior. Nature proclaims the will of God: from it can be derived standards, moral laws of nature, as it were. In the address at the inauguration of the Fourth Year of the Pontifical Academy of Sciences on December 3, 1939, Pope Pius XII said: "When our intellect does not conform to the reality of things or is deaf to the voice of nature, it wanders in the illusion of dreams and pursues a phantom. Between God and ourselves stands nature" (Wickler, *217*).

Anyone who seeks to take his bearings from nature and be guided by its ethical norms must not rely on incomplete information or he will be led astray. The current debate about the admissibility of various artificial contraceptive methods offers a good example of this. From the fact that the act of copulation in animals generally only serves the reproductive function, some theologians have concluded that this must also be the sole purpose willed by God in the case of human beings, and hence that all methods of contraception must be rejected as being contrary to the divine order. What they have overlooked is the fact that in man the sexual act fulfills a new function in maintaining the bond between partners (*50, 217*). Basically, then, this method of arriving at ethical norms is quite justifiable, provided one never loses sight of the fact that from the study of animals we can evolve hypotheses that will have only a varying degree of applicability to man. Their viability must always first be tested in studies of human beings. Anyone who derives norms for human behavior from the prevalence of a certain behavior in the animal kingdom is flouting the discipline of science. Nevertheless time and time again this is what happens; and then the choice of examples generally reflects the author's own inclinations. In his publication *APO und Establishment aus biologischer Sicht,* F. Frank (*62*) argues in this unscientific way. As he lays such stress on his career as a biologist, it must be said that very few biologists would derive general principles of human behavior solely from the habits of shrews, weasels, lemmings, field-voles, rabbits, and prairie dogs. This plea in favor of the "establishment," with its strongly zoological flavor, makes for somewhat painful reading.

There is a further point to be noted: nature does reveal the phenomenon of functional conflict. For example, it is advantageous for many animal species to eat as much as possible in a short time. But this makes proper chewing impossible, which is a disadvantage. To eat a lot and to chew it properly are two needs which clearly conflict with each other. The solution evolved by various ungulates is rumination. Many fish have striking species-recognition markings on their sides. These markings, often highly colorful, also make them easily visible to the fish that prey on them, so fish that live in open water or over sea beds where there is no cover cannot afford to be striking in appearance. The dual need to be able to signal to other members of the species and to be inconspicuous to predators has led to various compromises. Some fish have "invented" the ability to change color. They radiate bright colors when they are signaling to a conspecific, but immediately afterward resume their dull costume. Others keep their attention-catching signals hidden on fins that are normally folded up, and which they unfold only for the purpose of signaling (44, 46).

There are comparable conflicts in human behavior. Compassion can come into conflict with the need for obedience. Both are ethical values and there appears to be an innate disposition to both, as we shall see later. In such cases man cannot place absolute reliance on his "parliament of the instincts" and yield to the stronger impulse. He must seek to resolve the conflict by a process of examination. Examination of what? First of all, certainly, of what is expedient. Clearly anything detrimental to the survival of the species can be judged negatively. But is there, over and above this, a hierarchy of values? Can I place a higher value on one innate tendency over another? Is, say, compassion or love of one's fellow-man a nobler impulse to be valued more highly than aggressiveness? The problem is certainly a difficult one, for all these impulses are adaptive. If one human group exterminates another it could be said that the victorious group is biologically more successful than the defeated one and that it is quite right for the fitter to prevail in this way. In my opinion, however, it is possible to lay down a scale of values according to which such a view is inadmissible. My starting point is the fact of evolution. Scarcely any biologist really looks at nature impartially. We speak of a "higher" development of organisms in the course of evolutionary history and of "higher" and "lower" animals, by which we mean more or less differentiated. Those social drives, which are correlated with our love for our fellow-man, are not only of a more recent date than aggression; they have also led to a vast amount of differentiation in our social behavior. The astonishing development of human culture is based on cooperation and mutual assistance. With the capacity for love, the higher vertebrates have outgrown aggression and have reached an evolutionary stage that must be evaluated as "higher." Equipped with the aggressive impulse alone, we should not have advanced beyond the level of reptiles.

The biologist can use the same argument to support the argument for individual freedom. Our cultural development, and with it the acceleration and "rationalization" of evolution (see p. 40), is based upon it. And this is ultimately an evolutionary step, the consequences of which we cannot yet foretell.

In deriving ethical norms from nature we must note that many things can be a historical handicap. We have already mentioned those animals saddled with physical structures that were once evolved for a purpose, but which have lost their species-preserving value, thanks to changes in the environment (see p. 33). In the same way, many deeply rooted impulses may also become obsolete, that is to say, no longer adaptive. This is true, for example, of the impulses to conformity. People all over the world have a tendency to respond with violent hostility toward outsiders and minorities who deviate from the majority. Demagogues in all ages have always appealed to "sound national sentiment" when they wanted to incite feeling against a minority. This impulse can be seen even in small children who tease those of their playmates who limp or stutter. This behavior imposes conformity on those that are able to adapt, and this may earlier have been an advantage in the process of natural selection, for it strengthened the unity of the group. Today it is certainly no longer an advantage. The gifts of the outsider are of value to a society with a highly differentiated division of labor. Furthermore we have reached a level of awareness which enables us to recognize that even our fellow-men who may deviate from the norm resemble us in fundamentals. This awareness needs to be focused still more, for it is the only means of gaining mastery over our own obsolete intolerance. To establish that a tendency is innate to us is no reason to justify it.

The inclination to conformity also comes to light in various patterns of politeness. On specific occasions people dress in the same way, thus demonstrating their similarity. To be the odd man out is not good form. Even at table people have a tendency to order the same food, though in this case the drive to conformity is less strong.

A further pair of concepts closely related to those of "good" and "evil," though they are not synonymous, are the opposites "healthy"/"sick" or "normal"/"abnormal." If one wishes to establish what is the norm, one should not simply be guided by the numerical distribution of a characteristic in a population. Even if the number of diabetics amounted to over 80 per cent in the population, it would not occur to anyone to regard this diseased form of carbohydrate metabolism as normal. It can only be held in check by means of drugs and clearly constitutes a disadvantage in the natural selection process. Thus, in addition to the statistical norm, which simply gives information about the numerical distribution of characteristics present at the time of the investigation, there is also the ideal norm, which can be ascertained by considering the survival value of specific characteristics.

For this reason Kinsey (*110*) is wrong when he claims that the terms "normal" and "abnormal" are out of place in a scientific context. When the question of evaluating sexual aberrations arises, he himself, after all, makes full use of the concept of normality.*

INHIBITING AGGRESSION

The commandment "Thou shalt not kill" is found in some form or other among all peoples, even among headhunters and cannibals. General license to kill a fellow human being does not exist anywhere. This certainly makes sense from the viewpoint of expediency: without such a regulation it is scarcely possible to imagine human beings having a social life in common. But the interesting question is whether we observe this law solely by means of our reason or whether we are, in addi-

---

* On the subject of sodomy (in the sense of bestiality) Kinsey (*110*) writes: "There are histories of farm-bred males . . . who have lived in constant fear that their early histories will be discovered. The clinician who can reassure these individuals that such activities are biologically and psychologically part of the normal mammalian picture and that such contacts occur in as high a percentage of the farm population as we have already indicated, may contribute materially toward the resolution of these conflicts." Apart from the fact that this line of argument is unsound, it must also be pointed out that the statement that comparable behavior is a normal phenomenon in mammals is quite false. Among wild animals living free we have no knowledge either of mating between different species or of homosexuality. What we can do is to produce such phenomena artificially by means of imprinting (*185*).

tion to this, following innate tendencies. If the latter should prove valid our hope for a peaceful coexistence will have a firmer foundation than if compulsion and pure reason alone make us law-abiding.

We have already discussed the fact that among different animals the killing of conspecifics is prevented by observation of certain rules of combat and through the presence of certain aggression-inhibiting mechanisms. Many animals are able to submit to a conspecific in the course of a fight, and their gestures of submission inhibit any further attack. In animals these "behavioral analogies to morality," as Lorenz (*141*) calls them, are innate. Human beings, too, possess a rich repertoire of gestures of appeasement and submission, most of them innate. Thus people in the most varied cultures weep and lament in basically the same way—not only with the same gestures but with the same sounds. As already mentioned, even children born blind and deaf do weep. Even in those gestures of surrender that are culturally developed there is a residue of innate elements. Thus in submitting to another individual one makes oneself smaller, for example by prostrating oneself, kneeling or bowing.

Among !Ko Bushmen children, quarrels often end with the opponents staring at each other. One will finally give up, lower the head with a pouting expression on his face. This always inhibits attacks and may even release consoling (*52*). Helplessness, weakness, and childlike behavior equally arouse pity (p. 130).

Our most important signal of friendship is the smile. Equipped with this innate behavior pattern we are able to make friends with complete strangers. A smile disarms. I read only recently of an American sergeant who suddenly found himself face to face with two Vietcong soldiers. His gun misfired and he smiled, which inhibited his enemies. But mistrust and fear at once caused the established contact to fade away again. The American ejected the cartridge, recocked his gun and killed his opponents.

The characteristics of the small child (see the "infant schema" on p. 22) also have an appeasing effect in themselves. It is true that history has plenty of attested reports of acts of violence against defenseless children, but such events are always described by the chroniclers as something exceptional and terrible. It is significant that people everywhere were outraged by the massacre at My Lai, while the news of the anonymous murder of a far greater number of civilians by bombing attacks is received relatively calmly. The notion of someone gunning down women and children has always been horrifying, since it outrages our feelings. I shall discuss how things of this kind can nevertheless happen. Since a child inhibits aggressive acts just by its appearance, appeal via a child is very frequently used for appeasement. For example, if the Australian aborigines wanted to make contact with the white men, two high-ranking men would push a small child along in front of them, placing their hands on its shoulders. They relied upon the fact that no one would do anything to harm a small child (*12*). I shall give further examples in demonstration of this principle. Let me just state now that, in their means of inhibiting aggression, human beings are in no way out of step with the higher vertebrates. With a few signals we can appease our fellows within seconds. It is really amazing how quickly a person boiling with rage can be pacified with a smile, with submissive behavior (often with simulated helplessness—an "infant appeal"), or with a stammered apology.

Sympathy-arousing and pacifying appeals do not however always suffice to prevent the murder of a conspecific. And we are faced with the question of why this is so. Lorenz believes that our inhibitions against attacking fellow-men are only sufficient when they are personally known to us. Our reason can fully grasp the commandment to love all fellow-men, but, as we are now constructed, we are not capable of fulfilling this commandment. We experience warm feelings of love and friendship only as a bond with individuals; and, with the best will in the world, this cannot be altered. According to Lorenz, the only hope is that our descendants will alter genetically under the pressure of selection and thus acquire the capacity to love all men without respect of persons. Today's man, he believes, is not good enough for the requirements of modern social life. And this is indeed the impression one gains witnessing the ruthless warfare between nations.

By inclination we are certainly less inhibited vis-à-vis strangers. Every motorist knows how easily we grow annoyed with strangers who hold us up on the road. Only recently when I was driving my car an overtaking motorist cut in on me. I was just about to curse him when I recognized the driver as a close acquaintance and my mood at once altered; we smiled at each other, exchanged friendly waves, and my anger subsided. Toward strangers we are less tolerant.

In the latter we have an innate disposition which we share with those gregarious mammals that form closed groups. This includes most Old World apes and monkeys. Nevertheless aggressive encounters among all these animals do not normally lead to murder. Although gorillas, chimpanzees, and orangutans are physically very strong and have a powerful bite, there is so far only one written record of a male gorilla strangling another, and even in this case the reporter did not witness it himself but heard it from a game warden. Apart from this, to my knowledge, no observer has ever described a male ape killing another in the wild. In man the situation is quite different: according to the latest calculations, 25 per cent of all male Waika Indians are killed in battle (*30*). This fact about human aggression is not simply explained by lesser inhibitions with regard to strangers; there are two further factors involved.

Two conditions for the effectiveness of submissive gestures of appeasement are that the victim of the attack should have sufficient time to transmit his signals of subjection, and that his assailant can in turn take note of them. These conditions are generally no longer fulfilled when men attack one another with weapons. Even with the invention of the first prehistoric flint hand-ax man acquired the power to disable his opponent at a single blow and thereby to deprive him straightaway of all possibility of submission. It is certainly no accident that with the arrival of the first weapons we also discover the first smashed-in human skulls. Of the australopithecine skulls excavated by Raymond Dart in South Africa, most showed traces of the effects of violence.* Our innate means of inhibiting attack are adjusted to our biological equipment. So long as men attacked one an-

* The evidence about skull injuries in Pleistocene man has been compiled by M. K. Roper (*170*). Some cases have doubtlessly been wrongly interpreted as being caused by human hands, but enough cases remain to support the thesis.

other with bare hands, then one of them could end by submitting and thus arouse pity. With the invention of the first
weapon the situation was transformed overnight, and we must
realize that at that moment man found himself in a crisis similar to the one that confronts us today in the atomic age. Our
forefathers managed to adapt to it, but each new weapon confronted them yet again with the problem of inventing new
cultural controls; so the development of codes of chivalrous
behavior constantly limped behind weapons technology. I have
had recent personal experience in the Upper Orinoco of the
difficulties caused to men by newly introduced weapons. The
Waika Indians there have for some years been supplied with
chopping knives (machetes) from the missions. At one village
when I was there a man beat his wife with a machete, inflicting
deep cuts on her shoulders and arms. Only then did he realize
what he was doing and took her to be bandaged at the nearby
mission, looking after her most solicitously. Such accidents occur quite often. The danger of these machetes has obviously not
yet fully penetrated the Waikas' consciousness. Under the stress
of emotion they use them like cudgels. They would never use
their poison darts carelessly like this within their own group.

A weapon makes it possible to kill easily and quickly. Indeed
when firing from a distance a man with a gun is generally not
aware that he is on the point of killing a fellow human being.
He aims at a dark speck on the landscape and merely squeezes
with one finger. The fact that this has such terrible consequences for his fellow-man is something he simply cannot grasp
emotionally. And if one asked a bomber pilot to kill his victims
one by one, he would be outraged at the suggestion. That is the
extent to which our innate inhibitions are the dupe of technical
progress, and we must compensate for this with our understanding if we are to survive as a species. But the inhibitions—and
let us not forget this—are still present. Our means of appealing
and our innate capacity for pity are given to us as phylogenetic
adaptations.

Possibly even more serious than the invention of weapons
is man's ability to transform his opponent into a "devil."
Thanks to our highly developed intellect, human beings can
convince themselves that their opponents are not men but at

best beasts or highly dangerous monsters: such "vermin" not only may but must be killed. The Mundrucus of Brazil divide the world into themselves and "Pariwat"—all the rest. These others count as game and they are spoken of as animals [Murphy (*158*)]. On Java the same word is used for "human" and belonging to one's own group. A study of American war comics has shown that the death cries and shouts of terror uttered by Americans are different from those of the enemy (*203*). And in war, so as to prevent soldiers discovering, through contact with their opponents, that they, too, are fellow human beings, strict nonfraternization orders are issued, forbidding contact with the enemy even after defeat. Massive war propaganda would certainly not be necessary if man were not at bottom ready for contact and to a certain extent inhibited from attacking every fellow-man. The readiness to form a bond with one's fellow-man is in fact so great that there is always the "danger" that two hostile groups may fraternize if they face one another for long enough and at close enough quarters. In the First World War, the trenches on the western front were so close to one another that when the front remained at a standstill for months at a time the French and Germans could not help discovering the human qualities in their opponents; the simple realization that the fellow over there was just as hungry and suffering just the same daily privations was enough to "demoralize" the troops. When they reached the stage of exchanging cigarettes it was time for the general staff to replace them with reserves. In these cases the recognition that the others were human too sufficed to inhibit their readiness to attack and to arouse their readiness to form a bond. Thus the prior existence of an individualized bond is by no means a prerequisite for inhibiting aggression, though it helps considerably (see p. 125).

The process of transforming one's opponent into a devil does not consist simply in branding him as a monster, but much more in arousing fear and mistrust. And it is fear, as every traveler knows, that closes doors. Primitive peoples are often aggressive toward strangers only because of fear. If one visits such people in a fairly large group, one must make one's peaceful intentions very plain. Indeed among the aggressive Waikas friendly visits from village to village are tolerated only if the visitors bring women and children with them. On my many expeditions among these peoples I have very often been alone and I have never been approached by anyone with hostility. On my own I never released fear, only friendly curiosity, and this has given me the opportunity to make friends with these people by smiling and with the help of other contact-making behavior patterns (see p. 129).

The great significance attached to war propaganda shows how strongly men, left to themselves, incline toward peaceful contact. Once such contact is established between people, then there are strong inhibitions to aggression. Even in his day Darwin (36) was of the opinion that it is a crucial task of the civilized man to extend the feelings of sympathy that bind him to his acquaintances beyond the range of small-group loyalties to include all mankind:

"If man progresses in culture and smaller tribes are unified into larger societies, then the simplest consideration on the part of every individual will tell him that he must extend his social instincts and sympathies to all members of the same nation, even if they are unknown to him personally. Once this point is reached there is only an artificial barrier preventing him from extending his sympathies to all people of all nations and all races" (not quoted verbatim).*

Our discussion has shown that we are equipped with aggression-inhibitions, even vis-à-vis strangers, provided we do not erect barriers which prevent contact and do not employ weapons that so distance us from the enemy that we cannot take account of his human reactions. It is in the fact that these attack-inhibitions have not simply been created as a cultural superstructure that our greatest hope lies. If this were not so, a culture devoid of pity could all too easily be established—there would indeed be no norms of bond-forming behavior. As it is, for men everywhere killing our fellow-men cannot be undertaken without a sense of conflict.

Of the factors mentioned that enable man to overcome his

---

* This idea has also recently been taken up by A. Gehlen (73), who speaks of an enlarged "clan ethos" ("Sippenethos"): "The ethos of altruism is the family one; it first exists within the extended family but it is capable of extension until the idea embraces the whole of humanity" (p. 121).

innate inhibitions, I consider his capacity for mentally dehumanizing his fellow-men to be the most dangerous. In the last analysis it is this capacity to switch off pity that makes him into a cold-blooded murderer. It is with this in mind that Lorenz, too, has pointed out that the purely reasonable man of the future, predicted in the rationalists' utopias, who pays no attention to his inner voices, would certainly be no angel but much more likely the opposite.

OBEDIENCE AND LOYALTY

The capacity for pity is undoubtedly innate in us; but how far other basic ethical attitudes are determined by phylogenetic adaptations is much less certain. It is, however, noticeable that certain virtues prevail throughout the whole spectrum of cultures, for example, courage, loyalty to friends, altruism, self-sacrifice, helpfulness, respect, and obedience. These values held in common could, of course, result wholly from parallel cultural developments. But for obedience to authority there is experimental evidence pointing to the probability that this is a disposition innate to human beings.

Obedience to authority was and is an ethical value in a variety of cultures. Even today religious orders demand blind submission; indeed Abraham's willingness to murder his son still stands as a horrific symbol of our Western culture. Nevertheless, blind obedience to authority is being increasingly rejected. Obedience should derive only from understanding and should be withheld if one is ordered to harm a fellow-man. But even in cultures that support this ideal, in certain circumstances the readiness to obey can outweigh pity. This has been shown by S. Milgram (*149–151*) in a series of very striking experiments. He invited people from different walks of life to take part in a simulated learning experiment. The subjects were told that the purpose was to verify, by means of certain experiments, the effects of punitive stimuli on the learning process. They were then shown a person in the adjoining room who was strapped into a chair with electrodes fastened to his arms. Their task —they were told—consisted in transmitting punitive electric shocks, via a machine set up in the next room, whenever the man in the chair made a mistake. The strength of the shocks, moreover, was to be increased from mistake to mistake. For this purpose the machine had a series of thirty levers, graduated from 15 to 450 volts. The higher steps were also labeled as "dangerous." When a group of psychiatrists was asked about the likely outcome of an experiment constructed in this way they were unanimous in declaring that scarcely anyone would continue up to the highest electric shock level, and anyone who did so would certainly refuse to press the very last lever. Only 0.1 per cent would carry out the task obediently until the end. What actually happened deviated in an alarming fashion from this estimation of what was culturally probable. Although at the higher shock levels simulated cries of protest recorded on tape were heard from the next room ("It's hurting me," "Stop!" etc.), 62.5 per cent obeyed the experimenter's instructions. In so doing these obedient subjects experienced a distinct conflict. Their pity was aroused by the cries and they suggested to the experimenter that they should stop. But when the latter replied that they must continue, they did so, often laughing hysterically and insisting that they would take no responsibility. If the experimenter was not actually present in the room and gave his instructions by telephone, the subjects cheated. They pretended to increase the punishing stimuli from mistake to mistake as they were told, but they did not do so. This shows that they were not sadistically motivated. When the authority was less immediate, the subjects' willingness to obey was not so great. Some of the subjects came into the room and found an experiment already in progress: an accomplice of the experimenter's who was working the machine asked the experimenter if he was a doctor; if the latter replied that he was not, the number of people who subsequently refused to obey him was increased. Milgram's experiments show that innate dispositions prevail over cultural imprinting. The readiness to obey revealed by these experiments is a dangerous tendency in man. Willingness to obey and to subordinate oneself is certainly an ethical value. But it can also lead to people becoming tools of others, without a will of their own. In order to counteract this danger one must be aware of it.

A further human disposition is group allegiance. This, too,

is easily abused. The fact that we stand by our friends and are loyal to our group is certainly "good." Lorenz describes how people, particularly in case of danger from outside, will go to the aid of the members of their group and if necessary give their lives. This self-sacrifice is accompanied by the emotion of "enthusiasm" and by certain physical movements derived from our prehistory (see p. 16). We experience the sensation of our hair standing on end as a "divine thrill" (the *"heiliger Schauer"* of the German poets) running over our bodies. This drive to help one's fellows is easily exploited; every dictatorship knows how to activate assistance-behavior by invoking an imaginary danger, and in this way to unite the group. The group's aggressive feelings are then collectively directed against the enemy. When Arthur Koestler (in a paper at the fourteenth Nobel Symposium in Stockholm in 1969) commented on this in passing to the effect that the great catastrophes of human history are not to be traced back to man's fundamentally aggressive behavior but to the individual's excessive loyalty to the existing social order, he was doubtless conscious of making a debating point for effect. The fact of the matter is that excessive loyalty is only dangerous because fundamentally aggressive behavior *is* innate to man.

To summarize, then, we can state that there are in fact innate norms for our ethical behavior. All over the world it is murder if one kills a person with whom one is associated by a bond. What counts as a bond differs from culture to culture. Among many Polynesians the killing of a child was permitted so long as it had not yet taken suck from its mother. After this, however, it was held to be murder. On the Molucca Islands a headhunter was allowed to kill his enemy only from behind (202). If he had looked him in the face first and then killed him, it was murder. A greeting returned obliged the Rwala Bedouins to help one another (see p. 171). When a Papuan had eaten with another man he was this man's friend and was not allowed to kill him (*160*).

In addition to this, an innate inhibition against killing is demonstrable in man—its corollary being pity. Its effectiveness certainly depends on the degree of personal acquaintance, but it can also be activated by specific behavior on the part of strangers. The ability to "dehumanize" one's opponent and the invention of weapons have enabled man to override these inhibitions.

We should not follow all our innate inclinations unconditionally. This is particularly true of obedience and loyalty, both of which lend themselves to misuse by demagogues. They are therefore ethical values only in a restricted sense. Innate tendencies that counteract aggression are to be valued more highly. In my view the interpretation of evolutionary history justifies a hierarchy of values of this kind. And judged from this standpoint altruism also ranks more highly. The phylogenetic roots of this ethic will be shown in the following chapter.

7

Antidotes to Aggression

RITES WHICH ESTABLISH A BOND

Animals can be both sociable and aggressive. At first sight the two seem impossible to reconcile, for if a fellow species member can arouse both friendly impulses of attraction and those of repulsion one might expect the result to be insoluble conflict. And it is true that all animals living in closed groups have had to resolve this problem. In order to do so a number of inventions have proved necessary. Among other things, rites that appease and establish bonds had to be evolved. Aggressive animals that live in groups are always busy keeping the peace. A bull sea lion has to make peace many times a day. If two of his females quarrel, he quickly flops ashore and presses between the two of them, nodding to both sides. High-ranking baboons intervene in quarrels between members of the group, threatening in their turn. If this is of no avail they attack, which ends the fight at once. Greeting rites play a great part in the life of social animals, and their function in appeasing aggression in men and animals has been proved (see p. 108). If ever a night heron fails to greet its family when it lands on the nest, its offspring and mate will attack it with their beaks. And if we ourselves allow a long time to elapse without giving our friends some token greeting, we run the risk of falling out with them. If one observes gregarious animals, one notices that most of them make very similar use of their appeasement rites as we do of our smile. Potentially tense situations are relaxed by means of friendly gestures. We remember the hamadryas baboon (see

p. 76) that took possession of a female because it made first contact with it, and then appeased its empty-handed rival with gestures of "presenting" and lip-smacking. Human beings often take the sting out of unpleasant communications with an apology or some other friendly gesture. The appeasement of aggression, therefore, is a central function of social rites. But what do these look like in detail and how have they arisen?

The capacity to appease is already possessed by reptiles, which are not social animals. A sand lizard defeated by another will lie flat on its belly. This is the precise opposite of the threatening posture used in challenging. The fight-releasing signals are switched off and the fight ends because the animal is quite simply no longer eliciting a fighting response. It is hard to say in this case whether a positive inhibition to the fighting impulse is also released.* The principle of hiding the fight-eliciting signals so as to prevent further attacks is widespread. Many cichlids defeated in battle change from their bright colors to an inconspicuous hue, which at times resembles the coloration of the young. Rites that not only appease but also go on to establish a bond are generally somewhat more complicated.

A few years ago I was sitting on a volcanic rock on the shore of Narborough, one of the Galápagos Islands, watching the flightless cormorants, whose nesting ground this was. In front of me were two nests. On each was an adult bird shading its young from the sun with outstretched wings. They were panting noisily in the almost unbearable heat. From time to time one of the birds would sink down in a doze but at once the begging of the young birds or a movement from its neighbor would rouse it with a start. The two would then snap at each other with wide open beaks, but the nests were sufficiently far apart for the neighbors not to be able to reach each other. Their demonstrations of unsociability went no further.

The air shimmered over the black rocks and the volcanic island in the background was shrouded in haze. I was on the point of going off to find a place in the shade when I saw a soaking wet male cormorant come waddling up from the sea-

---

* In many reptiles submissive posture is the same as the female mating display. Occasionally male wall-lizards attempt to copulate with a rival that acknowledges defeat.

shore. From its beak dangled a bunch of seaweed. It made straight for one of the nests and woke its mate. She pointed her beak straight up at the sky and let out a deeply guttural "Cro cro"; the male bowed his head. The female took the opportunity to snatch the bunch of seaweed violently from him and built it into the side of the nest. Meanwhile the male dried off his wings and body plumage and five minutes later, when he had finished, he climbed onto the edge of the nest, briefly held his mate's beak in his own, then nibbled at her neck, and finally pointed down into the nest with his beak. At this invitation the female got up and moved off (Fig. 25) (47).

After that I watched several similar relief ceremonies and each time the returning bird brought a gift with it, generally a bunch of seaweed but sometimes a starfish or a piece of drift-

Fig. 25. Relief ceremony of the flightless cormorant. The returning male first gives the female a bunch of seaweed. He can now dry his feathers near her. By means of tentative nibbling movements (ritualized grooming), he then invites the female to give him charge of the nest (from photographs by the author).

wood. It never came without a gift, which suggested to me the experiment which I shall now describe.

On another occasion, when a male was waddling up with his gift, I went over and stole the gift from his beak. As these cormorants, like a great many of the Galápagos animals, are tame, this was not difficult. The cormorant looked round in momentary puzzlement, but he had obviously not quite grasped what had happened, for he waddled on up to the nest, where a little domestic drama was now acted out. Far from being met with a cry of greeting, the male received a pecking. He quickly made himself scarce, fetched a piece of driftwood, and tried approaching the nest again. This time it worked. The female took the gift and allowed the male to remain close to her.

In these birds, evidently, a conspecific releases strong aggressive feelings which can only be appeased by the offer of nesting material. One can observe how when this happens the bird taking the gift generally snatches it away violently. This suggests that the gift acts, among other things, as a lightning conductor for undischarged aggression. And this is entirely possible, for the motor sequence of thrusting and snatching has a formal resemblance to an aggressive act. Thus the discharge would take place by means of the appropriate motor sequences. We know, moreover, that animals can work off their aggressive feelings on substitute targets: if zoo animals cannot reach the object of their rage, because it is in the cage next door, they will often attack one of the occupants of their own cage. This also happens when an animal of middle rank has been attacked by a high-ranking animal. In such a case the animal attacked does not dare to strike back. However, it gets rid of the aggressive feelings that have been activated by attacking a third animal of a lower rank than itself. Grzimek (76) has aptly characterized this behavior as a "cyclist reaction." Birds frequently work off their aggressive feelings on inanimate objects in their vicinity. Oystercatchers, when fighting, peck up nesting material between rounds. Marsh tits tear moss from branches between bouts of quarreling, and herring gulls pull up tufts of grass during frontier disputes (206).

The passing of nesting material between cormorants when

function. And this could have been the phylogenetic starting point for the ritualization of such behavior into a greeting gesture. If the bird on the nest regularly snatched away the nesting material from its mate who came up to add to the nest and in so doing worked off its aggressive feelings, this could well suffice as the point of departure for a process of ritualization.

However this may have come about, the actions of passing over nesting materials are today common greeting gestures among birds: they have a clear appeasing function. I learned this as a student in a very dramatic way when I was working at the Wilhelminenberg Biological Station near Vienna. Otto Koenig, one of my colleagues, had brought a half-grown heron from nearby Lake Neusiedler which would not allow anyone to feed it. Whenever we approached, it drove us away with its beak. After several vain attempts to feed it, Koenig had an idea; he took a reed blade and held it out in front of the bird's beak. The heron lunged forward, as if to attack, snatched the reed, and built it into the nest on which it was sitting. After this its behavior toward us changed fundamentally. From now on the bird let us feed it. Gray herons pass one another reed blades when pairing, and our young bird had understood the gesture of friendship quite correctly.

Very many other birds pass one another nesting material when pairing. The male sarus crane pushes blades of straw toward its partner in courtship. Among skuas the females lay down grass in front of the male. Many male passerine birds mate with a blade of grass in their beaks, among them zebra finches. In the courtship of great crested grebes each partner holds a bundle of nesting material in its beak. Male greylag geese in the foreplay before mating dive for nesting material from the depths of the water in front of the female and make nest-building movements. Male diamond doves pass their females a blade of grass during copulation.

Adélie penguins lay a pebble at the feet of the female and many gannets do the same, including, interestingly, the blue-footed booby, which no longer builds a nest. In this case the expressive movement has survived the disappearance of the original behavior pattern. An instance of comparable behavior has been reported in the Central European cuckoo: a female held a twig in her beak when she was being courted by a male.

Red birds of paradise break off leaves during their courtship which they hold briefly in their beaks and then let fall to the ground. As a result of this, veritable carpets of leaves are formed under the trees where the courtship takes place. Perhaps it is from the offering of leaves that the habit of decorating a courtship platform with torn-off leaves evolved—a behavior pattern that is typical of various bower birds.

In the relief ceremony of the flightless cormorant, I also saw further behavior patterns of seizing the beak and nibbling at the neck feathers.

The seizing of the beak is a ritualized feeding gesture. It derives from brood-care behavior and its function is also to appease the mate. Such feeding gestures play a great part in the affectionate behavior of many animals. Often the partner is actually fed and the bond thus established by means of a reward. Male terns woo their females by offering them a fish. Tits, ravens, parrots, and many other passerine birds feed their partner as if it were a young bird (Fig. 26). The interpretation of this as a behavior pattern derived from the feeding of young

Fig. 26. *Above left: Common tern feeding its young; right: male tern, with fish, courting a female that is begging for food (from W. Wickler, 1969); below left: raven feeding its young; right: raven pair during courtship feeding (from photographs by E. Gwinner).*

Fig. 27. Above: Female woodpecker-finch begging from the male by fluttering her wings and opening her beak; below: male at entrance to the nest attracting the female by fluttering his wings (from film stills by H. Sielmann).

Fig. 28. Courting black-headed gull begging for food (from a photograph by N. Tinbergen).

is supported by the fact that the bird being fed often begs like a young bird. A male tit flutters his wings during courtship, as if he were a young bird: in this way he elicits the feeding response. Conversely, when the female transmits infantile signals the male will feed her. But the male's begging does not simply release the feeding response; it also attracts the female. On the Galápagos Islands we filmed a male woodpecker-finch attracting a female to the entrance of his nest by fluttering his wings (Figs. 27, 28) (*55*).

Feeding as a sign of affection has very often been ritualized into pure gesture. Thus bullfinches when they flirt with their beaks no longer exchange any food. They simply bill. Ritualized feeding can even continue as a friendly gesture when the parents have ceased to feed the young. The cuckoo feeds its female although it does not look after its own young. In one species of the equally parasitic wydahs, *Steganura obtusa,* the male "gives food" in front of the female in a ritualized fashion in midair. In the paradise wydah, *Steganura paradisaca,* however, we observe that the males carry out highly ritualized begging behavior in front of the females as a courtship display (*161*).

In mammals various forms of affectionate nuzzling have evolved from mouth-to-mouth feeding. Jackals, along with many other dog-like predators, feed their young direct from mouth to mouth or by regurgitating their food. In jackals and cape hunting dogs adults feed one another as well. A wolf or a domestic dog will appease a conspecific by pushing its nose against the corner of the mouth of the other animal, begging to be fed, and licking it, behavior which the other tolerates. In a whole number of predators the affectionate rubbing of noses has evolved out of such first steps. Female sea lions greet their young by rubbing snouts. This form of greeting has also been observed between male and female (Fig. 29). Later we shall be going into the origins of the human kiss (see p. 134).

Fig. 29. Affectionate nuzzling. Left: female seal greeting her young by rubbing snouts; right: male sea lion greeting a female (from photographs by the author).

A pacifying and bond-strengthening effect is also produced by the behavior patterns of social grooming. Many birds and mammals groom one another mutually, just as mothers clean their young; they lick their mate, rub it down, and comb through its fur or feathers. This is often no more than a fleeting gesture. The cormorant relieving his mate nibbles at her neck feathers only a few times. In other cases mutual grooming between adult animals is carried out at length and devotedly. Anyone can observe this in monkeys at the zoo. It is interesting that social grooming among members of a group of monkeys increases by leaps and bounds if young ones are present. My three marmosets groomed one another mutually three times as frequently after one of the females had given birth to young ones. This argues for the interpretation of social grooming as a derivative of parental care behavior. Clearly the marmosets were parentally motivated, for they also tried to approach the newborn babies, although the father would not allow this. Corresponding observations have also been made of lemurs. If a baby is born among monkey lemurs (*Propithecus verreauxi*), then the adult animals groom one another mutually four times as frequently as before (*106*).

The appeasing function of social grooming is supported by a series of observations. In the Schönbrunn Zoo in Vienna there was a wild onager stallion that always attacked the then director, Otto Antonius, when he approached its paddock. As Antonius always stayed out of reach, the stallion could never discharge its aggressive feelings on him. It would then regularly turn on a neighbor. On one occasion when this happened it was standing so that its hindquarters were turned toward Antonius. Antonius took his bunch of keys and scratched the stallion: "The result was staggering: as if he had received an electric shock, the stallion immediately left his neighbor alone, stood as quiet as a mouse, and surrendered himself, baring his teeth slightly, to the pleasure of this skin stimulation. After that his attitude to me was completely altered: whenever he saw or heard me he came up, turned round and presented his rump for me to scratch" (7, p. 300).

I have myself been able to make friends with an extremely timid bush-tailed galago by means of social grooming. Finally the animal lifted one arm, inviting me to scratch its armpit and chest. Clearly social grooming is experienced as pleasant by the animal being groomed.

In many cases the behavior patterns of social grooming have been ritualized into pure gesture. The mongoose lemur makes fur combing movements in the air with its lower jaw as a greeting, at the same time licking in the air with its tongue. Macaques chatter and show their tongues, even when they are greeting a human being whom they know. I have also seen this in a tame, collared mangabey (*Cerococebus torquatus*) and in a spider monkey (*Ateles geoffroyi*). I shall be referring later to movements in man that are outwardly extremely similar.

In the discussion of courtship feeding we mentioned that the animal being fed often begs like a young animal, making the first move for contact in this way. The fluttering of the young bird begging for food has been ritualized into a courtship movement in widely differing groups of birds. The male starling sings and flutters his wings, while the male great frigate bird displays himself with outspread wings and beats them if a female flies past. If the female lands beside him he puts his head back slightly and shakes it rapidly. This is yet another ritualized begging movement. Albatrosses bang their beaks together during courtship with rapid sideways movements. In doing this, they open and close them like young birds begging for food.

Young tree shrews lick saliva from their mother's mouth. In courtship the male licks the female's lips. Low-ranking dogs appease like puppies begging for food by pushing their muzzles against the corners of the mouths of high-ranking animals. Elements in adult behavior can even be taken over from that of the infant when being suckled. The friendly pawing of a dog, his gesture for making contact, is derived from the puppy's pawing movements when sucking milk. Dogs when submitting to another, appease, as we have mentioned, by presenting themselves on their backs like puppies. They urinate when doing this and this often releases the action of licking them dry, or at any rate such puppyish behavior inhibits aggression. The cape hunting dog or spotted hyena makes use of a form of "sucking-lick" in greeting which is derived from infant sucking

(*124*). The Uganda kob keeps the female with him after pairing by licking her udder (*28*). The female fallow deer approaches the buck with outstretched neck like a young deer coming to drink (*20*).* Chamois behave similarly (*120*). Young Grant's gazelle bucks submit to older ones in this posture.

The Chacma baboons' greeting of lip-smacking is also a part of their courtship foreplay. Anthoney (*6*) considers that the process here is one of rapidly repeated sucking movements from which lip-smacking evolves in continuous transition as the animal grows up. It is released by the sight of the pink nipples, the similarly colored penis, the female rump and the equally pink face of the young animal. These parts of the body have an attractive effect on baboons and thus contribute to the cohesion of the group.

It should now be clear that infantile behavior patterns are a quite normal part of the behavioral repertoire of adult animals. Use is made of them whenever the aim is to release appeasement and cherishing. My tame badger would suck at my elbow when frightened, long after it had been weaned. A male linnet that had broken a leg and begged like a young bird was fed by another. An adult frigate bird with only one wing and a blind adult pelican were found in a breeding colony. Both could have survived only because they were fed by conspecifics (*128*).

The reversion to infantile behavior patterns is described as "regression," and the infantile behavior patterns are described as "infantilisms" (see p. 130). The infantilisms in the repertoire of adults also include the cries of the young in the nest. When male hamsters pursue a female in courtship they emit cries like young animals that have fallen out of the nest (*42*). Male squirrels in the same situation employ the call of the young to their parents (*41*). The female roe deer in the rutting season attracts the buck with sounds like those used by the kids to call their mothers.

In the *Trachyphonus d'arnaudii*, an African species of barbet, both partners sing a melody together, each one taking turns

---

* Ewer (*59*), however, is of the opinion that this could be an intention movement for lying down, as fallow deer appease by lying on the ground with outstretched necks.

to sing specific sections. They sing so perfectly in tune with each other that one does not normally notice that two birds are singing together. During these duets the male will add a cry of "shrey" at a specific point, which is derived from the begging cries of the young (see Fig. 30) (*218*). There is an interesting parallel to this. The beak-snapping of the genera of weaverfinch, *Lonchura* and *Spermestes,* is a ritualized feeding process that occurs during courtship. In several species of *Lonchura*

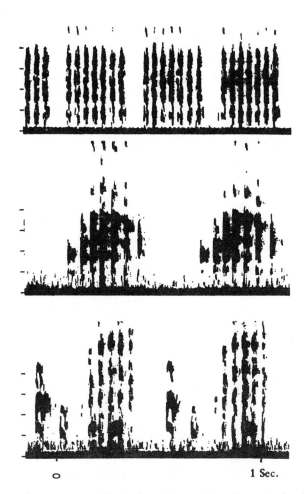

Fig. 30. Infantilisms in the greeting duet of the barbet, Trachyphonus d'arnaudii: *above: begging call of the young; middle: call of a young male; bottom: extract from a duet (from W. Wickler).*

(striated finches) this beak snapping is incorporated into the courtship song (*78*).

Male barbary apes appeal directly via the infant, just as men do (see p. 97). They will approach a high-ranking animal with a borrowed baby and in this way appease its aggression (Crook, verbal communication). It should also be mentioned that among Japanese macaques a male can increase its social rank by busying itself with a child. Itani (*104*) observed a male that managed to join the central group by cuddling an infant, at once increasing its rank. For the most part, however, infantile signals are not exploited so directly.

In the higher vertebrates most of these behavior patterns are modified infantilisms and actions derived from parental behavior. Of the eight known courtship movements of the weaver-finches three are derived from the begging of the young animal, two from feeding, and two from nest-building; the origin of the eighth movement is unknown (*78*). All the comforting gestures in the greeting repertoire of the chimpanzee (kissing, fingering, holding, embracing, and delousing) are derived from contact between mother and child.

It is noteworthy that even in social insects the behavior patterns of brood care are employed in the service of group cohesion. Ants, termites, and bees feed mutually one another. Bees and wasps on their return home are surrounded by their hive-fellows, who beg from them with animated movements of their feelers until they disgorge a drop of food. Those that are fed are then begged from in turn and in this way the food is shared out. The entomologist Forel has described the crops of the hymenoptera (ants, bees, and wasps) as a "social stomach" since the contents of the crop are indeed gradually shared out in this way among all the inhabitants of the hive or nest. In wasps and bees it is possible to establish that feeding does appease. A wasp will disgorge food as submissive behavior. Bees that get lost can be adopted into strange hives; initially they are liable to be attacked, but if they manage to distribute food quickly all round, they pacify their attackers and are accepted.

Among wasps and hornets the workers feed the larvae. They secrete a clear fluid between their jaws that is rich in protein and is eagerly taken by the latter. As long ago as 1928 W. M.

Wheeler (212) made the suggestion that the mutual exchange of food is one of the roots of the social life of insects. In his view, insect states are single permanent families, and the mutual exchange of food cements the group together. Only insects where the parents look after the young can feed one another mutually and only they form states.

Behavior patterns from the realm of parental care are particularly suited for group cohesion because cherishing behavior is primarily understood by the child as friendly. Conversely the mother is adjusted to the signals emitted by the young animal and reacts to them by looking after it. I shall go further into the corresponding relationships in man later on.

Appeasement and the establishing of a bond can also take place by means of sexual signals. The cichlid fish, *Tropheus moorei,* employs a shaking movement, also used by the male in courtship, as an appeasement gesture. Hamadryas baboons appease by presenting the rump. Even males make use of what was originally a female sexual gesture of presentation, and it sometimes happens that in response high-ranking males will mount them briefly and symbolically. This behavior pattern belongs to the greeting rites used on meeting. Low-ranking hamadryas baboons also greet high-ranking ones in passing with a brief presentation of the rump. In a number of primates that greet by means of female "presenting," the males have taken over more than the gesture into their repertoire of behavior; in the hamadryas baboon, for example, the males actually show a red swelling of the hindquarters as an intraspecific imitation of the female signal (217). Heterosexual "social" copulation which does not lead to ejaculation has also been observed in the hamadryas baboon.

BONDING DRIVES

The coming together of a number of animals into a group presupposes not only the existence of behavior patterns for appeasing aggression and establishing bonds but also the impulse to employ these means, a general appetitive behavior on the part of the individual animal to seek and maintain the proximity of another. This is true even of animals that live in open groups.

As a diver, one is always impressed by the large shoals of fish. To have thousands of silvery bodies come plunging up out of the blue depths of the sea, stream silently round one, and disappear into the far depths again is an unforgettable experience. I have spent many hours observing shoaling fish, and I have been particularly struck by their strong urge for cohesion. Individual fish separated from the shoal seek to return to it, darting this way and that as if in a real panic. Once back among the others they become quite calm, although they remained socially indifferent. The fish sought only the proximity of the others but paid no further attention to one another. Shoaling fish thus generally behave as if the conspecific were a refuge from danger. There are also fish living in quite small shoals which then know all the other members of the shoal individually, but these are exceptional. In the typical instance a shoal of fish.is an anonymous group.

Higher vertebrates initially seek refuge with their mothers. This is as true of chickens as it is of people. In baboons the young animal always turns to its mother during the first few months of its life, but later on looks to other high-ranking adults for protection. The most common goal-in-flight is the highest-ranking male, even—interestingly enough—when it is he that has elicited the flight response. If there is no high-ranking male available, then two young animals, or even two adults, may take flight toward and embrace one another. Left alone, a frightened young monkey will even embrace itself. Originally, however, the flight is always to the mother; the young monkey clings to her and may sometimes suck at her breast to calm itself (Fig. 31). The animal's readiness to take flight is then markedly decreased. What a moment ago released a flight response is now watched with interest from the position of safety. The calming effect of the mother can also be achieved by means of dummies. When frightened, young rhesus monkeys will run to a wire frame covered with cloth and cling to it tightly (*80*). Human children are soothed if one gives them a comforter and when they go to sleep they like to clutch soft objects like teddy bears or woolen blankets. A baby generally cries when it is put down and becomes quiet at once when picked up. As soon as a

Fig. 31. One source of the human urge for contact is going to the mother for protection. Frightened infants hide at their mothers' breasts and suck until they are soothed, or they may simply take the teat in their mouth like the infant rhesus monkey and the Negro baby in our pictures (from photographs by the author).

child can crawl or run, it will go to its mother and cling to her if anything upsets it (Figs. 32 and 33).

In all these cases we can establish appetitive behavior for security that is activated by the flight mood. Here the conspecific becomes what the mousehole is to the mouse or the hiding place in the reef is to the coral fish. The conspecific offers cover and protection and in this way to some extent acquires a "home valency." This is certainly one of the roots of the urge for contact. The conspecific becomes the "goal-in-flight"; its proximity means security. That is why the bond with a member of the group can be cemented by means of a fear motivation. Hess has reported that ducklings follow their mother even more closely the more one punishes them with electric shocks for doing so (*86*). If a female hamadryas baboon does not follow her mate closely, the male will run up to the female and give her a severe bite on the neck; after that she follows him again. It is often enough for the male to stare threateningly at the female (*125*). In men, too, fear often cements group cohesion, and political use is made of this fact (see p. 168).

Probably the formation of bonds via the flight drive is very old, for it is already at work in the open anonymous group. The child's action in going to its mother must originally have been motivated this way. The bond is instinctive and is not acquired merely secondarily via the feeding of the young, as is occasionally claimed (see p. 213). Children who grow up in foundling homes attach themselves to others of the same age and seek protection in one another, although they never feed one another. Young rhesus monkeys will cling in fear to a cloth dummy but not to a wire frame, although their milk bottle, which they look for when they want a drink, is fastened to the latter (*80*).

Fig. 32. Frightened creatures seek protection together. Above: the younger Sonjo child (right) clings to the older one, who clasps him protectively; below: rhesus monkey mother with half-grown young one. Contact with the mother soothes (from photographs by the author).

Fig. 33. The soothing effect of bodily contact is retained into adult life. Left: four-year-old female chimpanzee sheltering under the hand of a male (from a photograph by J. and H. van Lawick-Goodall); right: a human couple (from a photograph by the author).

On the other hand, the mother's attraction to her infant is motivated by the parental care drive. For the mother the infant does not represent the conspecific with a "home valency." It is primarily something to be cherished. In all mammals the young of the species transmit specific signals that release cherishing behavior. These can be olfactory, acoustic, or optical, although among primates optical infant signals acquire increasing significance. Young baboons have black coats up to their sixth month. The black coat elicits help and friendly interest from the adults. Even old males will take a young baboon to clean it and help it if it is attacked. Young vervet monkeys also have a coat coloration that distinguishes them from adults. Male vervets will even attack men who lay hands on a young one with this coat. They will not, however, come to the rescue if the conspecific caught is a young vervet that has lost its baby coat, or if it is an adult. The dark brown langur, *Presbytis obscurus,* has an almost golden yellow coat as an infant. So long as they are this color they will be cared for by all females.* Baby chim-

* But the inhibition of aggression effected by the langur's infant coat has no effect on males alien to the group. When a male overthrows the lead-

panzees possess a white tuft of fur on the hindquarters which is particularly noticeable when they "present." We have already discussed the infant signals in human beings.

Mothers often show extremely protective behavior. Mother baboons hold firmly onto their babies' tails as they make their first excursions and pull them back at once if there is danger. The females of anthropoid apes watch over the forays of their babies in the same way, retrieving them if they go too far away. Here, once again, we are dealing with genuine protective behavior which can occasionally be observed between adult animals. Galápagos sea lions bring back to the shore females that stray from their harems, using the same technique with which they drive young sea lions into the shallows when they venture too far out to sea (*43*). Gregarious birds also display protective behavior. Whether this should also be traced back to brood care behavior has yet to be proved. Lorenz (*141*) has described how jackdaws are brought back into the flock by members of the group. In 1929 when a group of jackdaws and crows settled near his jackdaw colony, the young birds born the previous year mingled with the strangers so that there was a risk that they would be absorbed into this migratory flock when it flew away. Two old males from the colony, however, brought the young birds back one by one in the course of a few hours by flying low over them from behind with outspread tails, emitting the "come home" call.

The mother's bond with her child is very frequently—but not always—individualized, that is to say, mothers recognize their own offspring individually. This is particularly true of mothers that lead their young and look after them for some time. In such animals it is certainly not adaptive for mothers to make no distinction between strange animals and their own young and to adopt young animals indiscriminately; this could lead to a female gathering too many young about her, which she would ultimately no longer be able to feed and look after. There is undoubtedly a selective pressure at work which de-

---

ership in a group of langurs he may sometimes kill all the young animals, though he spares the ones born after the takeover of the group, notwithstanding the fact that they, too, are not his progeny. This murderous behavior has so far been witnessed only by one scientist (*200*).

mands the cultivation of individualized relationships. Mothers often drive strange youngsters away fiercely. Female sea lions seize strange pups that are trying to suckle from them, frequently very roughly, and toss them to one side. Greylag geese attack strange goslings, and herring gulls even kill strange chicks that have strayed onto their territory (*206*). In such cases only acquaintanceship inhibits aggressive feelings. This pattern: "known = friend," "unknown = enemy" also generally determines the social life of the adults. Birds that are unknown to one another therefore have great difficulties in pair formation. Herring gulls and black-headed gulls must always begin by appeasing. Black-headed gulls, for example, in which both sexes have facial markings that release aggression, can never look straight at each other at the beginning of pair formation. They have to hide the aggression-releasing signal through a particularly emphasized turning away of the head known as "head flagging." At the beginning, they look at each other only out of the corners of their eyes. But as soon as they know each other individually they no longer need to do this. We have already referred to the aggression-inhibiting effect of personal acquaintance in human beings. In most cases the individual bond has probably arisen hand in hand with the development of parental care.

Konrad Lorenz (*141*) envisages an additional source of the individualized bond. He expresses the opinion that friendship—the coming together of two or several individuals into a defense community—was the starting point for the development of individualized relationships. "Doubtless the personal bond, love," he writes in *On Aggression*, "arose in many cases from intra-specific aggression, by way of ritualization of a redirected attack or threatening" (p. 217). This interpretation is based upon the observation that in many animals, threatening behavior patterns strengthen the bond with the partner and are made use of as greeting rites. The African jewel fish threatens a rival by swimming up to him, suddenly stopping very close to him, making a threat display and striking him with his tail. When greeting his mate, he shows the same behavior, with one difference: he carries out the tail-blow and the threat display as he swims past. Thus the orientation is different, a fact which indicates that the mate is not the object of the attack. Pairs of greylag geese greet each other with the "triumph ceremony," in which the geese threaten past each other with their necks. The two geese are, as it were, directing a threat against another party, and this unites the two partners. But in the greylag goose it is not only the male and female that are united by the triumph ceremony: the aggressive rite has become a general one for establishing a bond, one which unites groups of friendly individuals. Greylag geese also establish a bond with the mate during courtship by means of aggression. A gander begins either by actually attacking or by pretending to attack some conspecific—or even a human being standing on the shore—and then turns to the goose of his choice and greets her with the triumph cry. He repeats this until his chosen mate accepts his proposal and also utters the triumph cry. Later on, feigned attacks on some neighbor or other and the subsequent performance of the triumph ceremony with the partner serve to reinforce the bond (*141*).

A male rhesus monkey that wishes to make friends with another begins by remaining near him. He tries to win favor by offering to delouse him. In addition to this, he will make sudden attacks on passing monkeys; in other words, he tries to draw his prospective friend into a joint action, sometimes succeeding. Once the two of them have beaten up someone together they are good friends (222). We find comparable behavior in human beings (see p. 166).

Lorenz's (*141*) observations of greylag geese led him to the supposition that love is a child of aggression. In his opinion this is supported by the fact that intraspecific aggression is millions of years older than personal friendship and love. "During long epochs of the earth's history there have been animals that were certainly extraordinarily fierce and aggressive. Nearly all reptiles of the present day are aggressive, and it is unlikely that those of antiquity were less so. But the personal bond is known only in teleost fishes, birds, and mammals, that is, in groups that did not appear before the later Mesozoic period. Thus intra-specific aggression can certainly exist without its counterpart, love, but conversely there is no love without aggression" (*141*, p. 217).

There is no doubt whatever that this is so. But in all those cases in which it has been shown that redirected aggression serves to strengthen a bond, this effect could not occur without the prior existence of an individualized bond. Lorenz emphasizes that it is of the essence of this particular kind of appeasement ceremony that "it cannot be indiscriminately discharged at any anonymous fellow-member of the species but demands for its object the personally known partner" (p. 148). It can further be established that while there is no friendship without aggression, there is also, with few exceptions, no friendship without parental care. In addition, there is no case known to me in which animals have formed a bond via aggression alone, without parental care also playing some part in the process. This, just as much as the fact that the effectiveness of a "threat-greeting" in animals always presupposes the existence of a bond, seems to indicate that for the most part love is not primarily a child of aggression but has arisen with the evolution of parental care. Parental care includes defense of the young, and as the group can be regarded as an extended family, group defense, with its strong emotions, may well be derived from brood defense and family defense. Joint brood defense, or group defense, is a force for cohesion. Among the animals that do not look after their young, such as the reptiles or amphibians, we know of no group defense and no fighting partnerships. In this respect their aggression can be clearly distinguished from that of species that look after their young.

Brood care, on the other hand, calls very early on for individual partnerships and individualized cherishing of the young, and thereby offers the necessary basis for a differentiated social life. I know of no land vertebrate that bands together, forming a personal bond with other fellow species members in the process, and which has been proved to have no brood-tending ancestors. Secondarily, this type of banding together can acquire its own motivation completely. According to Tiger (*203*) this is true, for example, of the banding together of human males into all-male groups.

A strong motivation for contact-seeking results from the sexual drive. This drive is at least as old as aggression—perhaps even older, for even one-celled organisms are subject to it. It is therefore relevant to ask whether a lasting bond between conspecifics cannot be established via the sexual drive. Interestingly, this is more rarely the case than one would expect. One of the few exceptions is man. Social animals do indeed make use of rites borrowed from the sexual repertoire for appeasement, but a lasting union is established via the sexual drive really only in man and a few other primates (see p. 155), and this has certainly evolved, secondarily and additionally, to reinforce the original bond.

We can therefore answer the question we asked in the first chapter about the existence of innate "bonding drives" as follows. In vertebrates two principal roots of sociability can be proved. On the one hand contact-seeking is motivated via the flight drive. The conspecific is the "goal-in-flight": security is found in its vicinity. It has "home valency." This is already the case with shoaling fish and holds good right up to the higher primates. A second motivational root is the parental care drive. It unites the parents with their offspring and is clearly excellently suited to reinforcing the bond between adults. We drew attention to the fact that only animals that care for their young form closed groups. Only they have succeeded in forming a bond in spite of the "aggression barrier." They all do it by means of behavior patterns of cherishing which originate from parental care, and by making use of infantile signals, which activate this behavior.

Aggression plays only a secondary role in strengthening a bond and even then, this function—that of the "fighting community"—has evolved via the defense of the young and the family. To my knowledge no vertebrate has formed a bond with a conspecific primarily and exclusively via aggression. Even the individualized relationship—love—has evolved primarily from the parental care relationship. The sexual drive, on the other hand, is an extremely rarely used means of cohesion, although in the case of human beings it does play an important role. Despite the fact that it is one of the oldest drives it has, curiously enough, not given rise to the development of lasting individualized bonds, apart from a few rare exceptions. The roots of love are not in sexuality, although love makes use of it for the secondary strengthening of the bond.

8

What Keeps People Together?

As a social being with aggressive tendencies man, too, has to cope with the problem of controlling aggression. Within the group he avoids provocation and makes peace if two members quarrel. Conflicts that cannot be avoided are defused by the use of appeasing rites. If we find ourselves compelled to frustrate the wishes of a fellow human being, we excuse ourselves or we avoid saying so directly and say it "with flowers." This kind of indirect approach in our social manners reduces the harshness of any refusal and thereby preserves the social bond. This is clear in courtship customs, for example. In the Eifel district of the Rhine when a young man visits the girl of his choice he brings a bottle of wine and if she fetches a glass this indicates her acceptance. In Southern Germany and Switzerland men used to offer the girl a heart-shaped cake. If she accepted it she was announcing her interest in the suit. Request and refusal can also be made indirectly by means of an intermediary. In the Hirschberg area of Germany the suitor knocks on the parents' door and asks for a light. If he receives the reply: "I haven't got a light" then he knows his suit is unwanted (*193*). In our everyday life we sugar the bitter pill of refusal by expressing our regret. "I'm afraid I can't do it," we say, or in business letters: "We regret to have to inform you. . . ." We declare ourselves to be "much obliged" and in this way we keep the peace within the group. Do we first need to learn the means we use, or are they also partly innate to us, just as we know this to be the case with other vertebrates? What have we by way of phylogenetic adaptations to put at the service of group cohesion? How peaceful are we by nature, so to speak? And finally, can we, too, achieve cohesion via aggression? These questions will be my concern in this chapter.

APPEALS TO BE CHERISHED AND INFANTILE APPEALS IN HUMAN BEHAVIOR

I was recently looking at the cover picture of an illustrated magazine that carried a report on the war in Vietnam. The picture showed a young soldier who had obviously broken down under the shock of the events of the war, weeping with his face buried in the chest of a comrade. Another photo showed a soldier with his arms round his companion to comfort him (Fig. 34). Every mother behaves in this way toward her child and in so doing directly follows the comparable behavior patterns of the primates most closely related to us (see p. 120; Fig. 32). Among human beings, too, there are behavior patterns that are borrowed from the repertoire of the parent-child relationship— that is to say, there are parental care actions and infantile appeals. As I shall explain in what follows, they are fundamentally similar throughout a range of different cultures, and the fact that there are extremely similar behavior patterns in the

Fig. 34. A human being seeking comfort buries his face in the chest of his fellow-man as if he were a small child. The person comforting him embraces him like a mother. American soldiers in Korea, from a photograph by Al Chang (U.S. Signal Corps).

chimpanzees, the animals most closely related to us, is indicative of the innate basis of these behavior patterns.

The less "civilized" an ethnic group is the more direct and spontaneous are its gestures of inclination or rejection. A greeting I witnessed among the Waikas on the Upper Orinoco will remain an unforgettable memory for me. Our little group had arrived at the village of Yasubueteri and had established friendly contact by means of small gifts. We stood in the circular village, each one of us surrounded by a group of curious and friendly Indians. The women displayed a particular interest in my companion, Frau Elke Goetz. This was partly simple curiosity. They turned her blonde hair this way and that and felt her covered breast with their fingers. But one young Indian woman wanted to make friends with her. She nestled up to my companion, wrapped one foot round her legs, as children do when they want to climb up someone, and rubbed her forehead against her cheek with sideways movements of her head, while holding Elke's head still with her hands. I asked Elke not to stop her and just to keep smiling in a friendly manner. She complied with my request, and I filmed the behavior pattern with which this Indian woman sought to establish contact. As Elke merely smiled but did not respond any further to the Indian woman's advances, the latter tried out her entire repertoire of friendliness. First her forehead-rubbing became rougher and rougher: probably an aggressive form of plea and perhaps, too, a testing out of the tolerance of her partner. At intervals she would stop and look smilingly and inquiringly into Elke's face.

Once she touched Elke's cheek with her lips, as if kissing her. Then she rubbed her lips against her cheek with sideways movements of her head, and in between she would pucker up her lips and puff out her cheeks and blow—a behavior pattern that Waika mothers use to amuse their small children. She also rubbed noses (nose tip against nose tip), the action practiced among so many peoples. And again and again she would break off to smile at my companion. A charming picture was produced when she laid her head sideways on Elke's shoulder and draped Elke's long blonde hair over her own head, so that she was framed in it. In doing this she was probably following a spontaneous inspiration, for in contrast to all the other behavior patterns, she did this only once. Finally she began to bite Elke very gently on the cheeks, and this turned into a gentle nibbling (Figs. 35 and 36).

I have myself on one occasion been greeted in almost as friendly a fashion by a Waika Indian man. We had just reached the shore and I was still sitting in the boat when the friendly Indian began to feel me with his hands. I must have winced a little, as he was not very clean, for he at once washed his hands in the river and went cheerfully on with his greeting, his hands now dripping wet. When I gave him a trifle he embraced me,

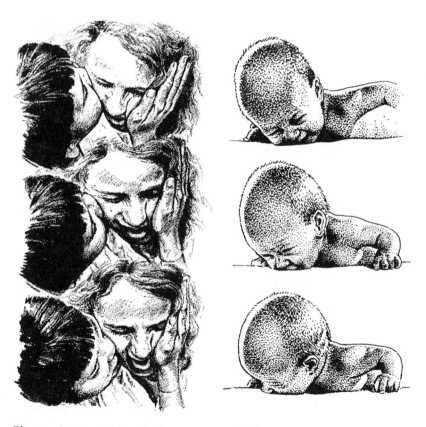

Fig. 35. Left: a Waika Indian woman rubs her mouth in greeting against a European woman's cheek (from film stills by the author); right: rhythmic search for the breast (searching automatism) in a baby.

Fig. 36. Friendly nose-rubbing and gentle nibbling of the partner in greeting (from film stills by the author).

patted my back, and finally kissed me on my cheek and rubbed his lips against it.

In these greetings a whole sequence of behavior patterns occurred—embracing, kissing, fingering and patting, rubbing noses, rubbing lips and nibbling—which I was able to observe again later among these Indians as friendly contact-making gestures. How is each to be interpreted? We will try to get to the bottom of this by means of a comparison between cultures.

The initiating of contact by rubbing with the forehead is something I have so far observed only among the Waikas. However, I recently saw a film of chimpanzees establishing physical contact with the head inclined. They invite social grooming with the same gesture, and it may be that one root of this behavior lies here (see p. 134).

Rubbing with the mouth I first took to be rubbing with the nose, but an examination of the film revealed that it was not the nose but the mouth that was rubbed on the partner's cheek. In doing this the Waika woman made rhythmical sideways oscillations with her head which had a formal resemblance to those of an infant searching for the breast (searching automatism). I consider this behavior to be ritualized searching for the breast. The same head movements are also made by people who bury their faces in another person's chest to be comforted. In both cases, in my opinion, it is a case of a recourse to childish behavior, a "borrowing" from the childish repertoire, designed to elicit the cherishing behavior of a parent.

The action of rubbing noses, on the other hand, is to be interpreted as a "kiss with the nose," the friendly sniffing of another person. Rubbing noses occurs as a greeting among many peoples (see p. 185). The starting point is a behavior pattern that we also practice in a nonritualized form. In the foreplay of love we inhale our partner's smell, and the normal German expression, "Man könne jemanden nicht riechen" (literally: "One can't stand the smell of someone") shows what a significant role the sense of smell plays in social intercourse.

The action of blowing against the cheek with pursed lips is noteworthy because here a behavior pattern (which has probably been handed down culturally) used by the Waikas to cheer up their children—in other words once again a cherishing action taken from the field of parental care—was being used as a friendly gesture.

Of particular interest are the behavior patterns similar to kissing. In human beings we can distinguish between a number of forms of kissing that probably have a common origin. The "love bite" takes the form either of rhythmically repeated nibbling or of a single controlled bite. Fairly large open areas of the partner's skin are touched, frequently the cheeks, more rarely the mouth. We know of a formally similar behavior pattern in the chimpanzee. The film by P. Marler mentioned earlier shows a chimpanzee living in the wild greeting another by inclining its head and touching it with the forehead; its partner responds to this with a "love bite" on the head. In so doing it opens its mouth wide but does not really bite. As this is the reply to a gesture of invitation to delousing, one can interpret the love bite as a ritualized grooming action. This interpretation finds support in man from the fact that in giving a love bite one nibbles a person's skin, and that in rare cases the teeth are still used in skin grooming. I have filmed a Waika woman biting impurities away from her husband's skin.

A second motivational origin of the love bite is certainly aggression. Sudden, occasionally quite hard biting can frequently be observed as a form of teasing in the love foreplay of human beings, often practiced by the woman as a reply to a mild provocation and also in defense (see p. 144 and Fig. 42). According to which of the two original impulses is dominant in the situation, one encounters a whole range of modulations ranging from gentle nibbling to biting in earnest. Chimpanzees take food with open mouths from their mother's mouth. However, the possibility that the love bite derives from this, and is therefore a ritualized food-reception movement, seems to me less likely. The actual movement sequence of nibbling and the transference of the movement onto parts of the body other than the partner's mouth are evidence against this interpretation. On the other hand kissing with lips and tongue by human beings is certainly a modification of feeding movements. Mouth-to-mouth feeding between mother and infant is practiced in widely differing cultures. Bushmen and Papuans feed their children with premasticated food, and this used to be customary even in Central Europe in some country districts (Fig. 37). It is reported, for example, of mothers in Schleswig-Holstein and in the Black Forest. R. Bilz (*21*) emphasizes that the children are adapted to this type of feeding and push their lips forward at the age of three months. If one touches their lips one can feel the tongue reaching forward, "as if it wanted to take something from there. If my wife . . . actually holds some semolina between her lips, the child takes this food into its mouth with its tongue. The baby possesses not only the ability to suck as an innate feeding function, but also the ability to take food from its mother's mouth" (p. 238).

We can observe mouth-to-mouth feeding among the anthropoid apes (gorilla, chimpanzee, orangutan), and among animals generally, as parental care behavior (Fig. 38). Suma, a mother orangutan in the Dresden zoo, would pass her baby premasticated bananas from mouth to mouth. Even adult chim-

Fig. 37. Papuan mother feeding her baby (from a photograph by Dupeyrat, in W. Wickler, 1969).

panzees will feed one another from mouth to mouth as a friendly gesture. Observations of them in the wild have shown that they greet one another when they meet by touching lips, but without passing on food, which can be regarded as a ritualized form of feeding (Fig. 38). M. Rothmann and E. Teuber (*172*) and also R. Bilz (*20, 21*) have argued on these lines for a derivation of the human kiss from parental feeding of the young.

The interpretation of kissing with lips and tongue as ritual-

Fig. 38. Left: mother chimpanzee feeding her baby from mouth to mouth; right: two chimpanzees greeting with a kiss (from a photograph by H. and J. van Lawick-Goodall, in W. Wickler, 1969).

ized feeding is supported by the fact that lovers sometimes exchange delicacies when kissing. In former times inhabitants of the Hinterzillertal in the Tyrol used to chew resin. The boys would offer it to their girls. L. v. Hörmann (*97*) described it this way: "In the chewing of resin the custom of mutual exchange is usual as with chewing tobacco. It plays a great role among lovers in particular and also especially in dancing. 'Go on, then, bite it off me' says the boy to the girl, letting the tip of a piece of pitch appear between his clenched teeth. Now the girl has to press her mouth close against his and try to take hold of the end that is showing and pull out the 'plug.' The boy, for his part, tries to make this difficult undertaking as hard as possible—in order to prolong the love play. If the dancing partner accepts the boy's challenge, it is a sign that she likes him and often even more than that" (p. 99).

The close connection between kissing and feeding is also clear in the following Hungarian custom: on the middle reaches of the Tisza, on Sunday afternoons when wedding banns are published, the "kissing" between the engaged couple takes place. The young man going to "kissing" brings his fiancée a small bag filled with tiny apples, which they eat together "in such a way that first the boy takes a bite and then the girl, and each bite must be seasoned with a kiss. At the same time the wedding day is fixed" [Baksay (*11*), p. 75].

The *Kama-Sutra* (the Indian love manual) instructs the lover to take wine in his mouth and to pass it on to the loved one with his lips. But even without actual feeding, the movements of food transmission are as widespread as tongue movements. Thus in kissing we can observe both ritualized food transmission movements (tongue-kiss) and food receiving movements (sucking). People kissing push forward their lips toward each other like small children waiting to be fed. This childishly puckered mouth has a very strong appeal and is especially exaggerated in drawings as a childlike feminine characteristic (see p. 21). The Göttingen Institute for Scientific Film has a reel in the archive that shows a male Ituri pygmy cutting off pieces of an animal killed on a hunt, putting them between his lips, and passing them on to his companions, who receive the gift with their mouths. A full description of this ritual is not available

Fig. 39. Ituri pyg-
mies: the man sitting
on the dead elephant
is distributing strips
of elephant fat with
his mouth to his com-
panions (from a film
still taken from film
number C-567 at the
Göttingen Institute
for Scientific Film;
reproduced in W.
Wickler, 1969).

(Figs. 39 and 40). The friendly effect of mutual feeding is often used to give an attractive appeal to advertisements for chocolate, biscuits, cheese, toothpaste, and the like. These show children putting things in their mouths, mothers feeding their children, and frequently lovers feeding one another with tidbits, often, significantly, from mouth to mouth (Fig. 40).

If kissing is indeed a ritualized feeding gesture handed down to us by our primate ancestors we should expect to encounter this

Fig. 40. Mutual feeding as a friendly gesture: biscuit advertisement
(from **Bunte Illustrierte 20,** *1968).*

behavior pattern all over the world. But in the view of a number of authors this is not the case. Darwin (*35*) remarked on the subject: "We Europeans are so accustomed to kissing as a mark of affection that it might be thought to be innate in mankind; but this is not the case . . . Jimmy Button, the Fuegian, told me that this practice was unknown in his land. It is equally unknown with the New Zealanders, Tahitians, Papuans, Australians, Somals of Africa and the Esquimeaux. But it is so far innate or natural that it apparently depends on pleasure from close contact with a beloved person; and it is replaced in various parts of the world by the rubbing of noses . . ." (p. 216).

If one checks these statements carefully one has to conclude that they are unreliable. A number of writers have shown that Papuans do in fact kiss one another. Sorenson and Gajdusek (*192*) have published a picture of children from Fore, Papua, kissing each other on the mouth (Fig. 41).

Fig. 41. Above: Fore, Papua: siblings kissing one another (from a photograph in E. R. Sorenson and D. C. Gajdusek); below: Nikita Khrushchev, the former Russian party leader, greeting his American host with a kiss on the cheek (from a photograph by U.P.I.).

According to T. Schultze-Westrum (*183*) Papuan mothers of the Mount Bosavi district kiss their children on the mouth. Among the inhabitants of the central Waligi Valley, the Woitapmin and the Kukukuku, I have myself observed mothers kissing their children on cheek and head and among the Kukukuku a father greeting his son by kissing him on the cheek. In the case of the Woitapmin, the Kukukuku, and the inhabitants of the Bosavi district, these are village communities that have only very recently been discovered by the government patrols and which are broadly speaking still at the Stone Age level. In previous investigations, far too much reliance has been placed on asking questions, probably only asking about kissing between man and wife in sexual foreplay, which is hard to observe among many peoples. If one asks the Japanese, for example, how widespread kissing is one generally receives no clear reply, or one is informed that the kiss was introduced by Europeans. The fact that this is not so can be learned from ancient Japanese sources. In one medieval text, for example, there is a warning to men against kissing with the tongue while the woman is experiencing her orgasm, since at that moment she might bite off the tip of one's tongue (*121*). From this it can be assumed that kissing has always been practiced there. Equally unreliable is the information obtained from primitive peoples. Many aspects of intimate life are taboo and are not discussed. It is also possible, finally, for an innate impulse to be suppressed, so that for this reason the kiss could be absent from adult heterosexual relations. It is therefore advisable to study mother-child relationships (which are much less hedged about with prohibitions) and greeting rites.

In this connection an observation of the ethnologist Bernatzik (*18*) is instructive. He writes that the Akha in Indochina are unfamiliar with kissing in the European sense, "that is, if one excludes the kiss of the Akha mother who touches the cheeks of her baby with her lips" (p. 96). Among the Semang in Malaya the same author observed a father cuddling his son, smiling at him to cheer him up, making grimaces, and giving him "snorting kisses on his little face."

Human beings often kiss other parts of the body. It is not only in European culture that kissing hands is common. The

Barotse in South Africa take one another's hands and kiss them on greeting [Lang (*131*); Fig. 60]. The feet are kissed in many different cultures as a sign of respectful submission (Fig. 52). One can also greet someone by kissing one's own hand (blowing a kiss). In ancient Rome travelers greeted the images of the gods in this way. In addition to this when a high-ranking chimpanzee stretches out its hand to permit contact, low-ranking chimpanzees will occasionally touch it with their mouths in a "love bite," as one can learn from one of Jane van Lawick-Goodall's films.

In these various forms the kiss is very common. I have observed kissing with the lips among the Samoans, the Balinese, the Masai, the highland and rainforest Indians of South America, and the Japanese. Hottentots embrace and kiss one another in greeting. In the West the kiss can already be found in antiquity. Herodotus reports that Persians of equal rank kissed each other on the mouth when they met. If one of the two was of inferior rank he kissed the man of higher rank on the cheek. There are countless mentions of kissing in the Old and New Testaments. In Germany kissing is mentioned in medieval accounts. In Mexico too it was practiced before the advent of the Europeans. Montezuma greeted Cortez by blowing a kind of kiss. Cortez approached the ruler and made a deep bow, "to which the Mexican then replied after the common custom of his country by dropping his hand to the ground and then bringing it up to his lips" [Prévost (*166*), 13, p. 334]. The easiest kind of kiss to observe is the kiss with the lips. Kissing with the tongue and love bites are more intimate forms of making contact, and one therefore has fewer opportunities to see them.

Children are not always fed by their parents from mouth to mouth. Among the Waikas the food is premasticated and handed to the child. Bond-establishing rites are also derived from this. Among several peoples of Africa it is customary to chew up food for the guest and hand it to him—or even to put it into his mouth with one's hand. And the widespread custom of establishing friendship with gifts of food is also derived from it (see p. 205). Even at the age of one children attempt to do this quite spontaneously. This behavior pattern is so normal that one is inclined to assume an innate basis. But an investiga-

tion by means of cultural comparisons has not yet been undertaken. Small children very often make use of the offering of
food (or other gifts) in order to establish contact with strangers.
I experienced an example of this when a young couple with a
little girl, aged three years and two months, were staying at our
house. In these unfamiliar surroundings the child was reserved
and shy. She watched carefully to see how her parents were be-
having toward us. We had lunch together. After the meal coffee
was served on the terrace. Suddenly the child, who had been
playing at some distance from us, ran up to the table, took a
biscuit and offered it to me, smiling bashfully. When I took
it and ate it her whole face lighted up; she took another one at
once and gave it to me as well. In this way she fed me a number
of times and then also took one for herself, which I invited her
to do. From now on the ice was broken; the child became trusting and happy. I have also recently met a ten-month-old girl
who repeatedly thrust her toy into my mouth.

Children also display a pronounced need to eat if their parents take some food, and the way this happens makes it clear
that this is a case of the appetitive behavior for strengthening a
bond.* The child who is not hungry at all but who wants a bite
from the piece of bread or the apple that its father or mother is
eating is releasing parental feeding behavior that strengthens
the bond between them. At the same time it is reassuring itself
that everything is all right.

The giving of food as gifts has undoubtedly a bond-forming
and aggression-appeasing function in human beings. An acquaintance of mine experienced a shattering example of this
during the war. He was given the task of capturing enemy sen-
tries from the trenches for interrogation, and carried it out
successfully several times. But once when he again jumped into
an enemy trench, pointed his pistol, and tried to take the sen-
try he had surprised, the soldier, who was eating at the time,
held out a piece of bread to him. My friend took the bread and
found himself so inhibited in his attack that he withdrew. After
that, he told me, he was no longer capable of carrying out mis-

---

* In a number of mammals the knowledge of what kinds of food are edible
is passed on traditionally by the young animal eating food from its mother's mouth. This could still be playing a role here.

sions of this kind. In ordinary life, tense situations can be relieved in a similar manner. Lévi-Strauss [quoted by E. Goffman (75)] describes the tense situation that arises when two Frenchmen who are not on speaking terms find themselves opposite each other at a table in a restaurant. The conventional way for tension of this kind to be resolved is for each man to pour wine from his own carafe into the other's glass. This exchange of civilities makes it possible for them to hold a conversation.

Eating together forms a bond of friendship among many primitive peoples, and this fact is made use of in many bond-forming rites. H. Nevermann (*160*) describes an experience he had among the Makleuga in New Guinea. "When ginger was mentioned Mitu pulled up a plant with its root, knocked some of the earth off it and took a hearty bite from the root. Then he thrust the rest of it into my mouth. Later, on quite a different occasion, the conversation turned to head hunting among the Makleuga and I asked in parting whether in that case I had been right to sleep as peacefully as I had done among them. Mitu gave a covert sigh and said to me in a tone of regret: 'I should have liked to have your head, even if it is not very beautiful any more, but we have eaten together and now you are not a stranger' " (p. 44).

In discussing greeting rites I shall be mentioning further examples of points of comparison between cultures. We can for the moment record that rites derived from parental feeding are generally used for forming a bond. In this process kissing and gifts (see p. 205) are certainly the most widely ritualized forms of feeding.

"Tongue-flicking" is not to be confused with kissing. Here the tongue is put out fleetingly, sometimes with a brief licking motion in the air. It is indeed a ritualized form of licking. In our society this gesture is considered indecent. In Central Europe girls of easy virtue signal their sexual readiness in this way. But apart from this use one can also see the gesture in people who are flirting—often only fleetingly and not so much directed at the partner as slipping out unconsciously. In Western Europe people who are flirting will sometimes lick each other's faces. Waika girls showed their tongues as an invitation to me to flirt with them. Waika men made similar proposals quite uninhib-

Fig. 42. Flirting Frenchman licking the corner of his girl-friend's mouth and receiving a controlled bite on his cheek in reply (from film stills by the author).

itedly to my female companion (Figs. 42–45). In this case the gesture is a heterosexual invitation. Tongue-play—like the love bite—must be derived from an action of social grooming. Many mammals lick their partners in mating foreplay, the males particularly the genital region, which a mother animal also makes

Fig. 43. Tongue-play: North German shopgirl (from a photograph in Brigitte, *Oct. 21, 1969, p. 85).*

Fig. 44. Tongue-play: Waika Indian woman, left: tongue-play; right: inviting a kiss (from film stills by the author).

a particular point of cleaning. We have mentioned that a dog, when submitting, offers itself for this purpose, just like a puppy, to the victor and urinates, which releases the action of licking it dry. In some monkeys, too, licking movements in the air occur as greeting gestures (see p. 115).

The whole complex of social grooming actions serves among human beings—also in their nonritualized form—for the maintenance of friendly relationships. Papuans remove lice from one another as devotedly as Balinese or South American Indians.

Fig. 45. Tongue-play: Waika Indian (from a film still by the author).

Fig. 46. Social grooming. Above: Balinese women; below: rhesus monkeys (from photographs by the author).

The behavior pattern is also practiced between couples as love foreplay. In Europe, too, lovers still like ruffling each other's hair, the erotic significance of which is extremely great. On a Mediterranean beach I filmed a girl who was patiently scratching away and squeezing out small pimples for her male companion. Caressing and rubbing certainly belong in this complex of social grooming actions. Monkeys part the hairs in their coat with their hands in order to expose the roots, and people do the same thing when they are delousing the hair of the head. By running their hands over their male partner's skin, girls at once discover any small irregularities. In this sense caressing fulfills yet another task in the service of body care. I know of no culture in which people do not caress one another. We stroke the heads of both children and adult friends in order to comfort them when they are in distress. Laying one's hand comfortingly on the head is sufficient. In some cultures this has

Fig. 47. Comforting by stroking—or simply laying the hand on the head (from a photograph by W. Eugene Smith, in Life *magazine).*

also become the gesture of blessing and healing. In its most ritualized form the palms of the hands are no longer laid upon the head, but simply spread out in blessing (Figs. 46–48).

Fig. 48. Gestures of blessing derived from the human gesture of comforting: laying on of hands and blessing with outstretched hands (from press photographs of the ordination of priests).

A widespread gesture of comforting and soothing is the embrace. It is not hard to recognize this as a protective gesture on the mother's part which has been ritualized into a gesture of comforting and greeting; it also plays an important part in love foreplay (Fig. 49). Often the person embracing pats the back of the person embraced. In this repetition of release from the embrace and clasping anew, the gesture follows a widespread pattern of ritualization. By this means its effect as a signal is reinforced. Interestingly enough chimpanzees also pat each other on the back when they embrace in greeting. And, as is the case with humans, the movement is often simply performed as a pat on the shoulder in passing without a full embrace, or even on occasion simply a fleeting touch on some part of the body (see "holding out hands," p. 179). All these are transitional variations. When an animal touches or pats some part of its partner's body in passing, one can no longer determine whether this represents a fleeting intention to embrace or to caress.

The person embraced can respond by embracing his partner

Fig. 49. Left: Andamese greeting one another (from a photograph by Heywood Seton-Karr, in K. Lang, 1926); right: at the palm fruit festival of the Waikas (see p. 200) the host and guest embrace each other while singing promises to give each other gifts (from a film by the author).

in return. But very often we can observe him hiding his face in his partner's breast, especially when he is seeking comfort and protection. At the same time we may sometimes observe a sideways oscillation of the head—as in an infant searching for the breast—and the manner of speaking reverts to a childish level. There is no doubt that true functional regressions, i.e., infantile appeals, are present. In love foreplay men like to nuzzle up to the girl's breast. In this process sucking movements are also activated. This activity is directed toward the woman's breast, and sometimes also her neck, the lobes of her ears, or other parts of her body.

In women, too, the sucking drive is activated; it is, however, directed not toward men's breasts but toward areas of exposed skin or the ear lobes. Desmond Morris (*155*) believes that ear lobes have evolved as erogenous zones exclusively in order to meet the partner's need for something to suck. The female breast has undoubtedly become a "signaling apparatus" over and above its milk-dispensing function. And this is primarily—though not exclusively—in the service of the sexual bond.

A number of noteworthy observations have been made which show that the offering of the breast can serve on occasion as a greeting and appeasement ritual. Erika Kulnig of the Austrian Embassy in Djakarta has told me that on visiting a Papuan village in West Irian Indonesian acquaintances must first briefly take a welcoming suck from the breast of the wife of the village headman. Rasmussen (*168*) has reported a similar greeting ritual among Polar Eskimos. And in Kropotkin's book (*122*) I found the following note: "Even today, when feuds are ended in the Caucasus the guilty party touches the breast of the eldest woman in the tribe with his lips and becomes the 'milk brother' of all the men in the injured family" (p. 137).

There are various views about the phylogenetic development of the woman's breast as a signal. Morris (*155*) has evolved the hypothesis that the woman's breast is a copy, projected onto the front of the body, of the buttock. He starts from the fact that our primate ancestors, in the manner of all apes and monkeys, copulated by mounting from behind and must therefore also have responded to sexual signals that were visible from

behind—according to Morris the "fleshy, hemispherical buttocks" and "a pair of bright red genital lips, or labia." With
the upright posture and the individualization of relationships
a frontal mating posture came to be adopted, and this created
the need to bring sexual signals onto the front of the woman's
body. The man's innate readiness to respond to the signals
just mentioned led to the evolving on the front of the woman's
body of copies of these signals.

I have already raised objections to this elsewhere (*48*). To
begin with, the similarity between the female breast and the
buttock is really not very great. And then we can see—and
Wickler (*217*) has recently documented it with a series of examples—that sucking from the female teat in a variety of
carnivores, ungulates, and primates (p. 115) has evolved into
a bond-forming signal that also plays a substantial role in the
sexual behavior of some of these animals. The starting point
for this development was the placing of behavior patterns of
parental care at the service of group cohesion. It is unlikely
that man is exceptional in this respect, particularly since even
for the child the female breast fulfills a socially cohesive function over and above the feeding function. We have mentioned
that frightened children flee to their mother's breast, take her
nipple in their mouths, and then survey their surroundings
from this comforting position (Fig. 31). The same is true of
primates. J. Bowlby (*24*) has emphasized that taking the nipple in the lips and sucking have two quite separate functions:
the latter is for feeding and the former for establishing a bond.
He says: "Both these findings are consistent with the conclusion,
that the non-nutritional sucking of human infants is an activity
in its own right and separate from nutritional sucking; and that
in man's environment of evolutionary adeptness, non-nutritional sucking is an integral part of attachment behavior . . ."
(p. 250). Morris's thesis is not wholly to be dismissed—especially
since there are primates with sexual signals projected onto the
front of their bodies—but his hypothesis is less probable than
the assumption that the woman's breast acquired its signaling
function in connection with parental care. And his theory that
the lips are copies of the labia does not stand up under examination. The human lips must have evolved as signals (for

kissing) hand in hand with the evolution of mouth-to-mouth feeding. This explains why both men and women have them.

These last examples show that in human beings too, with the differentiation of behavior patterns of cherishing into signals, certain organs, by means of which cherishing is offered, evolve into releasers.

From what has been said so far it should be clear that many behavior patterns that are regarded as typically sexual, such as kissing and caressing, are actually in origin actions of parental care. We remind the reader of this because Sigmund Freud, in a strikingly topsy-turvy interpretation, once observed that a mother would certainly be shocked if she realized how she was lavishing sexual behavior patterns on her child. In this case Freud had got things reversed. A mother looks after her children with the actions of parental care; these she also uses to woo her husband.

Ritualized parental care is also expressed verbally. Protective assurances and soothing remarks belong to the repertoire of affectionate conversation, which—from its content—seems in this respect to be preprogrammed by phylogenetic adaptations. The vocabulary changes from culture to culture; but what is said—to judge by our investigations so far—appears to remain constant as a stereotype.

We can observe how in human beings conversation is practiced as a bond-forming ritual. In such conversations hardly any factual information is passed on, as they consist largely of extremely banal, constantly repeated statements concerning such matters as the weather. Nevertheless the conversation does convey the social information that one is interested in one's partner and his concerns, insofar as one is willing to listen to him and reply to him. Morris (*155*) has very aptly called this kind of conversation "grooming talk" since its function, as in mutual delousing, is the establishment of friendly contact. I consider it likely that such conversations also have their root in the mother-child relationship and indeed in the simple voice-testing conversation, the sole purpose of which is the inquiry "Are you there?" and the reply "Yes, I'm here." When a child is playing in a room and its mother is working in the room next door the child will call out to her repeatedly, but it will be completely satisfied with the simple confirmation of its mother's presence ("Mummy!" "Ye-es."—"Mummy!" "Ye-es." Etc.).

The cherishing behavior patterns of parental care have their natural counterpart in the signals that release them, which have been taken over into the repertoire of contact-making and aggression-inhibiting behavior patterns as "infantile appeals." In certain situations the adult behaves as if he were a child and, as we have already mentioned, such regressive manifestations belong to the normal behavioral repertoire of animals. In man it is the same. People who need help or who wish, as in courtship, to elicit affectionate behavior relapse quite involuntarily into the role of a small child. Regression of this kind is not at all pathological, a fact that should be emphasized, for in the writings of psychoanalysts the impression is often created that this is an abnormal phenomenon. This is true only in the case of people who cannot find their way out of this role.

Regression can often be observed in women who have recently lost their husbands, in old people in the presence of others, and also in small children when a newborn sibling occupies an excessive amount of the parents' attention so that the child feels neglected. It is known that in such cases many children suddenly begin to wet their beds again and that their speech reverts to the level of baby talk.

In the process known as "brainwashing," in which the personality is altered, the Chinese force their prisoners to regress. A relationship of extreme dependence is created by putting fetters on prisoners who are resistant to the new teaching, so that they cannot attend for themselves to even the simplest physical needs. They have to be fed and cleaned by fellow prisoners who have progressed further; in this way a bond evolves and ultimately the readiness to adopt the views of the others (*209*).

Withdrawn (autistic) children have no relationships with their fellow human beings. In the course of a sensitive period (see p. 223) they have omitted to learn how to establish social contact with other people. They can be cured by being fed repeatedly with little tidbits. By means of social feeding a bond is established, and the children learn to love the person who cares for them. After this one can begin to educate them as well by means of praise and blame.

Regressive phenomena can also be observed in speech. Lovers talk to each other in a childish way, making copious use of diminutives. Girls like to pretend to be helpless in the presence of men, and their childlike behavior releases the impulse to cherish them. They may also readily pretend to be somewhat less intelligent than they are and allow things to be explained to them that they already know. Childlike behavior belongs to a girl's natural repertoire, and interestingly she also retains physical "baby signals." A girl's forehead is more protruding, her cheeks are rounder, and her facial bone structure is in its total effect neater and smaller. Make-up is used to emphasize the babyish traits of the face. The cheeks are colored, the lips shaped into a small mouth pursed for sucking, and the size of the eyes is exaggerated. These traits are particularly exaggerated in the many drawings in illustrated magazines (Fig. 7).

Finally it must be reiterated that appeals to cherishing and appeasement appeals are frequently made directly via a child (see p. 96). People appease aggressive feelings by taking a child with them; they beg through the medium of a child (Figs. 50 and 63). On our travels through East Africa the Masai begged for sweets from us. The people begging often thrust

Fig. 50. The appeal via a child—Masai children begging. Left: using the hand of a small sibling to beg; right: pointing to the baby (from film stills by H. Hass; see also p. 201).

small children forward, holding up their hands. The Waikas also begged via their children's hands. Masai mothers, when begging, would point to their baby in the sling on their back although it was too young to eat sweets. The fact that professional beggars in different parts of the world make use of children is well known.

We have mentioned that Australian aborigines who want to make contact with Europeans will thrust a child along in front of them in order to put the strangers in a friendly mood. The research worker to whom we are indebted for this report also reports how once in Central Australia he surprised three women in the act of cooking a snake. Two of them fled when they saw the strangers, while the third seized hold of both of her breasts, an expression of extreme terror on her face, and squirted milk at the white people. When questioned later she explained that she had done this in order to show that she was the mother of a child, hoping that in these circumstances they would do nothing to her. A female acquaintance has told me that after the Russian occupation of Danzig women were safe from rape by the occupying forces if they had small children. In that case the soldiers showed themselves to be kindly disposed and often even gave them presents. In order to protect themselves the women worked out a regular traffic in lending babies. Waika warriors when visiting a friendly village take their children and let them dance along with them (see p. 200).

Politicians in all ages have used children to establish a bond. Parliamentary candidates, dictators, and monarchs are fond of patting children's cheeks in public and use this means to build a human bridge to the people. Christianity has been highly successful in elevating the child into a symbol of unity. In this connection an idea of F. Fremont-Smith is noteworthy (*68*). At a conference in Russia he asked himself what common interest there was that could unite the factions of humanity over and above their differences, and the answer he found was the defense of the child. In his speech before his Russian hosts he made this proposal: "We have now reached that point in our history when no nation can any longer protect its own children. No government, may it be ever so powerful, can any longer guarantee the safety of its most precious possession, the safety of its children. If a nuclear holocaust should come New York, London, and Moscow will perish and with it all its children. If the nations could, however, agree to protect the children of the others then the children could be saved. If the USSR would guarantee the safety of all American children, then all children could be saved."

Out of this common interest a common symbol could also be formed: the needy child. In the strongly emotional—because innate—basis of our parental care behavior there can in fact be found a strong motivation for peaceful coexistence, and peace research should certainly pay attention to these dispositions.

THE SEXUAL BOND

Sigmund Freud derived all man's social relationships from sexual relationships. From the preceding section it should be clear that expressed in such general terms this is certainly not the case. On the other hand, it is true that in human beings in particular the maintaining of a bond between the sexes by means of the sexual relationship plays an exceptional role which is without parallel in the animal kingdom. The full significance of this role has often not been clearly recognized—especially not in the present debate about birth control—and it therefore merits discussion.*

The teaching of the Roman Catholic Church asserts that the union of man and wife and the reproductive function are inseparably linked by natural law, and that an act of coition from which the possibility of reproduction is excluded is therefore contrary to nature. But this appeal to natural law is defective insofar as the statement does not even hold good for all animals. In one-celled animals, union does not lead to the procreation of offspring, but only to an exchange of genes. Still more relevant is the fact that in vertebrates sexual behavior patterns have undergone a variety of changes of sig-

---

* On this subject a detailed investigation by Wolfgang Wickler, *Sind wir Sünder?* Munich, 1969, has recently been published.

nificance and, like parental care behavior, have been placed at the service of group cohesion. This is particularly the case with primates living in groups. In baboons and some other primates the female mating display—the "presenting" of the rump—has become a gesture of greeting and appeasement. In the hamadryas baboon this applies to the male copulation movement, which gives the lie to the statement that in the animal kingdom copulation only serves reproduction. Social mounting serves this social purpose exclusively and no ejaculation takes place.

If we now investigate these matters in man, we find that nature has apparently used up all the possible means of forming and maintaining a bond. Apart from the group-uniting mechanisms already mentioned, nature has made considerable use of sexual behavior for the purpose of maintaining heterosexual partnerships. The need to make use of this possibility probably arose because of the length of the period of ontogenetic development in man. Children generally have to be looked after up to their fourteenth year, and in their first years they are almost wholly dependent on the care that a mother completely provides. She, in her turn, needs the division of labor in which the man gives her help in the procuring of food and, in particular, protection. For this reason she must tie him to her emotionally for a long time. The tie afforded by the sexual drive is therefore particularly suited to this because it is very strong. On the basis of the fulfillment of a sexual desire a bond can easily be cemented. This presupposes, however, that the woman can respond to the man's sexual desires most of the time, something that calls for new and special adaptations in the physiology of the woman.

In mammals, with a few rare exceptions, readiness for copulation and readiness to conceive coincide with the few fertile days when the female is in heat. The act of copulation among mammals nearly always serves only the purpose of reproduction. If it was to sustain the additional function of maintaining a bond between partners, the rigid dependence on reproductive cycles would have to be eliminated. Thanks to a series of physiological peculiarities, a woman has the ability to respond to a man's sexual desires even outside the days when she is fertile. Most of the time she is capable of being sexually aroused and ready to give herself to the man of her choice. She can thereby maintain a tie with him by means of sexual reward (50). Even in the first months of pregnancy this readiness is not wholly extinguished. But a certain individual variability suggests that in the case of this extended readiness we are dealing with a recent phylogenetic acquisition. Some women can be aroused and experience an orgasm only during ovulation, which reminds us that it is also at this time that women are especially receptive to certain odors (see p. 24). In our own ancestors readiness for copulation must have been limited, as it is in most other mammals, to the time of readiness to conceive. This close physiological link was later abandoned. At the same time the human female developed the ability to experience an orgasm, increasing her readiness to copulate. It is not hard to see that this strengthens the mutual bond. A further adaptation, finally, in the service of maintaining the bond between partners is the increased sexual potency of the man (50). Not only does he have a constant sexual readiness at his disposal—it is even retained into old age. Misunderstanding its biological significance, moralists have repeatedly bewailed this "hypersexuality" as evidence of decadence, and the debate about "the pill" suffers from the fact that the function of sexuality in maintaining the bond between partners is not recognized by the religious authorities who make decisions.

There is no doubt that sexual union in human beings has the function of maintaining the bond between partners and reproducing the species. The two functions can be looked at separately. Biological adaptations specifically ensure that coitus takes place outside the fertile periods, which demonstrates the great importance of the pair-maintaining function of sexuality. From the point of view of the selective process, this makes complete sense. Once several children have been born in a family, it is certainly in the interests of species preservation for the man to remain with his wife and to look after the growing children even when the reproductive capacity of the woman is extinguished.

Although we have recognized the two functions of human

sexual behavior we still have to discuss whether either one should be valued more highly than the other. This question must be answered before we can decide whether the conscious elimination of one function, namely, that of procreating offspring, while retaining the other function, is against nature or not. First we must put on record that even among some animals the maintenance of a bond with the partner plays a more important role than the procreation of offspring. In many animals that mate for life the partnership is maintained right through the periods of sexual inactivity, even when the mate has become infertile.

When we turn to the human situation, one source of knowledge is indispensable—namely, our own subjective experience. Wolfgang Wickler (*217*) has insisted on the importance of this path to understanding and has emphasized the fact that this is the very avenue to value judgments not open to celibate theologians. "What is harmful here," he writes, "is not so much the—in itself astonishing—state of affairs in which the priests are the only members of the Church apart from the monastic orders who are excluded from one of the sacraments and from the grace it brings. It is a fact that they exercise supreme authority over the natural moral law although in this field they have insufficient access to knowledge, as is quite evident from a number of passages in the encyclical.* For example, paragraph 17 contains not only the much-criticized fears of a variety of abuses (free will can also be abused but the Church tolerates it), but the following sentence: 'Another effect that gives cause for alarm is that a man who grows accustomed to the use of contraceptive methods may forget the reverence due to a woman.' This could only be such a remote possibility—and among people of a low moral calibre —that as a crucial argument it would appear to be irrelevant; but since it is there one can only assume that, in the opinion of the Church's teachers, reverence for one's marriage partner rests substantially on fear of the consequences of the sexual act. Husbands and wives united by a deep love must find this an imputation only to be excused by ignorance. Equally dan-

* *Humanae Vitae,* 1968 (tr.).

gerous is the assertion in paragraph 21 that periodic continence has no harmful effects on conjugal love" (p. 291 f.).

All married experience equally belies the statement of the papal commission that love between man and wife (if it is true love) is above all spiritual and calls for no specific gesture —still less its repetition with any particular frequency. The conjugal act has a deep significance for the maintenance of a bond between man and wife and can certainly be performed without any concern whatever being experienced for offspring. It can be based entirely on the mutual self-giving of the two partners. When this is the case the act is not in any way experienced subjectively as being less valuable. And since no criterion can be inferred from the natural order that contradicts this subjective evaluation, there is really no well-founded objection to the standpoint that not every conjugal act has to serve the transmission of life. On the other hand, an act performed with the aim of begetting a child but in hatred against the partner certainly does run counter to the natural moral law. "Perhaps this is clearer to natural sentiment than to a particular moral theology" [Wickler (*217*), p. 299]. Total personal devotion to the partner seems a much more essential prerequisite for loving union. This is so important for the maintenance of the bond with the partner that any holding back is inadmissible if one wishes to maintain the marriage. On the other hand, if circumstances demand a limitation on the number of children, then one must approve of contraceptive devices. This is as little contrary to a natural moral law as, say, those interventions of medicine into the individual life that serve to prolong it.

The great significance of the act for maintenance of the partner bond has brought with it in certain respects a "hypersexualization" of man, that is to say, in the course of his phylogeny he has evolved an increased sexual drive and an increased sensuality. Once we have grasped that this hypersexualization is in no way pathological, the realization must lead to a fundamental acceptance of human sexuality, even when conception is excluded in advance by use of contraceptive devices. But the fact that sexuality serves to maintain a bond between partners presupposes the existence of an individualized pair bond, that is, love. To say this is, in effect, to say that passing relations with constantly changing partners are at most to be regarded as natural during a transitory phase of youthful exploration and experimentation but not as a lasting attitude. Love is an individualized relationship between partners, and a constant changing of partners is a contradiction of this. To fall in love means to tie the bond with one specific partner. And this need is a part of our nature. In this sense we have innate dispositions for lasting partnerships of a conjugal type.

This does not mean, however, that we are bound to any specific form of matrimony. The findings of the ethnologists offer evidence to the contrary, for they show that monogamy and polygamy are more or less equally common, the number of cultures which permit polygamy* being the greater. This suggests that man is polygamous by inclination. Indeed the existence of this tendency has recently become undeniable even in monogamous societies, where it simply dons the mask of a succession of monogamous marriages. The percentage of divorces is relatively high in our Western culture, and the question often arises whether the demand for divorce, simply in order to remain faithful to an ideal of monogamy, is really humane. Divorces do not always take place with the full agreement of both partners. Generally one of the partners suffers in the process and so, as a rule, do the children. For this reason everything that serves to preserve a family once started should be used. If it should turn out that the legalization of a type of conjugal relations with a second partner can contribute to this, then such possibilities should also be considered. For ultimately polygamy does not mean a constant change of partners: it means a conjugal bond.** The argument that the ideal individualized relationship is fulfilled only in monogamy, be-

---

* In most cases of polygamy a man is united with a number of wives in lasting partnership (polygynic). Cultures in which one woman marries a number of husbands are rare exceptions. We find them, for example, as an extreme form of ecological adaptation in the blind valley-ends of the Himalayas where no expansion is possible, and therefore the population must not increase.

** The harem in a polygamous society is just as degenerate as the rapid succession of marriages in Western civilization.

cause it is limited to a single person, has the ring of conviction
and a general trend toward monogamy can be observed. In
answer to this, however, it can be objected that we have extremely individualized and deep relationships with our children, and that these feelings do not become in any way shal-
lower when there is more than one child. Scarcely anyone could
seriously propose to campaign for the one-child family, so
that the parents could have a particularly deep relationship
with a single child.

My pursuit of the question of what are the natural, or innate rules that regulate our sexual behavior brings me to
the incest taboo. Sexual relationships in the nuclear family
are allowed only between man and wife, not between parents
and children or between siblings. No culture makes an exception to this, and a great many investigators have striven to
explain this phenomenon without so far having arrived at
a convincing answer. One biological theory claims that there
is an innate inhibition against marrying the people with whom
one grows up in one's narrowest group. The selective advantage
in this is supposed, first of all, to consist in the fact that it
ensures an exchange of heredity between members of a population who are as genetically varied as possible, and the genetic
consequences of inbreeding are thus avoided. To this it has
been objected that the pure civilization of a line is not necessarily harmful and is often practiced in the breeding of domestic animals. One can reply to this, however, that it is
generally avoided in nature. In the plant kingdom the most
complicated devices exist to prevent self-pollination. Some
plants are self-sterile; in others self-fertilization is avoided by
stamens and stigmas ripening at differing times or being physically remote from one another. The phenomenon of hetero-
morphism described by Darwin (plants with pistils and stamens
of differing lengths) is well known. Briefly it can be considered
proven that the prime function of fertilization is to serve the
exchange of genes. In plants, where thanks to their often bisex-
ual flowers and their stationary positions, the danger of self-fertilization exists, arrangements have evolved to prevent this,
thus offering fairly clear proof of the positive selective value
of fertilization by another. In animals such incest-preventing

devices are generally not necessary, since a more thorough mixing up of animal populations is achieved through their greater mobility. It therefore does no harm if a mouse or a squirrel occasionally mates with a sibling. Generally the family is dispersed when the young are weaned. In many cases, as for example the Central European squirrel, the mother actually drives her children away after they are weaned. And, as families do not remain together, the genetic exchange within the population is generally assured. Only where family ties are very strongly developed is there a danger of regular inbreeding and it is in such cases that we find an innate inhibition against mating with parents or siblings. A classic example of this is offered by the greylag goose, which does not mate with conspecifics it has grown up with, even when they are not actual siblings (*115*). Recently a kind of mother-son incest taboo has been demonstrated in Japanese macaques. Jane van Lawick-Goodall (*133*) observed that two sexually mature chimpanzee sons, although they were the only males in the group, did not mate with their mother. She watched this through two periods of oestrus. A young male copulated repeatedly with his sister while she had her first and as yet incomplete swellings. But at the first proper oestrus she drove her brother away and offered herself only to other males. An examination of the literature shows that on this most interesting point we know far too little, because higher mammals have simply not been observed through the generations under natural conditions. Individual examples show, however, that there are sometimes innate inhibitions in animals against mating with close relatives, and we can reckon accordingly with the same possibility in man.

In man there is an additional selective advantage in the social sector for a prohibition on incest. If fathers were to marry their daughters and sons their mothers, then, given the great age differences, this would soon lead to the widowing of the younger partners. A marriage outside the family, on the other hand, makes possible the selection of a suitable partner of the same age and also forges alliances beyond the limited framework of the family.

Opposition to the hypothesis that the incest taboo is innate in man comes from various psychoanalysts who believe they have detected the sexual desires of children vis-à-vis their parents and of parents vis-à-vis their children. The boy is supposed to feel sexual desire for his mother, which arouses fear of the punishment he may receive from his father: this appears in the literature of psychoanalysis as fear of castration. But a great deal of what Freud and his pupils have interpreted as sexual (caressing, kissing, and so on, see p. 130) is primarily not sexual, but derived from parental care behavior. To attribute sexual desire to a son who embraces and kisses his mother is simply false. While recognizing the contributions made by psychoanalysis, one must in this case reproach some of its exponents with proceeding unscientifically. A plausible interpretation has all too readily been adopted as a casual explanation, and the Oedipus complex, castration fears, and penis envy in girls are now built upon as if they were proven facts. Nothing of the kind has been proved. What is true is that here and there a girl very much wants to be a boy and a son experiences premature conflicts with his father. These things can be just as plausibly explained, outside the sexual context, as maturing dominance disputes.

For the moment the question of whether an incest taboo is innate in us or handed down culturally must still be left open. There are, however, substantial arguments to support the theory of an innate basis to it. These we have set down, and as a further argument we can once again draw on our own subjective experience. We are certainly aware of a very strong and powerfully emotional bond with our children. But sexual feelings do not enter in. Ethnologists who have asked in the most varied cultures why people do not marry their siblings or their children have noted again and again that they were met with a complete lack of comprehension. The question had simply never occurred to those they asked. Sexual games occur between siblings when they are children, but with puberty a strong, emotional, sexual barrier develops; this occurs without any particular educational pressure. It simply happens this way, and hence it looks like the coming to fruition of innate inhibitions.

As a result of our investigation we can state that, in addition to the reproductive function, sexual behavior patterns in man are also called upon to fulfill an important task in maintaining a bond with a partner of the opposite sex. Normal partnerships between individuals of the same sex are not, however, cemented sexually; this is also true of the parent-child bond and of the bond between brothers and sisters, which essentially takes place via parental care actions and their derivatives. The moralistic misunderstanding of sexuality—in particular on the part of Catholic teaching—carries with it the danger of trivializing relationships between the sexes, which, in having their sexual content repressed, are being robbed of their most specifically human values. Furthermore every repression in this field, as Plack (*163*) shows convincingly, leads to increased aggression. Many a sadistic perversion has its roots in such repression. In this connection Plack refers both to the persecution of witches in the Middle Ages and to the fact that the sadists of the SS were supporters of a puritanical sexual ethic. Certainly repression also leads to feelings of guilt and these may quite well have been cultivated to a certain degree in the past in order to maintain a relationship of dependence. Feelings of guilt make men easily led. The untenable doctrine of original sin was cultivated for centuries largely for this reason. During the past decades we have witnessed a growing liberalization in the sexual field as well as in others. It is interesting that this has coincided with the world-wide movement directed against war and aggression. Evidently we are striving quite unconsciously for the activation of all those forces that are socially cohesive and which sublimate aggression, including those that reside in sexuality. There is certainly a possibility in this but also the danger already mentioned of a depersonalization of sexual relationships. That would spell the death of love.

BONDING VIA JOINT AGGRESSION

In all ages the cohesiveness of human groups has been strengthened by a common danger. And in all ages the leaders of states or tribes have understood how to cement the community if need be, and often to inspire them to collective aggression, through the decoy device of an enemy. In such cases aggression aroused against a common enemy clearly has a cohesive force: a "fighting community" is formed.

This disposition, present in a number of social primates, has also developed quite independently among birds and teleost fishes. The classical example has been described by Konrad Lorenz (*141*). When a greylag gander is courting a female he behaves most strikingly. He struts up and down, with feathers slightly ruffled, in front of the goose of his choice and goes in for unnecessary displays of strength, such as flying over quite short distances, despite the effort involved in taking wing and landing, which would therefore not normally (that is, if no female were present) be worth it. The gander will even, unprovoked, attack humans standing on the shore or other feared beings. Then he will return to his chosen one, landing in front of her and uttering a "triumph cry" while stretching his neck forward, as in threatening. The threat is directed not against her, however, as we have already mentioned, but past her. He repeats this behavior over several days, always attacking someone or other and then returning as if in the role of protector and hero, until the female joins in with his "triumph ceremony" and holds out her beak in turn, threatening and uttering loud cries. In the process the two birds become so oriented that they threaten past each other with their necks. They can now be regarded as "betrothed." They have formed a fighting community, a prerequisite for the successful rearing of the brood. Further courtship, in the course of which ritualized nest-building movements are carried out, is nevertheless necessary before mating takes place (see p. 125). Basically, however, the courting gander has established the bond via aggression. We have already explained that aggression could first become a force for cohesion via the defense of the young. We can observe that defense communities are formed only by animals that look after their young. We are dealing, therefore, with a particular form of aggression that is not encountered, for instance, in reptiles—which do not look after their young. So far as we know there are no species which do not look after their young and which can be proved to be bound together via aggression alone. Aggression becomes group cement only via brood defense. In this form it also unites many social primates. Among marmosets that live in conjugal pairs, the nuclear family (father, mother, children) forms a fighting community. They defend their territory in common. Among the higher primates the males carry the chief burden of group defense. In rhesus monkeys the females also fight when disputes between groups arise. The males are the more active, however, and it is they that form a bond of friendship with another monkey by trying to involve the potential friend in a joint aggressive action (see p. 126).

The parallels with human beings are certainly more than mere analogies. As primates living in closed groups we are disposed to close our ranks in danger. Common defense or common aggression establishes an exceptionally strong bond. This is true of primitive peoples, and there is no question that we follow the same pattern. Groups are even united by ritualized battle-games (football, etc.). It is also noticeable that the emblems to which anonymous groups of people rally are generally of an aggressive kind. This is as true of heraldic animals (bear, lion, cock, wolf, eagle, etc.) as of monuments erected to celebrate victories or the liberation of new nations. Parental care motifs (mothers with children, protective fathers, and so on) are often associated with them too, but tend to be secondary.

Aggressive symbolism also plays a significant role in human greeting behavior. In addition to the "threat-greeting" intended as a demonstration of one's own strength, there are also "gestures of threat-greeting" expressing readiness for the common fight, for example, the salute with the clenched fist. The individuals greeting one another feel themselves bound together as a fighting community. One form of ritualized threat that has a cohesive effect is actually innate, namely, laughter. This expressive movement probably arose from a form of behavior that we describe as "mobbing." Very many social animals threaten jointly against an enemy, whether of the same or a different species. Many apes and monkeys that live in groups show their teeth when they do this and emit rhythmic threat sounds. Both these elements are still retained in our laughter, and there is no doubt that it is often very aggressively motivated. People laugh *about* someone or they may laugh *at* them, and we like doing this together with others. The person who is laughed at experiences the laughter as aggressive. But the people laughing together feel themselves bound together by this ritualized mobbing.

Scapegoats are often used to give a group cohesion by means of aggression. Sometimes when new states are formed they are deliberately included to strengthen the new group, as, for example, the Chinese in Singapore and Malaya, the Indians in Kenya. At moments of internal crisis aggressive feelings can be deflected onto them, and they are used as dummy enemies in order to strengthen the group through fear (see p. 168). In the Christian world the Jews played this role for a long time, and it was made impossible for them to adapt to society because they were needed for the role of scapegoats (73).

A sense of identity achieved via aggression is dangerous on account of the strong emotional commitment involved. We often defend our ideals with a commitment similar to that with which we defend our children, and in a certain sense our ideals *are* our spiritual children. It will depend upon man's reason whether this capacity for enthusiastic commitment benefits or harms him. It is dangerous if we unite aggressively against fellow human beings. But we can commit ourselves just as emotionally to a common cause that is not directed against another group of people. The thesis that a humanity, if it could ever unite, would once again split up into warring factions, "Mankind being, alas, what it is" as von Holst maintains (95), is by no means substantiated. Natural catastrophes and other events unite people for joint action. The capacity of human beings to come togther constructively has been demonstrated.

Interestingly, men in particular seem to be gifted for this kind of association, as has been recently investigated by Tiger (203). Men experience a clear inclination to get together with their fellow males and like to exclude women. We have probably evolved this capacity for male friendships from the necessity for hunting and fighting together, for which the woman, because of her physiological and psychic traits, is less suited. This disposition lives on in men's clubs, bars, and fraternal societies. The bond between friends has a strongly emotional tinge that is not sexual. It is strengthened by adventures experienced together (hunting, fighting). Eating and drinking together are also a part of this, which suggests roots of sociability even more deeply seated than aggression.

FEAR AS A MEANS OF BONDING

A young animal runs to its mother when danger threatens, and we have mentioned how adults will also run to one another when they are afraid. Fear unites in a twofold manner: firstly through the activation of flight to one another, and secondly through the releasing of collective aggression, as we have just discussed. The bond through fear is probably the oldest in vertebrates. We have pointed out that even in a shoal of fish the conspecific becomes the goal-in-flight with a "home valency" (see p. 120). Right up to man fear has remained a strong force for cohesion, which has been used, amongst others, by politicians and religious leaders. Politicians arouse both fear of enemies and fear of chaos—for order gives us orientation and with it security. That is a point to be noted. If we watch a young hamster leaving its burrow for the first time, we can observe how initially it learns the escape route back to the burrow by running back there again and again. Only gradually does it increase its range of activity. If we put down an adult hamster in a strange place, it will begin by orientating itself and learning the way home. Only then will it feel safe and embark on other activities. Our own desire for order has its roots in flight motivation. Order means orientation in time and space and not just in relation to events outside our species. It also gives us a sense of security if we can tell in advance what other people will do, and if we know what we should do. Even a small child will ask firmly what it should and should not do: in this way it acquires social orientation and with this a sense of security. The need, motivated by fear, to know for sure how one stands can even lead to extreme forms of subjection. In a self-governing group of fourteen-year-old boys who lived in a home, a group of tyrants was formed, to whom the others each had to give one of his rolls of bread at breakfast. And the contributors entirely accepted this arrangement; they had achieved security through order (*164*). The readiness with which we accept the dominance of individuals has a further root in our need for security. A parent-child relationship is also induced via fear: the dominant individual acts in a fatherly manner and the subordinate in a childishly dependent manner. The bond through fear plays a great part in the Christian religion. Original sin and the threat of eternal damnation are used to establish a bond between human beings and God the Father.

Establishing a bond through terror is, in conclusion, a strategy for tyrants. Just as the whipped dog crawls whining to its master's feet and licks the hand that holds the whip, so human beings submit to the cruel ruler and give him their allegiance.

9
More About
Bond-establishing Rites

In the preceding chapters we tried to show that the behavior patterns utilized for group cohesion are in the first place adaptations that have been phylogenetically acquired. Some of them we share with other mammals, others have developed independently by a process of parallel evolution. Critical readers may object that my examples have been especially selected and that in a comparative examination of cultures, taking, for example, greeting customs, one might well establish a great degree of variability. In such a situation one could scarcely speak of rigid preprogramming, but rather of culturally transmitted patterns. Let us deal with this justifiable objection by working through two examples and making cultural comparisons. For this purpose I have selected patterns of greeting and festivals.

GREETING

"Anyone who sought to list all the different national forms of greeting could easily fill a book with them. But the scientific gain would be small. One would be confronted by enormous variety, one would come across apparently more or less inexplicable peculiarities, and one would be left amazed at the subtly cultivated etiquette of forms of greeting" [Andree (4)].

Human greeting behavior certainly displays a great number of astonishing peculiarities and great variation. But with our knowledge of animal behavior these rites are for the most part explicable. One key to the interpretation of these phenomena is offered by the understanding of their function in establishing a bond and appeasing aggression. And a further one by our knowledge of the process of phylogenetic ritualization and the recognition that the majority of bond-establishing rites are derived from the field of parental care, that many others are derived from sexual behavior and a few, finally, from aggression itself. It is the diversity of these origins of the rites employed to establish bonds that causes the multiplicity of forms of greeting. Furthermore, since some individual components can be culturally emphasized while others can be suppressed, significant differences often occur. This factor, just as much as the fact that even fixed action patterns that are innate can produce a variable outward appearance through superposition (see p. 44), makes more difficult the search for constants. Nevertheless, by taking as a basis the equipment we have so far fashioned for ourselves, it should be possible to track them down. I shall attempt to do this in the following pages.

The universal function of a greeting is to establish or maintain a bond and to appease aggressive feelings. One greets friends and acquaintances not only at the first meeting of the day but often repeatedly after only a brief separation. Leave-taking is also a part of the complex of greeting behavior. In taking leave of someone we are once more strengthening the bond for the future by means of friendly rites. From the moment of departure a person walking away is in a dangerous situation. He cannot keep his eye on his partner. The latter might very well throw something after him. Anyone who leaves the presence of a superior bowing deeply and walking backward out of the room is showing this fear motivation quite clearly. Leave-taking of this kind does not to my knowledge exist in animals.

The peacemaking significance of a greeting in our daily life is evident. Not greeting someone releases aggression even within the family circle. Conversely we all know how a friendly gesture of greeting can relax a tense situation. The reply to a greeting is an important confirmation of one's willingness for contact and to a certain extent it implies a pledge. For this reason a greeting returned is generally a guarantee of security. Traveling alone through the country of the Rwala Bedouin, a stranger who crosses the territory of a tribe unknown to him and greets someone there—even if it is only a little girl—and has his greeting returned, can be sure that he will neither be attacked nor robbed, for even a little girl, with her relatives, will protect him. If a member of the little girl's tribe should attack him, he needs only to turn to her family for help and it will be granted to him. Even enemies can count upon this protection if they succeed, perhaps in flight, in tricking a member of the enemy family into returning a greeting. For this reason adult Bedouin are extremely wary in replying to a greeting [Musil (*159*)].

A greeting creates and confirms unity. In the U.S., blacks who are strangers to one another can be observed exchanging greetings at bus stops, thus giving evidence of a feeling of solidarity. This is also done by the owners of the same make of car when they pass on the road, especially if the make in question is an uncommon one (*75*).

In our daily life we do not by any means greet everyone. In large cities we hurry past our fellow-men without a word. But as soon as we want something of a person good manners demand that we begin by greeting him. We also offer greetings when we enter a shop or a strange house; the Japanese do this too. In addition, we will greet a stranger if we meet him alone somewhere out in the open. If we do not, we experience an unpleasant feeling of tension. As soon as we step out of the anonymous crowd, in order, say, to make a particularly active individual contact, we have an urge to greet, an inner "greeting impulse."

The forms greeting takes are at first sight very diverse. Even in one country there are many different forms of greeting. Thus (in Germany or Austria) if we meet a stranger somewhere in the mountains we will smile at him, give a friendly nod, raise our hats, and probably also say *"Guten Tag"* ("Hello"). If we meet in a very lonely place we may also feel the need to add a few friendly embellishments to the exchange. But generally we stick to the greeting formula that offers good wishes. If we are not wearing hats we may still touch the side of our heads with our hands, or briefly raise an open hand. If we meet a friend we behave in basically the same manner but we momentarily and involuntarily raise our eyebrows at the moment of friendly recognition (see p. 16). We also hold out our hand to friends in greetings and shake hands, each according to his temperament. If we are wearing gloves, then good manners dictate we remove them—but that goes only for men. Women may retain their gloves. We may slap close friends on the back and we embrace and kiss close relatives. We will then talk with our friend and give evidence of our concern by asking how he feels, where he has come from, and where he is going.

If we are visiting someone in his house the "contact greeting" (handshake, embrace, or kiss) and the greeting formula will be the same. But, as visitors, we are prepared for the meeting and bring gifts—a box of chocolates, candy for the children, flowers, or a bottle of wine. After coming in, we remove our hats. In our own greeting behavior, therefore, very many different patterns can be observed. What specific function does each fulfill, and how far can we observe outward or functional correspondences in other peoples? I will go through the individual behavior patterns that occur in greeting from this point of view, making comparisons between different cultures.

We have already mentioned the smile. This expressive movement is specific to man and evolves even in people born deaf and blind. We do not know its origin, but we know its function in appeasing aggression: a smile disarms. Since we show our teeth in smiling it has been suggested that what we have here might be a ritualized threat movement whose original meaning became reversed in the course of evolution. There is, however, the fact that in threatening we show our teeth quite differently. We threaten by opening the corners of our mouth and drawing down the corners of our lower lip especially far, probably so as to expose the full extent of the long upper canine teeth that we no longer possess, as various primates still do (see p. 18). It is furthermore not easy to imagine how, of all things, a threat to bite which is directed straight at the partner (there is no question here of a redirected threat like that of the greeting rite of the greylag goose) should have evolved into such an exceptionally pacifying gesture. It might possibly be derived from a defensive fear-threat. In various primates we find a "grin of fear" in subordinates, in which the front teeth are bared (5). But there is one other possible derivation. Many primates groom the coats of group members and we have mentioned that ritualized grooming movements are carried out in the air. In this process the incisors, which are used in grooming, are bared. This is a thoroughly friendly signal with the teeth, and I consider it likely that smiling has evolved in this way. Its interpretation is made more difficult by the lack of film documents showing corresponding behavior patterns in those primates most closely related to us. Thus we can speak with certainty about the function and the distribution of smiling but not about its origins.

"Greeting with the eyes," as we have already mentioned, where the eyebrows are quickly flashed upward, occurs among the most varied peoples (see p. 15). The movement is an extremely friendly signal and is probably a ritualization of the expression of pleased surprise. When surprised we raise our eyebrows. This has also been ritualized into a threat; for example, if a child uses incorrect table manners one often sees its parents giving a threatening look. In this case the eyebrows are held up for quite a long time and the eyes are fixed on the transgressor. Various apes and monkeys do the same thing. In the eyebrow flash, on the other hand, the expression of surprise has been ritualized into a friendly signal in a different fashion. The eyebrows are raised only briefly, signaling recognition and surprise. The threatening stare is absent and the appearance of the smile denotes pleasure in seeing the other person.

Nodding with the head is known to us not only from the greeting situation but also as a gesture of affirmation. In both cases there is consent—in greeting, the consent to friendly contact. In its origin nodding is a ritualized bowing gesture and therefore one of submission.* When nodding agreement in conversation we are submitting, as listeners, to the ideas of the speaker. I have filmed people nodding in a greeting situation among the most varied ethnic groups—Stone-Age Papuans (Kukukuku, Woitapmin), among Waika Indians of the Upper

---

* Chimpanzees invite their conspecifics to groom them socially with a deep bow. They are thus using, in order to approach one another, the posture that is the antithesis of the threatening posture (see Fig. 51).

Fig. 51. Female chimpanzee greeting a male. The bow is probably a ritualized form of invitation to social grooming (from a photograph by the author).

Orinoco, among Nilotohamites (Turkana, Karamojo), Bantus, Balinese, Samoans, and Japanese. So far I have not discovered any culture in which people do not nod when greeting. The people I have named also nod when affirming, but there are in addition other forms of affirmation (see p. 54).

Less ritualized forms of submission are bowing, falling to one's knees, and prostrating oneself (see Figs. 52–55). As a respectful greeting, bowing can still be found among Europeans. The teachings of the Egyptian sage Ptahotep contain the following precept: "Bend your back before your chief, your superior, and the administration of the king; and your house and your goods will endure and you will receive your just rewards." * In ancient Egypt people used to fling themselves on the ground in front of their lord and either sniff at or kiss the earth. As a particular favor the subject was permitted to kiss the king's feet instead of the earth. In Japan people greet one another with a deep bow. Old explorers' accounts carry reports of extreme submission among Africans. Heinzelmann (*84*) de-

* "Die Lehren des altägyptischen Weisen Ptahotep," *Völkerkunde* **6**, 259.

Fig. 52. Greeting
an Egyptian dig-
nitary (from K.
Lang, 1926, p.
201).

scribes a greeting of this kind: "Here in the capital city
Katunga the King Mansola held sway. His subjects greeted him
as follows: they threw themselves on the ground at some distance from him and smeared their heads twice with earth. Then
they dragged themselves closer and remained lying with their
faces in the dust. When they were close to the King they kissed
the ground as well and laid each cheek on it. By now head, face,
lips and chest were properly soiled with red earth and they received permission to sit near their king and converse with him.
But a few officials distinguished themselves still more in dem-

Fig. 53. Laotian
greeting (from C.
Bock, Im Reiche des
Weissen Elefanten,
Leipzig, 1885, p.
128).

Fig. 54. Ife people (Yoruba) greeting their ruler (from O. Frobenius, in K. Lang, 1926, p. 265).

onstrating their subjection by rolling about this way and that on the ground" (p. 228).

These examples should suffice to show that one encounters every gradation of submissive behavior from nodding to self-prostration. In principle this behavior follows essentially that observed in other vertebrates: one makes oneself small, and this is the precise opposite of threatening behavior.

A particular form of greeting bow is practiced by Fulah women. They turn their backsides toward the person greeted

Fig. 55. German police-man greeting President de Gaulle of France (from a press photo-graph).

Fig. 56. Fulah women greeting (taken by Passarge, in K. Lang, 1926, p. 203).

and bow deeply (Fig. 56). This behavior pattern is uncommonly reminiscent of the appeasement "presenting" of various apes and monkeys. Perhaps it represents the persistence of a behavioral root. It is certainly noticeable in Europe that on the outside of old fortress and city gateways bared buttocks are often shown. From Japan I know protective amulets that show the same thing, which could be a portrayal of appeasement "presenting." In this connection Wickler mentions that, among the Germanic tribes, both men and women stuck their bared bottoms out of their front doors to propitiate Wotan (*217*). In Japan men and women warded off spirits by lining up and parting their kimonos to show their sexual organs (*29*). In this case there was both appeasement by means of the female mating-invitation and a phallic threat to the evil spirits. Such presentation often occurs, as men threaten spirits as well as appease them. The principle of linking a phallic threat with female "presenting" is also seen in the common marmoset of South America. In these monkeys both males and females "present" when making threats against strangers. They turn their rumps toward the enemy in the female mating-invitation gesture. But at the same time the males also show the typical male genital presentation: they stick out their testicles in a remarkable manner and also have an erection. This is threat and appeasement at the same time.

Let us return to human greeting behavior. I have mentioned the habit of raising our hats in greeting and removing our gloves. These are of course conventional customs but what is their origin? In order to understand the raising of the hat one needs to know that originally in greeting the helmet or protective head covering was removed. One was to a certain extent giving up one's protection, and this proof of trust has developed into today's gesture. The same is true of the removal of the gloves when greeting. In the Middle Ages these were made of steel and afforded the warrior protection. This explains why only men remove their gloves. In the same way putting aside one's weapon in greeting is giving up one's protection. Demonstrations of trust of this kind can once again be observed among the greatest variety of peoples. The ancient Germans laid down their weapons before an audience outside the castle gates. If two nomadic Obbos from East Africa meet they put down their bows and arrows. The Wasindja do the same. The Kaffitsho put their spears down beside them, bend their knees, and fold their outstretched hands (*131*). Masais, when greeting, stick their spears in front of them in the ground. In ancient Japan a person of low rank removed his sandals when greeting and, as a sign that he was unarmed, thrust his right hand into his left sleeve. After that he let his arms fall slowly to his sides; walking past the person of high rank he called out, "Do me no harm" and mimed a gesture of fear [Lang (*131*)]. Unlike the greeting behavior patterns we discussed earlier (smiling, greeting with the eyes, nodding, bowing), these demonstrations of trust just mentioned are culturally formed. They take account of the fact that a threat display with weapons activates feelings of aggression, and this is a trait specific to all human beings— hence the parallels.

The handshake is a most remarkable form of greeting, occurring in the most varied cultural areas. Papuans, who had had their first contact with a European only seven months before my visit, greeted me in this way (*49*). Children and adults of the Kukukuku and Woitapmin tribes came thronging up to me specifically in order to give me their hands—holding their hands outstretched with the palm upward, as if begging. At first I believed this to be the European influence, but when I ques-

tioned them the natives explained that they had always greeted
one another in this way. Patrol officers assured me of the same
thing; even at their first meetings the Papuans had greeted
them by taking their hands (Fig. 57). In Europe the custom of
giving one's hand has been described as early as Homer. In
Africa it is widespread as a greeting, for example among the
Nilotohamites (Masai), the Bantu, and the Bushmen. Among
the Bajangi in West Africa one holds out one's right hand to
the partner while taking hold of his wrist with the left (*131*).
Shaking hands has also been reported among Eskimos, American Indians, Guatemalans, and in Central Asia. Of the Dayaks
on Borneo, Selenka (*187*) writes: "All the Dayaks whom we
met came up to me with a friendly expression and held out
their hands to me" (p. 39). Of the Wedda he reports: "I held
out both my hands to the brown fellows and they gave me theirs
in all simplicity as if it were the most natural thing in the
world. I was extremely struck by this willing grasping and
stretching out of the hands, which is certainly not a custom

*Fig. 57. Papuans
(Dugum Dani) greeting
one another (from the
film "Dead Birds" by R.
Gardner).*

Fig. 58. Female chimpanzee (left) inviting a male to give her his hand (from a photograph by J. and H. van Lawick-Goodall, in W. Wickler, 1969).

among such primitive peoples, even in my Dayaks who have scarcely rubbed shoulders at all with white people, and their culture. There must be something natural and easy to grasp in the movement" (p. 328).

The ease with which the movement is picked up must initially rest on the fact that we hold out our hands to our children to help them and thus seek physical contact. We will further remember that even high-ranking chimpanzees will hold out their hands to subordinates to encourage them and that subordinate chimps sometimes beg for contact. Chimps place their hand on the hand held out to them and many human beings do the same (Fig. 58). If a dominant chimp lying in the grass is feeling really lazy, he will often stretch out only a foot to the begging subordinate. But this has a reassuring effect just like the extended hand—indeed like any contact; both young and adult anthropoid apes experience a need for this in time of danger. Kortlandt (*114*) observed wild chimpanzees attacking a stuffed leopard. At intervals they would draw back again and hold hands with one another, thus giving one another mutual encouragement before returning to the attack. They drew courage from one another quite literally. The action of a chimpanzee seeking contact resembles the movement of begging for food. As chimpanzees will also hand food to a begging chimp, it is conceivable that the whole complex of extending and taking the hand could be interpreted as ritualized feeding. Instead of food, contact is given, which both rewards and re-assures. The begging movement is undoubtedly identical in both cases, but contact is given in a different way from food, so these two acts of giving must have two distinct origins. Not all people give their hands as we do. They often hold one another by the shoulders, hips, elbows, or other parts of the body. Among some Papuan tribes it is customary to touch the man one is greeting on the tip of his penis. Whether there are people who lack any kind of contact greeting I do not know. I have never come across any express mention of such a thing. There must be a primary need for such contact. It reassures and encourages us and this we seek. The actions of seeking and granting contact, however, can be highly ritualized, so that no actual touching is needed. A speaker who feels unsure of himself will look inquiringly at his friends and wait for a sign of encouragement; a nod or a wink will suffice.

There are other elements in the handshake that are worthy of note. We do not simply hold out our hands and make contact. We take hold of our partner's hand, press and shake it—actions that can be observed in different variants in other peoples. This form of establishing contact includes a demonstration of strength and enables people to size each other up. We feel ashamed when we cannot return a handshake properly, perhaps because the other person has taken hold of our hand too near to the fingertips. In this respect the greeting undoubtedly contains an element of aggression: shaking and squeezing hands is often a kind of sporting contest.

Aggressive elements are inherent in many male greeting rites and are described as "warrior greetings" in the literature of ethnology. These are demonstrations of one's skill as a warrior, by means of which one seeks to win respect on the one hand, while also clearly expressing that one has no hostile intentions. In some Indian tribes of the Amazon rainforest there is for example the "arrow greeting." The Indians shoot arrows at the people approaching them, but the aim is so accurate that the arrows fall into the ground just in front of the visitors. (Many visitors have misunderstood this as hostile!) This is a form of greeting that is highly comparable to our own gun salutes, which were not always fired from empty guns. Baker (*10*) describes how he was greeted by Turkish troops in Northeast Africa: "After we had travelled for an hour, always following on the trail of the company, we saw in the distance a great Latuka city and as we drew closer we discovered crowds of people who were gathered under two huge trees. At once the guns crackled, the drums sounded and as we came nearer we noticed the Turkish flags at the head of a troop of about a hundred men who were approaching us with the usual greetings, in which each man fired off ball cartridges as fast as he could load . . . They marched up to me in order to salute me, which process ended with them pointing the muzzles of their guns downwards and almost discharging them at my feet" (p. 173).

Among the North American Indians similarly aggressive greetings were customary. In Central Australia a high-ranking person from a friendly tribe was received with raised weapons as if his greeters wanted to ward him off. The visitor then made a mock attack which the others repulsed with their shields. After that the guest was embraced, led into the camp, and entertained by the women with food [Howitt (*99*)]. Sometimes whole traveling groups greeted one another fully armed and this often led to accidents among the Central Australians because their emotions got out of control [Spencer and Gillen (*194*)].

The Maoris of New Zealand greeted an unknown visitor by throwing a spear in his direction. After that both men sat down on the ground, rubbed noses, and the stranger was entertained. Comparable rites are known among Africans. In Uganda, for example, warriors made greetings with a spear held at the ready (Fig. 59). The greeting rites of Central Eskimo tribes are particularly noteworthy. The inhabitants of the village stand in a row and one of them steps forward. The stranger goes up to him with arms folded and his head inclined to the right: he now receives a powerful slap from the local man on his proffered cheek. But the latter must then hold out his own cheek and receive a slap from the stranger. This slapping duel can continue until one of them falls to the ground. Generally such

Fig. 59. Threat greeting by a warrior from Uganda (from J. A. Grant, A Walk Across Africa, *London, 1864, p. 191).*

greeting duels end peacefully; the stranger is considered to have been accepted and may take a wife. The object of the duel is for the stranger to prove that he is worthy of acceptance (*131*).

Such aggressive demonstrations, however, are virtually confined to greetings between men, who also have the tendency to establish a fighting community via aggression. Later in this chapter I shall present a further example.

Aggressive demonstrations constitute a remarkable elaboration of the greeting process—the actual function of which is to appease aggressive feelings and to emphasize what unites people. It is true that when a good marksman places his arrow just in front of his visitor's nose or shoots between his horse's legs, what he is doing is precisely giving an assurance of his friendly intentions. But misunderstandings can still occur.

Embracing and the various forms of touching, patting, caressing, and also kissing can be counted among the exceptionally friendly gestures of greeting. We have already mentioned the wide distribution of kissing and the occurrence of clearly homologous behavior patterns in chimpanzees. The nineteenth-century Austrian poet, Grillparzer, wrote a poem about kissing:

"Respect kisses the hands, friendship the open brow, pleasure the cheek, and blissful love the mouth." Other peoples appear to make similar distinctions about where they kiss. We have already mentioned that some Africans were often allowed only to kiss the ground in front of their ruler, or as a special favor his feet. Greetings between the ancient Persians differed according to rank. Equals kissed each other on the mouth, but if one ranked lower than the other both would kiss each other on the cheek. In the case of very great differences of rank the subordinate flung himself to the ground before the other. Detailed information about other peoples is unfortunately not available. Human beings will kiss the hand, feet, shoulder, cheeks, brow, eyes, the hem of the coat (Fig. 60). In the Egyptian Sudan each person kisses the palm of his own hand before extending it to the other person. Kissing oneself and then extending one's hand recurs frequently. When we blow a kiss we first kiss our own hands. The Bedouin smack their kisses in the air while shaking hands with a guest [Lang (*131*)]. Kissing with the lips is, as we have said (p. 135), a ritualized mouth-to-mouth feeding action. We have already shown that this behavior pattern is probably innate to man. The kiss taking the form of a "love-bite" is only rarely used as a greeting (see p. 134).

Many peoples greet with their noses in a manner superficially similar to kissing. This is a friendly sniffing action in which the nose is pressed on the cheek or nose of the partner and lightly rubbed against it. In Burma this form of greeting is called "namtschui" [from "nam" (smell) and "tschut" (to inhale)].

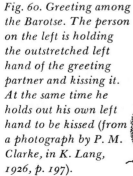

Fig. 60. Greeting among the Barotse. The person on the left is holding the outstretched left hand of the greeting partner and kissing it. At the same time he holds out his own left hand to be kissed (from a photograph by P. M. Clarke, in K. Lang, 1926, p. 197).

Sometimes the person greeting simply takes the other person's hand and rubs his own nose with it, as Cook (*31*) reports of the New Zealanders and Wilkes (*221*) of the Samoans. We find greeting by rubbing noses amongst the Lapps, Eskimos, Waikas, and Malayans; on Madagascar, on New Guinea, and in the Polynesian area. Greetings taking the form of friendly sniffing can also occur in other ways. Prince zu Wied (*219*) mentions that the Botocudos of the Brazilian jungle sniff one another's wrists.

The movements of embracing and caressing occur in the greeting behavior of many peoples. The derivation of this behavior from the realm of parental care has already been discussed. Prévost (*166*) has described the King of Loanga (West Africa) being greeted by his chief men in the following way: "They clap their hands two or three times and throw themselves at His Majesty's feet, rolling over and over in the sand to demonstrate their submissiveness. After this performance the particular favourites run right up to the king and lean on his knees with both hands, so that their heads rest on his bosom" (4, p. 677).

The raising of the open hand in greeting cannot be shown to be universal but it is certainly very widespread, so that one may assume a disposition for this gesture. I have observed it in Papuans, in the Shom Pen on Great Nicobar Island, and among the Karamojos and Turkanas of East Africa (*49*). The gesture is a clear demonstration of peaceful intent. One is in fact showing that one is not holding a weapon in the right hand. Occasionally it is combined with a wave. In Japan I have seen mothers watching their children riding on a roundabout waving to them in this way. People lamenting often raise both hands with outward-facing palms somewhat higher than their shoulders. Whether there is any connection between the two gestures is something that merits investigation (Figs. 61 and 62).

"It can be said that it is the custom all over the world to invite strangers to partake of a meal or to send them presents of food. We ourselves regard eating as something different from anything else and are pleased to accept an invitation to lunch even if we would be glad of the price of the meal" [Birket-Smith (22), p. 363].

Fig. 61. Little Neapolitan girl greeting by raising her open hand; at the same time she puts a protective arm round her little sibling (from a photograph by H. List, in Leica Fotografie **6**, *1960).*

Fig. 62. Shom Pen islander (Great Nicobar) giving a greeting by raising his open hand (from a photograph by the author).

Food and gifts are offered in greeting to guests among the most varied peoples. One drinks to the guest in friendship and hands him a drink of welcome. And even if it is not a universal custom for wives to come on their knees, bringing a drink of water for their returning husbands, as the Mandigoans of the west coast of Africa did [Prévost (*166*)], nevertheless in principle the same means of demonstrating friendship are used everywhere. Rasmussen (*168*) describes how as soon as he arrived at a Polar Eskimo village he would always have to eat with the various families in turn until he could simply swallow no more of the frozen walrus liver. It took him days to recover from friendly greetings of this kind.

When a stranger visits a Masai kraal he first sits outside the village under a shady tree and waits until an old woman brings him milk. The guest drinks a few swallows and hands back the vessel and the woman returns home. Now a man comes and spits in front of the guest—which the guest returns. After this exchange of greeting formulas he is taken into the village.

When the Walbiri of Central Australia arrive in the territory of another tribe, they always bring gifts of kangaroo meat, grain, or tobacco. Often this is no more than a gesture if the visitors themselves have nothing (*148*).

This custom is not confined to primitive peoples. In Central Europe when we visit a family for the first time in their new home we bring bread and salt. In the Ukraine these are always given to a visitor in greeting. When making formal visits we take candy with us; we offer our guests food and raise our glasses to them. At all feasts and festivals [in German "Fest"], the ultimate significance of which is the strengthening [or "Festigung"] of the bond between people, eating and drinking together play a great part, whether the affairs are family or work parties, the palm-fruit feasts of the Waikas, or a Papuan "Singsing." We reinforce the bond for life with a wedding cake, while the Patasiva on the Molucca Islands do the same by eating a dish of popeda together—only then is the marriage considered to be sealed. Our own family ties are strengthened by eating a birthday cake together as well as, for example, an "Easter ham" (in Central Europe).

One of the motives for trade is the exchange of gifts that

form a bond. "We are inclined to regard trading and the exchange of goods as purely economic questions and economic motives are certainly not absent even from the trading of primitive peoples. But this aspect is not always the most important. Often trade is regarded as a means of tying bonds of friendship between individuals and clans, which is far more important than the actual exchange of goods. Amongst the Central Eskimos a man will often have a good friend in the neighbouring group with whom he is accustomed to exchange gifts with ceremonial drumming and song and dancing. In Alaska the Eskimos used to invite the inhabitants of friendly settlements to splendid feasts at which they exchanged gifts in accordance with a ceremonial which was both complicated and strictly adhered to" [Birket-Smith (22), p. 187].

The refusal of an invitation to communal eating and drinking can constitute a mortal insult. Bernatzik (17) mentions an incident which can serve as an example. A French forest engineer was murdered by the Radé (an Indochinese tribe). A punitive expedition was sent out which succeeded in capturing the culprits. At the trial the latter stated indignantly: "The white man insulted us in a way we could not tolerate. We offered him our drink of welcome and the meat of a pig which we had sacrificed to the spirits in his honour. But he refused to accept our gifts and we had to watch him being fed by his Annamese slave. So we decided to avenge this insult and to kill him."

If two Arapesh are seriously angry with each other then, according to Margaret Mead (147), one will hang a bunch of croton leaves as a reminder on his front door, which signifies that he will never again eat with the other man. The breach can only be healed if the one who put up the sign slaughters a pig.

The giving of other gifts is probably derived from the giving of food. In Japan, it was formerly the custom, when tying a gift parcel, to include a small dried herring. The function of any gift in establishing a bond is completely equivalent to that of a gift of food. When Rasmussen (168) gave an Eskimo orphan a knife, he had won a reliable friend. "It was assuredly the first time in his life," writes Rasmussen, "that the orphan had had such an experience as to receive a present. He looked me up and down and shook his head. I assured him that I really meant it. Then, without a change of expression, he snatched the knife out of my hand and ran off. I did not think I should see any more of him for the present and was just going into our tent, when he came running up with a piece of walrus meat, which he pressed into my hand. 'Thou gavest, see: I give too,' said he and his face shone with grease and pride. Of course he had stolen the walrus meat. But from that day forth we were friends" (p. 51).

An Eskimo of the east coast of Greenland will offer a visitor the use of his snuffhorn, whereupon the latter offers his own. They also do this when taking their leave.

Finally we also offer objects as gifts. In the Upper Austrian *Mühlviertel* district, when a woman marries into a farm she must give every member of the family a gift as her entrance fee.

The gifts can also be symbolic. Thus, among very different peoples there is an equivalent to the olive branch of peace. Green twigs, leaves, bundles of grass, palm fronds, and so on are presented among the Waikas of the Upper Orinoco, the Masai, and the inhabitants of the Polynesian Islands, to name but a few. On the *Xarifa* expedition to the Indian Ocean (46) one of the Shom Pen who approached our ship gave us a green leaf. It was his first contact with a white man.

The ritualization of giving has progressed furthest when we give the other person our good wishes. A good wish is a verbal gift exchanged in greeting when we meet—or perhaps sent on a postcard.

Thus far we have mainly been talking about greeting rites that are in principle very similar to our own. But there are greeting customs among some primitive peoples that differ from our own and which it is hard to interpret. Thus in several places it is customary for the person greeted to be rubbed with or to come into contact with a substance that comes from the person greeting. Among the Nilotohamites one spits at the partner or spits in front of his feet.

The Wakikuyu spit into their hands before holding them out in greeting [v. Höhnel (90)]. Two Wakikuyu seal a friendship by fetching water and sprinkling it over each other's head.

They catch the water in their right hands as it runs down and drink it.

The "spittle greeting" of the Eskimos is also well known. Kotzebue (*118*) describes the greeting he received in the Bering Strait as follows: "Here a dirty skin was spread out on the boards, on which I had to sit down and then one after another of them came up to me, embraced me, rubbed his nose hard against mine and ended his caresses by spitting in his hands and wiping them several times over my face" (p. 196). Among the Kanum-Irebe of New Guinea it is a display of friendliness if one takes something of the smell of the departing man and transfers it to oneself. The person saying good-bye takes hold of the person who is going by the armpit, sniffs at his hand, and rubs the smell on himself. Urine, too, has this bond-forming function for some tribes. Among the Dama in South Africa the parting blessing uttered by an adult runs: "May you be pissed upon by the fathers, my uncles!" As far as I could gather from the sources, this remains a figure of speech. When a man takes his leave one of the old men remaining behind takes a vessel of water, drinks from it, and spits it out at the parting man. This ceremony is also carried out when someone returns. Old men and young as well as women are greeted in this way. But the greeting can only be given by old men (*131*).

Rites actually involving urine occur among the Hottentots. If a man has killed a lion, an elephant, or a rhinoceros, his heroic deed is celebrated in the following way: he retires to his hut until an old man fetches him out of the kraal and invites him to come and be honored. The older man leads him to the center of the village where all the men are gathered, waiting for his arrival. The hero now crouches down on a mat and all the men squat down round him in a circle. The old man goes up to him and urinates over him from head to toe. If he is a good friend of the hero, he will deluge him with urine—this makes the honor all the greater. After circumcision the boys are urinated on by the person who performs the operation. The same thing is done when youths are received into the community of men. Urine ceremonies, finally, also occur at marriages. The men squat round in a circle with the bride and bridegroom in the middle. The master of ceremonies, a man from the bridegroom's village, urinates first on the bridegroom, next on the bride, and finally directs his attention to each of the spectators in turn until his supply is exhausted [Kolbe (*113*)]. The whole procedure is uncommonly reminiscent of the marking rites of various mammals. Many rodents mark members of their pack with urine to identify them as belonging to the group. It is possible that what we have seen in this very primitive human group is an analogous (though not related!) behavior pattern, which in the course of time was transformed by other races into rites in which water is used, such as baptism in our own culture. Anointing people with spittle and other substances may be based upon the same motivation—that of establishing a bond by means of a common substance. Rüppell (*174*) writes about the greeting he received from the Hammer-Arabs: "When I arrived at the Well of Nedjer with the chief of the Hammer-Arabs, Hadgi Minhin, his three wives welcomed him with solicitous insistence; they pressed his legs and smeared them with butter; each desired that he should enjoy the half-acid drink she had herself prepared . . . The slave women crawled towards him on their hands and knees and embraced his knees until he had laid his hand on the head of each one of them; they seemed to take no notice whatever of me" (p. 148). The Ovambo go in for a similar anointing with butter in greeting [Andersson (*3*)]. Being anointed with other substances fell to the lot of all high-ranking persons in antiquity.

There are many other forms of bidding farewell, as for instance the greeting with tears that was customary in a number of North American Indian tribes and also on the Solomon Islands. There is a little more to be said, however, about greeting formulas. In principle they express the same as the greeting gestures, namely, peaceful intentions, sympathy, submission and the desire to establish a bond. People also wish one another all good things, and this is a ritualized form of giving gifts. Good wishes are a gift. We wish one another a "good day," "good fishing" [in German "Petri Heil!"] "good hunting," "peace be with you," etc. One bids a person "welcome" and wishes him "good-bye." One signs letters "sincerely." If we compare the greeting formulas of various peoples we can confirm that in principle they are similar.

A Waruvu tribesman in East Africa will ask a series of friendly questions to which the person addressed replies "Hm"; the first man then replies in the same way [v. Höhnel (90), p. 70].

	Then	
A says to *B*	*B* replies	*A* replies
Kilo vedi? (Have you had a good night?)	Hm!	Hm!
Sie vedi? (Have you had a good day?)	Hm!	Hm!
Ho kaja? (How are things at home?)	Hm!	Hm!
Ho kaja kilo vedi? (Did you have a good night?)	Hm!	Hm!
Mzima? (Are you well?)	Hm!	Hm!
Sana? (Very?)	Hm!	Hm!
Jambo! (Greetings!)	Hm!	Hm!

Two Tuaregs who are strangers greet one another when they meet in the following manner:* they stop and the higher-ranking person (the "respect person" or "RP") holds out his right hand to the other one. Both rub the palms of their hands together in a pulling movement, in which the hand, as soon as the fingertips break contact, is quickly withdrawn upward.

> The RP says: *Salam Aleikum!*   (Peace be with you!)
> Reply: *Aleikum salam!*   (With you be peace!)
> RP: *Matulit?*   (How are you?)
> Reply: *El Cheròs.*   (Well.)

The RP begins with the introduction: "I am the son of — and — from the tribe of —." The other replies in the same manner. Then they ask for and exchange news, and gather information about where each is bound for. Finally the RP wishes *"Aerr Sarchat"* ("Until we meet again") and receives the reply *"Inshallah"* ("If Allah wishes it"). The greeting formula is repeated

* I am indebted to my friend Markus Krebser for this information.

with the roles reversed: once again they rub hands and then move on. If both are riding on dromedaries, they remain seated on them throughout. But if they know each other personally, then the lower-ranking person dismounts and gives the RP his hand and they shake hands as we do. The RP then dismounts. The other prepares tea or a meal appropriate to the time of day, while the RP asks questions of a general nature, to which the other replies without asking questions himself. The RP is accompanied for another hundred yards after the exchange of parting formulas already described. They then shake hands and part.

When a Masai takes his leave of a guest he says: "Live well, pray to God, speak only with things that are certain and meet only blind people." To this the guest replies: "May God give you always milk and honey wine" [Fuchs, p. 92, quoted in Lang (*131*)].

Often sympathetic inquiries are made as to whether the other has eaten well. The Chinese coolies would formerly never forget to ask *"Che fan la moa?"* ("Have you eaten rice?"). And the Germans would say *"Wünsche wohl gespeist zu haben"* ("I hope you have eaten well").

The Waikas use the word *"Shori"* (brother-in-law) in greeting. In this way they express their willingness to become related to the person they are greeting.

What is remarkable about these greeting formulas is the fact, which to my knowledge has been little noticed, that people in certain situations always say the same things, which is indicative of innate dispositions. This is particularly marked in talk between lovers. Just as in their behavior patterns, in the words they speak lovers also make use of infantile appeals to be cherished.

The behavior patterns observed in greeting rites frequently occur in religious rites as well. People commune with spirits and gods as if the latter were a kind of human being. They are given rice and other foodstuffs; they are offered flowers and scents in sacrifice, and people bow down before them. T ᴗ communal meal also plays a great part in the religious life of many peoples. Christ's Last Supper performed the function, at the moment of parting, of establishing a bond symbolically for the future. If we survey the multiplicity of human greeting gestures, it becomes very clear that they follow essentially the same patterns everywhere. This arises in part from their function of making peace, so that even culturally transmitted rites display similarities. But there are a whole number of similarities of principle and formal sequence which can be interpreted reasonably only on the assumption that common phylogenetic adaptations are present.

Various gestures of granting contact, such as extending the hand, feeling and patting, embracing and caressing, are derived from parental care behavior. Ritualized feeding occurs in greeting in the form of kissing, offering the breast, offering food and drink and, by derivation from this, the exchange of gifts. All these things can be expressed verbally by giving the partner good wishes and by expressions of interest and sympathy.

The origins of man's innate peace signal, smiling, cannot yet be determined with certainty. We have referred to the possibility of a derivation from social grooming. If true then this behavior pattern, too, is derived from the complex of maternal cherishing actions.

Infantilisms are also manifested in the striving for contact by the person greeting when he holds out his hand. The action of greeting when a person buries his face in the chest of a high-ranking person is equally an infantile behavior trait. Occasionally he even sucks at the breast. The sideways oscillations of the head in rubbing noses and in nestling up to the breast are certainly also to be interpreted as infantilisms. Occasionally the appeasing appeal is not made by means of childish behavior but directly via a child. In our own culture it is customary for children to present bouquets to guests on state visits.

Certain appeasement gestures (presenting the buttocks) can be interpreted as ritualized behavior patterns from the sexual field, which are directly related to the presenting gestures of female primates. We have mentioned the greeting of the Fulah women; it is likely that this behavior pattern is not confined to them, especially since the gesture is widespread elsewhere as a protective gesture of appeasement.

Demonstrations of peaceful intent in which one abandons one's protection (laying down weapons, removing the helmet, etc.) and submissive postures (bowing, prostration, nodding) are universal practice. These gestures are partly culturally formed, and partly innate (nodding), and have probably developed independently as an antidote to threatening behavior.

Aggressive in origin and indeed still aggressively motivated today are demonstrations of strength expressed, for example, in the firm handshake or in the various forms of "threat-greeting" (gun salutes, presenting arms).

The greeting with the eyes which is common to all cultures is a ritualized expression of pleased surprise. Greeting with the nose is derived from friendly sniffing. The derivation of greetings with tears is uncertain. It could be a ritualized expression of concern or else a form of ritualized begging to be cherished. I am inclined to the first of these views, because grief experienced in common has a very strong cohesive effect (see p. 202).

The origin of the rites in which people smear one another mutually with various substances is also puzzling. These customs are startlingly reminiscent of various forms of mutual scent-marking in mammals.

For all their multiplicity, all forms of greeting behavior really amount to one fundamentally quite uniform type of behavior in which the same behavioral elements recur again and again across the spectrum of cultures. Their function is essentially appeasement, the establishing of a bond, and self-presenting threat display. So in the case of many greeting rituals we can certainly assume an innate basis.

THE PALM FRUIT FEAST OF THE WAIKAS

The average person, when asked why people come together from time to time for small celebrations, would probably reply that *he* does it to have a thoroughly good time. At feasts and festivals people eat, drink, flirt, and dance—and all these things are fun.

When, however, one has acquired the habit of inquiring

what particular function given behavior patterns have in the preservation of the species, one soon discovers that feasts and festivals have a central importance in human social life. They are rituals which strengthen the bonds between people and which are in many aspects related to greeting rituals. This can best be clarified with an example.

I recently visited the Waika Indians on the Upper Orinoco.* This ancient Indian group, which is probably descended from the first wave of settlers who migrated into the Americas via the Bering Strait, has remained until today in its original state, thanks to the remoteness of the region where they live. These Indians live as hunters and food-gatherers. They do, however, cultivate bananas. Both men and women wear only a cord round their waists. The men use this cord to bind up their penises. On festive occasions they decorate themselves with paint and feathers and many also wear strips of cloth acquired by means of bartering from the missions. Their fighting and hunting weapons are bow and arrows, the arrows being poisoned with curare. The Waikas live in village communities that rarely comprise more than a hundred persons. A village consists of wind-shelters set up in a circle round a large open space. These lean inward and the hammocks of the various families are slung between the supporting posts. Thus the whole village community lives to a certain extent under one roof, while each family occupies a sector of this wind-shelter with its own hearth.

These Indians are extremely warlike and impulsive and live in a constant state of feud with the neighboring villages. The survival of the smaller village communities depends on whether they can make alliances with other villages who will grant them refuge and assistance if need be. And these alliances are concluded and strengthened at feasts. Since the guests have to be entertained and given gifts by the hosts, the feasting generally takes place at the season when the palm fruit

* I am particularly indebted to Dr. Inga Steinvorth de Goetz and to her daughter, Elke Fuhrmeister de Goetz, in this connection. Dr. Goetz arranged for me to be flown in by one of her pilots and her daughter acted as my guide. Dr. Goetz knows the Waika Indians and has recently published a remarkable book about this tribe (*199*). [See also Zerries (*224*).]

is ripe.* We were staying in this region just at that season, and shortly after our arrival at the Ocamo mission station we learned that inhabitants of a nearby Indian village had received an invitation from the village of Shiparioteri on the river Ocamo.

We made the acquaintance of this group, gave them presents and were able to join them on their two days' journey to the neighboring village. Women and children went with them and, as I later learned, this is an important detail, for in this way they demonstrate their peaceful intentions. Without women and children such a troop of armed warriors would never be admitted into a strange village. We began by traveling upriver in boats. This voyage was an extraordinary experience. Elke Goetz and I sat in one of the great dugout canoes facing an Indian family of four. The two boys were aged about nine months and five years. All day we traveled up the constantly winding brown river past a marvelous backdrop of forest with flowering trees and half-uprooted forest giants that leaned right out over the water. Here and there a flock of parrots took flight. We made good progress, for we had been given powerful outboard motors from the mission. Our hosts were mutually attentive throughout the voyage, spending most of the time delousing one another. First the husband would delouse his wife; then he would lay his head in her lap and was deloused in his turn. Sometimes a whole delousing chain was set up: the father deloused the mother, the mother deloused the five-year-old son, and the latter played with the baby. Whatever the man caught he offered her as tidbits on his outstretched palm. She, on the other hand, did not share her pickings but immediately ate everything she found. She searched her husband's body as well, biting away small impurities with her teeth. At other times they ate provisions and offered some to us with friendly smiles. By means of simple gestures they asked us if we had a baby like theirs; they were probably quietly amazed that we did not delouse one another at all. The baby was the center of attention. When he was not being

* The mealy fruits of the Pijiguao palms are an important source of food for the Waikas.

suckled or held over the side to do his business, his parents and brother played with him. His mother could make him laugh by pressing her lips hard against his stomach and blowing with puffed-out cheeks. The baby would shout with delight and she looked round proudly. She also sucked the baby's penis and so did his brother from time to time. I later saw other mothers who cheered up their boy babies in this way. During this long journey by boat I only once saw an angry reaction. When the baby wetted the little boy as they were playing, his expression changed to one of disgust and annoyance and he passed the baby back to his mother. When the baby wanted to crawl back to him, he pushed him away. But this did not last long. After a few minutes the two were playing together again. Even the father joked with the children.

We repeatedly passed sandbanks where the boats stopped. Everyone grubbed in the sand for turtles' eggs and the delight was great when we found some. Before nightfall we made camp in the forest. The undergrowth was cleared away, the hammocks were slung, and small fires were kindled. Each family has its own fire. The effect of them in the dark night was very cozy. The villagers were never all asleep at once. Repeatedly in the night one would call out something and another would reply. It seemed as if they were keeping one another's spirits up in this way. A traveling group of Waikas always has to reckon with the possibility of being attacked; for this reason they always travel armed.

After breakfast we continued our journey by water but only for a short way. Then we went on foot through the forest down a path that we should never have recognized as such. But our traveling companions ran confidently along it and we followed. Elke took off her shoes in order to run more comfortably, but she would have been better advised not to, for I started up a snake which flashed in alarm backward between my legs straight towards Elke. I called out: "Look out, a snake!" Elke leaped in the air as if bitten by a tarantula and landed first with one foot and then with the other right on top of the reptile, which was fortunately concerned only with escaping and wriggled violently away. I have never before or since seen anyone hopping up and down on one spot so fast.

The snake got away, and for that reason I still do not know to this day what species of snake Elke danced on. It was probably entirely harmless but after this adventure we felt somewhat subdued.

On the afternoon of the second day's traveling, emissaries from the village of our hosts-to-be came out to meet us. The leader of our group and a man from the host village squatted down on the ground facing each other and each made a speech, gesticulating, which we did not understand. The upshot was that we pitched our camp there for the night and moved on into the village only the following day. But already that evening we were richly entertained by our hosts with cooked palm fruits, smoked monkey and bird meat.

The following morning we went on until we were just outside the village. There we were once again fed by our hosts. Then all our group decorated themselves. Even the children and dogs were painted with squiggles, spots, and wavy lines.* While everyone was decorating himself, we moved off into the shadow of the village and waited to see what would happen.

As a prelude to the feast the guest warriors each danced once round the village. Many of them had on their war paint and brandished bows and arrows. Stamping, with chests flung out and with heroic expressions, they displayed themselves before their hosts. Their heroic poses demonstrated that they were fine fellows whose friendship was worth having, a principle we have already encountered in the threat greeting. But threat displays and the show of weapons release aggressive feelings that must be appeased. This was done here by means of a child; behind each arrogant warrior generally danced a child, waving ragged palm fronds in its hands. Threat display and appeasement, the two basic functions of human social behavior, were here combined in a striking picture (Fig. 63). Alternating with the weapon-brandishing warriors were figures without weapons, brandishing green leafy whisks. What

---

* I was recently showing a dog specialist some of my transparencies. The first one showed a white dog with round rust-red spots all over its body. My colleague was delighted. The next dog he saw had squiggles and stripes on its legs, and he became extremely excited about this rare breed. When I finally showed him one covered with spots, squiggles and wavy lines he threw the ashtray at me.

Fig. 63. Threat displays and appeasement, two basic functions of human expressive behavior. The Waika warrior who is a guest at the palm-fruit feast dances in front of his hosts, making an aggressive display. But he documents his peaceful intentions by means of the child dancing behind him. The sight of the child creates a friendly mood (from a photograph by the author).

the origin of this ceremony is nobody knows. It is striking the way the display of the green parts of plants is employed for demonstrations of peaceful intentions right across the cultural spectrum. It recalls the display of nesting material by birds when courting and greeting. But in the primates which are our closest relatives we find nothing comparable.

At the close of the introductory dance some girls pranced in a ring, holding up palm fronds and waving them high in the air. After the dance the guests slung their hammocks between those of their hosts and began by lying down. In the course of the afternoon small groups then separated off and sniffed *yopa* with the hosts. This very strong narcotic—a brownish powder—is blown right up the partner's nose by means of a blowpipe. The effect is astonishing. The person sniffing it first of all winces as if he had had an electric shock, then he scratches his head and there is considerable mucous secretion from the nose. Sometimes the person even vomits. After a short time the drug takes effect and induces an exaggerated feeling of strength and self-awareness. The intoxicated person dances and sings until he is exhausted. The drug has no protracted aftereffects. Later in the afternoon the hosts decorated themselves and danced in their turn, and everyone danced together as a larger group. Meanwhile the women had made a banana soup which hosts and guests drank together, scooping it out of a bark vessel; but only the men did this. The women remained, as they had done so far, in the background. In essence the feast was a man's affair—a point we shall return to. One exception to this was a small mourning ceremony in the evening and on the following morning. In the evening, after a communal round dance the natives lamented those who had died during the year. The women of both villages gathered round the chief of the host village; they wept and mourned the dead of both villages. All displayed mutual concern, and their mutual grief increased their feeling of solidarity.

Thus far the feast had served to strengthen the alliance at village level: it was a communal celebration. But with the arrival of nightfall a new phase of the feast arrived. Everyone had withdrawn into his hammock, the fires glowed, and the talk died away. Then suddenly two men interrupted the peace of the night with a loud dialogue that gradually turned into a sung duet. It began with one of the guests scrambling out of his hammock and speaking. A man from the host village replied briefly, climbed out of his hammock as well, and squatted down beside him. And now the dialogue changed into a not very melodious song. To begin with, the guest sang whole sentences, then only more or less fragments of words, and the host replied to each call with a short melodic grunting noise which can be expressed roughly as an unvoiced "m, m, m" repeated three times quickly. The song lasted a good half-hour, and the more time passed the more violently the singers gesticulated. After a while they swapped roles. Then they spoke a few words in conclusion and crept back into their hammocks. Scarcely had they finished when two others began their duet.

As I do not understand the language of these people, I could not understand the words they were singing, but I recorded them on tape and Padre Berno of the Salesian Mission was kind enough to translate parts of them for me. This is a ritual known as "Uayamou," which one can translate as "sung contract." In this song promises—in other words, verbal gifts— and verbal assurances of friendship are exchanged. I have not been able to find any translations in the literature on the subject and I therefore want to include a section, especially since the conjecture has been voiced (*184*) that these songs are fragments of longer "mythical" texts.* In point of fact these "mythical" texts are thoroughly down-to-earth and realistic, as emerges from the translation that follows. In this song the guest—a man from Patanoueteri**—is speaking. The host replies after each sentence with the brief sound just described, which I have noted only in the first few sentences, and afterward omitted.

The guest begins: "I will speak"—(host murmurs)—"We are friends"—(host murmurs)—"I speak the truth"—(host murmurs). "We are poor, because we live far away, you are rich because you live near the foreign mission."—"The Mapeyomas are here, the Salesian nuns and the Nape, the lay brother Iglesias.—They give you many things.—We have no one we can ask for things from; but they give you machetes, pots, hammocks, clothes, glass beads."—Pause—"The Pissasaiteri

---

* Since writing this statement I have come upon a publication by E. Biocca (1969) in which some contract songs are translated. (E. Biocca, *Mondo Yanoama*, De Donato editore.)

** I recorded this song at a second feast in Platanal.

came to us Patanoueteri and attacked us with bows and arrows, they are very evil and wicked. They killed one of our men and my wife. I am very sad about that and very angry.

"You are a friend, get me a machete which the lay brother has given you and pots which you receive from the nuns."— Pause—"I have no dog and am very angry about it. You have many. I need one for hunting tapirs, so I ask for one of yours. Give it to me, I will pay you and I will be able to hunt tapirs.

"I never want to go away from here for you are my friends. I will stay in your houses which are in the forest. Give me a dog, even if it's a thin one, I will feed him up and will hunt tapirs with him. You have many dogs and you also have a bitch which will have puppies. So give me a dog."—Both embrace one another and the man thus addressed replies: "I promise you I will give you a piece of tapir, for I have dogs to hunt more. So you can eat bananas with meat. I will also give you the dog so that you can later hunt, and bananas, meat and piyiguao palm fruit."

In exchange he asks for rajaca (sticks for making arrows) for they have many enemies and they could then send out all their friends to fight.

"Give me and I will give you": that is the essential content of these "mythical" exchanges. They were carried on loudly all through the night and once again this was a men's affair. And with good reason. Essentially what was settled on the village level and during the night on an individual basis were military alliances, friendships binding the men to mutual aid in battle.

The following morning a group of women and men once again assembled for communal mourning.* They lamented and wept heartrendingly. The women sobbed as they held the gourds containing the ashes of their loved ones high in the air and then handed them to the chief who sat in the middle. The latter stirred the ashes into a banana broth and handed it to a young warrior to drink. Thus they consumed the ashes

---

* In our culture, too, bonds are cemented through communal mourning for the dead, for example by the laying of wreaths at state visits or by annual reunions of associations at which we rise to our feet for a minute's silence in memory of the dead.

of their people in a communal funeral ceremony. Finally the men sniffed *yopa*. There followed a communal dance by the men, who ended by facing one another in pairs in a squatting position, embraced one another, and once more—this time all together—sang their contracts.

Meanwhile the women had laid out banana leaves and spread them with baskets containing piyiguao palm fruits, bananas, smoked armadillos, monkeys, crocodiles, birds, and other game. These were gifts for the guests, who now in turn gave gifts. As they lived near the mission they gave strips of material, machetes, and the like. After that they shouldered the gifts they had received and left heavily laden.

The Waikas' palm-fruit feast serves to strengthen an alliance, and it is interesting that this goal is achieved by means of mutual feeding and gift giving, the exchange of promises, shared mourning, and shared threat-displaying dancing. Substantial elements of greeting behavior thus recur in these rites.

Comparable feasts, by means of which an alliance is strengthened, also occur in a wide variety of peoples. They are always associated with aggressive exhibitions and feasting. At one festival in the highlands of New Guinea I watched several thousand Papuans coming together in the central Wahge Valley. Armed, decorated with the feathers of birds of paradise and brightly painted, the men began by dancing. They had cleared a dancing floor several hundred yards long down which they stormed, dancing. At their head was a group of about forty drummers; after them came several hundred fantastically decorated dancers, brandishing long wooden spears and stamping their feet on the earth, pawing the ground violently at every step so that earth and stones flew and dust shrouded the scene. It was a gripping, aggressive demonstration. The drummers with their hand drumming made a powerful, dully reverberating sound. Each time they started up suddenly, almost all together, then they would stop in the same way. Then the dancers also crouched on the ground for a short rest, only to go storming forward again in their dance, with the drums beating once more, toward the place where the pigs killed for the feast lay on the ground outside a small round spirit-house. An enormous banquet followed in the course of which several hundred pigs were consumed. The young men competed with one another in trying to climb trees whose bark had been removed, and which were smeared with pig fat and to the tops of which trophies had been fastened. Sporting competitions often have a place in feasts. These serve to work off aggressive feelings in a ritualized form. Our own German shooting-matches, which make for social cohesion at the clan or village level, have the same character. One drinks, feasts, and demonstrates one's worth by showing off.

The demonstration of one's own worth often leads to strange and extravagant growths. Hosts and guests sometimes try to surpass one another in hospitality. Surely the most perverse development of this was shown at the feasts of the Kwaikutl Indians of Vancouver Island. Their so-called "potlatch" feast in essence represented a demonstration on one's own superiority in the face of the invited guests. The host chief glorified himself in his songs and at the same time had no qualms about ridiculing the guest as a poor wretch.

"I am the great chief who makes people ashamed.
I am the great chief who makes people ashamed.
Our chief brings shame to the faces.
Our chief brings jealousy to the faces.
Our chief makes people cover their faces by what he is
*   continually doing in this world,*
Giving again and again oil feasts to all the tribes.

"I am the only great tree, I am the chief!
I am the only great tree, I am the chief!
You are my subordinates, tribes.
You sit in the middle of the rear of the house, tribes.
I am the first to give you property, tribes.
I am your eagle, tribes!

"Bring your counter of property, tribes, that he may try
*   in vain to count the property that is to be given away*
*   by the great copper maker, the chief. . . .*

"I search among all the invited chiefs for greatness like
*   mine.*

I cannot find one chief among the guests.
They never return feasts,
The orphans, poor people, chiefs of the tribes!
They disgrace themselves.
I am he who gives these sea otters to the chiefs, the guests,
    the chiefs of the tribes.
I am he who gives canoes to the chiefs, the guests, the
    chiefs of the tribes."

[Ruth Benedict (*13*), p. 148 f.]

The hosts tried to surpass the guests in every possible way. They entertained them in an extravagant manner, even poured oil onto the fire, destroyed boats, killed a slave, or broke "coppers" (etched sheets of copper) of great value. "Furthermore, such is my pride," announced one host on such an occasion, "that I will kill on this fire my copper Dandalayu, which is groaning in my house. You all know how much I paid for it. I bought it for four thousand blankets. Now I will break it in order to vanquish my rival. I will make my house a fighting place for you, my tribe. Be happy, chiefs, this is the first time that so great a potlatch has been given" [Benedict (*13*), p. 195].

The guests, thus challenged, had, if possible, to destroy even more property at the return feast, in order to save face. When such a point is reached the feast has a markedly aggressive character. It almost becomes a tournament, a safety-valve custom for working off aggression. The escalating status contest of the potlatch rivalry is, however, by no means the only decisive aspect of these feasts. It does not always predominate, and even when it does, it concerns only a few people, generally two. For the guests and spectators this spectacle affords entertainment. They are also the judges, a factor that helps to maintain the institutionally established forms of the contest. What Ruth Benedict does not sufficiently emphasize is the further fact that the giving of a potlatch is not only self-aggrandizement; it is also evidence of regard for the guests. Its consequence therefore is not only rivalry but also, as Rudolph (*173*) has argued, mutual gratitude. It is true that such a feast can lead to strife on occasion, via an escalation of mutual competitiveness, but generally it remains "sporting." The cohesion of the temporary group—guests and hosts—is strengthened by such displays of power. The aggressive element of ostentation can basically be demonstrated at every cocktail party, at every state reception, and at the Olympic Games. As at the potlatch of the Kwakiutl, every host tries to surpass his predecessors in some way. At Munich they have rigged up a particularly expensive Olympic stadium. One can say that a considerable proportion of the state's income is thrown away in what ethnologists call the "prestige economy."

It should not be overlooked, however, that display at a feast honors the guests as well. Ostentatious display is a reflection of regard for those invited and it is a common feature of patterns of expressions of esteem that a high-ranking position is assigned to the guest, as evidenced in magnificent shows, preferential service, and so on. We do the same in everyday life. We give a guest preferential status, we let him go first, we give him the place of honor, we serve him first and in so doing we are following the basic patterns of politeness which one encounters in a similar fashion almost everywhere.

Self-glorification is also an important element in all national days of celebration. In a wide variety of countries people celebrate acts of aggression by their own community (provided the outcome was successful), and in this way the group activates experiences that reinforce its solidarity. This can even be observed in quite small groups. A few years ago I made a journey with my friend Hans Hass in a Land Rover through northern Uganda and Kenya. After a fairly long journey through the wilds, we arrived one evening at a Karamojo village, which consisted simply of a kraal with a few huts. The men were naked except for shoulder cloths and wore ostrich feathers in their hair, which was modeled with clay and other decorations. The women were ornamented with countless metal rings on their necks and arms. We had come upon a region still untouched by civilization. After we had introduced ourselves with gifts, we pitched tent. Until nightfall we were surrounded by curious villagers; then they scattered.

We had already crawled into the tent when the deep sound of singing and humming drew us out again. Not far from the camp stood a group of warriors; some were clapping their hands, others were throwing their spears in the air, points upward, and catching them again in the same rhythm. One warrior was leaping as high as he could in time with the beat, and in the pauses the young men sang. They took no notice of us when we approached them and said a few friendly words. This gave us an uncanny feeling. We returned to our tent and slept for a short while. Soon their singing woke us again, for a new, high, piercing trilling had been added to the sound which really alarmed us. After I made a few tape recordings, we slipped out of the tent. As nothing happened, we crept back into our sleeping bags after awhile, our limbs numb with cold. In the morning the villagers came to see us, and we played their singing back to them, which entertained them hugely. When they sang again that evening we felt braver than the night before and watched their dance.

Once again the group of dancers were out in the open on their own. Girls kept away from them. The only spectators were small boys with sticks held like spears; they watched the warriors with fascination and tried to leap like them on their little bow legs. They quite clearly identified themselves with the warriors. The women sat apart, as if none of this concerned them. But gradually they came up, some of them mingling, leaping with the dancers and giving out those high trilling notes that had frightened us the previous evening. During the course of that expedition we learned that the village communities assembled every evening for dances like this. The same was true of the neighboring tribes, the Turkana and Samburu. The warriors sing about their cattle and their exploits and win the admiration of their fellows, as well as of the girls and children.

In general the elements of threat display are less marked in the celebrations of small groups, particularly family celebrations. At christenings, weddings, birthdays, Christmas, and on many other occasions people eat, drink, and give presents to one another.

Eating and drinking together is generally the core of the ceremony. It occurs, for instance, in most marriage rites. If two Wapare in East Africa want to marry each other, they take a small vessel of beer, milk, or meat broth, pare some pieces off their fingernails, and mix these in too. After exchanging a few oaths they hand each other the pot and both drink from it. The man begins the oath-taking something like this: "If you break the marriage bond let our marriage-drink kill you; but if you are true, it will be like oil upon your body. If I see you gossiping with other men and become jealous and beat you, let the marriage-drink kill me, for not trusting you, for henceforward it shall be the guardian of your virtue." The woman replies: "We are making a vow because we love each other. If you beat me when I have not been untrue, let the marriage-drink kill you; but if I go with another man, the accursed drink will kill me" [E. Kotz (*117*), p. 161].

In the Salzburg area a man coming to pay his respects formally to his betrothed for the first time used to bring several coins as "Drangeld," or suitor's money, whereupon both of them would eat together out of one dish. In the German provinces a whole variety of occasions provide the excuse for a celebration: family events such as christenings, birthdays, name-days, weddings, Easter, and Christmas, to name but a few. The last of these often extend beyond the family, but they remain essentially family celebrations. "Shooting matches," harvest festivals, or solstice celebrations, on the other hand, are the affair of the community at large. At all these festivals people eat and drink together, and this unifying element is dominant in family celebrations. The more official a celebration is, and the larger the number of people taking part, the more it will also be a display. Such celebrations, too, serve to strengthen bonds among people. Communal showing off vis-à-vis the others also unites a group. The greater the group celebrating, the more marked the collective group aggression becomes—and thereby unites the group. This is particularly evident on days of national celebration. Elements of a contest can also be observed in family celebrations, particularly in the way we celebrate Christmas. But at the same time one must not forget the extraordinarily positive aspects of family celebrations. One sends greeting cards to friends and relations all round the world. To dismiss this as part of the Christmas "racket" is to oversimplify too much. Celebrations of this kind promote good will—and everything which helps that must be welcomed today more than ever. Suspect only are national days celebrating aggressive events, which unite groups through hostility to another group. These sow mistrust, arouse fear, and fan the flames of hatred and intolerance.

The comparisons we have made between different customs used in greeting and at feasts and festivals have brought to light many points in common, which can be explained by the common function of establishing a bond. The same means in principle are used, and in the case of many rites they can be shown to have a phylogenetic root.

With this we conclude our discussion of the phylogenetic and functional aspects of bond-establishing behavior and turn to the following questions: How do our experiences in the course of growing up affect our social behavior? How do our friendly social relationships evolve during childhood? In the ontogeny of animals, as we mentioned at the beginning of this book, certain basic social attitudes are often fixated as in imprinting in the course of sensitive periods. Is the lack of charity which can often be observed in modern city dwellers the result of "deficiencies in upbringing"? Are there circumstances in which human beings can be imprinted with the basic attitude of a lack of charity?

10

The Development of the Personal Bond and Basic Trust

The ability to make friends develops only gradually as a human being grows up. Initially a baby is tied to its mother by certain innate reactions. Inborn impulses make the infant seek contact: it has gripping reflexes with which it can hold onto her as though she still had a hairy coat. When it drinks, the baby's fists are very tightly closed, and this is undoubtedly something we have inherited from our primate ancestors, whose babies had to hold on to their mother's coats quite actively. In the first place, the mother is an object one can cling tightly to and suck from. In addition to this, she offers protection and is therefore an object with "home valency" (see p. 121). It is well known that a baby who is not hungry will start to scream and cry if put down gently, but will calm down at once if it is picked up or if one gives it the illusion of being carried around by rocking its cradle. Many young mammals emit such cries at being abandoned when they have fallen out of the nest or lost contact with their mother. A baby monkey is not normally put down at all, and to lose contact with its mother spells the greatest danger. In a similar manner man is by nature a "parent-clinger," "Elternhocker" as W. Wickler (217) calls it. We are not only programmed to these conditions by numerous behavior patterns, we are also equipped with appetitive behavior for restoring contact—to begin with by crying out and later through active seeking. Our drive activities of clinging and snuggling are adapted to the mother as object. It is this appetitive behavior for contact that is the true root of the bond between mother and child.

We emphasize this because the learning theory is sometimes used to explain this bond as a secondary one. According to this theory, the primary need is for nourishment and as the mother fulfills this need the child learns, secondarily, to attach itself to its mother. The idea goes back to Freud, who wrote: "Love has its origin in attachment to the satisfied need for nourishment" (Vol. 23, 1940, p. 188). But this hypothesis cannot be upheld. Even in the first days of its life a child calms down if caressed, picked up or spoken to. Being fed and kept clean are not prerequisites for this.

In a kibbutz the children are cared for most of the time by a communal nurse. The nurse feeds and washes the children and their parents spend only one or two hours a day with them, except on Saturday, which is a holiday. Nevertheless the bond between children and parents is stronger than that with the nurse who feeds them. By playing with their children the parents give them love and security, things which count far more than nourishment. The bond with the nurse is a transitory relationship that changes with the object that satisfies their needs; the bond with the parents is a deep individualized social relationship. The bond with the parents is stronger the more promptly they respond to the baby's crying and the more frequently they initiate social contact themselves [Bowlby (24)]. We know from orphanages that one child may also snuggle up closely to a second child, as if to a mother-substitute, even when the second child has done nothing to satisfy the first's normal physiological needs. And we know from animals as well that the bond with the mother is not only established via feeding rewards. Harlow (80) reared rhesus monkeys from birth in isolation with only wire dummies. The baby monkeys could choose between a dummy covered with cloth and a plain wire one. Food was obtainable only from the bare dummy. In danger, however, this dummy which provided food was not the one to which the monkeys fled. The baby monkeys ran much more frequently to the cloth-covered dummy which afforded good contact. It is not the food reward but other stimuli that tie the young animal to its mother, before any conditioning has taken place. We have discussed (see p. 120) the fact that the mother probably begins by being the "goal-in-flight." We should also mention the psychoanalytical interpretation that the child resents being thrust out into the world at birth and strives to return to the mother's womb. Melanie Klein, who evolved this theory, traces all our striving for contact back to this starting point. This is a thoroughly contrived interpretation that is generally rejected even in psychoanalytical circles.

The mother too is primarily bound to her child by means of a number of signals that release cherishing behavior. But on her side the relationship very quickly becomes individualized. A mother soon recognizes her own baby and will decisively reject others. This is the case with a great many mammals. A ewe licks and sniffs her lamb thoroughly after it is born and then will not let any other one push under her. A female sea lion rubs her muzzle against her baby's and, like the ewe, recognizes it as an individual soon after it is born and will not tolerate any strange baby near her. Greylag geese attack strange goslings and herring gulls actually kill young that are not their own. All animals in which this rejection of strange young is so pronounced are the "precocial type." Those in which the young grow up in the nest ("altricial" type) will generally adopt strange birds without hesitation. One can, for instance, put more babies under a female house mouse or brown rat than it can feed. Nevertheless, in experiments where they can choose, these animals frequently show a preference for their own young. There is thus a remarkable individual variation. But the young of animals reared in the nest do not normally run any danger of being swapped for others, so no special measures to avoid this have proved necessary.

In any case, one might ask: Why should it be prevented? What is the selective advantage? One important point, certainly, is that a mother can look after and feed only a limited number of young. If she adopted babies indiscriminately a point could be reached at which her family became too big. The young ones would not be properly fed and looked after and under certain circumstances none would survive. Furthermore the brood-tending cycle is a physiological process, the course of which is governed by hormones. The brood-tending phase can be extended by sensory stimuli, but there are limits to this. If a female adopted a young one at the end of a brood-tending cycle the chances of her really being able to suckle it would be small. If young were adopted freely, mixed families would also arise in which young animals of different ages were competing for milk which would certainly endanger the small-est. Finally, if gregarious animals had a tendency to rob one another of their young, this could lead to the disruption of their social life. For these reasons it is thoroughly comprehensible that in cases where the young might easily be exchanged —that is, in those that leave the nest and those that cling to their parents—an individualized bond between mother and child has proved to be an advantage.

The human mother's fear of her child being swapped and the strong emotional revulsion at the very idea of exchanging her own child for a strange one probably has a biological root —it corresponds to an innate disposition.

Initially the child does not care who looks after it. But it soon directs its attention onto its mother's face, a process which itself facilitates individualized contact. Experiments with dummies have shown that babies stare at the pattern of a human face: the eyes are particularly important. When a baby begins to look at its mother it is well known that the mother reacts very strongly. Mothers experience an extremely positive feeling and generally at once begin a friendly little game with the child. When this process begins—sometimes as early as the fourth week—a very strong relationship of trust evolves between the mother and her child. Robson (*169*) suggests that this behavior on the part of the baby rewards the mother for all her efforts in the same way as the smile. "The human mother" he writes, "is subject to an extended, exceedingly trying and often unrewarding period of caring for her infant. Her neonate has a remarkably limited repertoire with which to sustain her. Indeed, his total helplessness, crying, elimination behavior and physical appearance, frequently elicit aversive reactions. Thus, in dealing with the human species, nature has been wise in making both eye-to-eye contact, and the social smile that it often releases in these early months, behaviors that at this stage of development generally foster positive maternal feelings and a sense of payment for 'services rendered.' . . . Hence, though a mother's response to these achievements may be an illusion, from an evolutionary point of view it is an illusion with survival value" (p. 15).

The great importance of this staring reaction of the baby for the development of social contact also emerges from the fact that it is innate. Even a baby born blind will "stare" at its mother (the source of sound); if she bends over it and speaks, the restless eye movements of the blind come to a stop. This must be the result of a basic staring process at work, since the child can see nothing [Freedman (*64*)]. By means of its smile and its staring reaction a baby at first quite unconsciously and automatically establishes contact with its mother. During the second half-year of life further behavior patterns of contact-making mature. The baby's babbling releases replies from the mother, and now babbling dialogues take place in which one can perhaps detect the origins of the bond-establishing conversational exchanges we discussed on page 151. When a baby crows with joy this has a particularly cheering effect. Within the first year the child begins of its own accord to hold out objects or playthings invitingly to its mother. It expects one to take things but also to give them back. It throws things out of its crib and expects them to be picked up again and brought back. At about the same time the child begins to point to objects in its surroundings with outstretched hand and index finger. According to all the observations I have made so far in comparing different cultures, this gesture is common to all peoples. Finally, toward the end of the first year the social contact gesture of giving food evolves. The child begins to put food in its mother's mouth of its own accord—or also to feed its brothers and sisters.

We can therefore observe that even at a very early stage children, by means of specific initiative gestures, elicit and strengthen social contact, start conversations, and invite others to mutual physical manipulation of objects from their environment (play). Children make an astonishingly large number of initiatives, and the fact that these invitations meet with so little response in the case of children reared institutionally may well be the reason for the social and intellectual stunting they undergo.

Certainly human development, like that of any other organism, is based on processes of maturing, growth, and differentiation, the program for which is inscribed in the genetic inheritance of the species. Among other things, the child is so programmed that, as we have just explained, it invites contact with its environment and puts questions to it; but these contacts must be facilitated and the dialogue with the outside world must be granted. A married couple named Dennis (37) undertook an experiment shortly before the Second World War which was as interesting as its approach was ruthless. They wanted to know how children develop when they grow up with a minimum of social contact. Two five-weeks-old twin girls were kept during their first six months under conditions of relatively strict deprivation of experience; later these were somewhat relaxed. The children were not allowed to see each other and the experimenters treated them completely unemotionally. They fed them, bathed them, changed them, and made certain experiments with them. Apart from this they left the babies in their cradles and took no notice of their crying when they left the room. They avoided any signs of sympathy such as smiling, caressing, and cuddling.

At seven weeks the children began to follow the experimenters with their eyes, and sometimes they smiled at them when they came in. Once they began looking at the adults their attention was directed more toward their faces than other parts of the body. Between the ninth and twelfth weeks they began to laugh and to coquette, and between the thirteenth and sixteenth weeks they cried when the adults left their bedside. About the sixth month the children reacted with alarm to sounds, and they now smiled steadily when someone went up to them and when they had had enough to eat. They frequently gurgled a great deal at the same time. In the eighth month one of the children managed to touch the face and hair of the experimenter and in this way to break through the atmosphere of indifference. From then on the Dennises gave in to the children's striving for contact. They spoke to the babies a little every day, played with them, and allowed the twins to play with one another. It was the children's constant attempts at contact that had prevailed upon the experimenters to soften their inhuman experiment. Nevertheless they still kept them under strict conditions of deprivation of experience until their fourteenth month. The motor development of the children was held back. Neither of them could stand before the end of the first year. Then, with a little help, they managed to stand up for a few seconds on the first day if the experimenters held them and after four days' practice they could stand up with help for several minutes. Their development was markedly retarded, but this was quickly normalized, the experimenters assure us, when they offered the opportunities for practice.

What was remarkable was the way in which the twins reacted positively toward the experimenters; the latter were unable to film their negative reactions: every time they approached, the crying stopped and the children smiled. The fact that these experiments did no harm to the children's welfare is almost certainly due only to the way their own initiatives for contact broke through the armor of the experimenters' indifference. In the second half-year of life, social contact plays a decisive role in the child's further development.

Toward the end of the first six months the child can distinguish between strangers and people it knows and shows an innate tendency to approach only people it knows, one of whom it quite specifically prefers. Even when a child is surrounded by several friendly people, all of whom are inviting contact, one of them is clearly preferred. J. Bowlby (24) has coined the term "monotropy" for the phenomenon of the child seeking contact only with one person. He writes: "It is a mistake to suppose that a young child diffuses his attachment over many figures in such a way that he gets along with no strong attachment to anyone and consequently without missing any particular person when that person is away. On the contrary, such evidence as is at present available supports a hypothesis advanced in an earlier paper . . . namely that there is a strong bias for attachment behaviour to become directed mainly towards one particular person and for a child to become strongly possessive of that person. In support of that view attention was drawn to the way in which young children in a residential nursery tend, when given any opportunity, to latch themselves onto a particular nurse. . . . Because the bias of a child to attach himself especially to one figure seems to be well established and also to have far-reaching implications for psychopathology, I believe it merits a special term. In the earlier paper I referred to it as 'monotropy' " (p. 308).

This innate tendency toward an individualized tie is of some significance with regard to the occasional attempts that are made to depersonalize the human relationships (see p. 238). In the second year of life, finally, the fear of strangers gradually develops. R. A. Spitz (*195*) has explained this as the fear of separation from the mother, but Bowlby (*24*) emphasizes that this interpretation really explains nothing. One cannot really prove that children are specifically afraid of separation. They simply fear strangers and this fear seems to be innate, for in my own experience the rejection and fear of strangers is to be observed even in children born deaf and blind. In this case the attitude evolves absolutely counter to the direction of the children's upbringing. Every effort is made to convey to these children that they have nothing to fear and that everyone is their friend.

With the maturing of the fear of strangers in the child's second year the strength of the personal bond increases, and the capacity to form such ties is a prerequisite for the continued healthy development of the human being. If a child in a hospital is parted from its mother for a long period, this brings on a bitter shock. At first the child protests and cries a great deal. Gradually it calms down and seeks to establish contact with a nurse. If a bond with a mother-substitute such as this is successfully formed, the prospects for the child's future development are favorable; but this possibility is made more difficult by the fact that a nurse generally has no time to give the child. Apart from this nurses are constantly changing because of time off and night shifts and every loss of the mother-substitute inflicts a fresh shock on the child. In the end the child will shut itself off from the outside world and fall into a state of apathy. If it is taken back into a family after three or four months' stay in the hospital it will then recover. But after a longer stay in institutional conditions the damage done is extremely resistant to therapy. In a children's home, despite the best hygienic care and good feeding, the children's physical and mental development is retarded. Since nurses are constantly changing, such children have given up the attempt to seek social contact. And the overworked staff, for their part, have no time to play with the children and to comfort them. According to Spitz (*196*) about one-third of such children die before the end of the second year.* The development quotient of those that survive reaches about 45 per cent of the normal. If such children deprived of love survive, they remain shy of contact in later life and have a strong tendency to follow a criminal path. Spitz also compared the development of the children in a foundling hospital and those in a home for children whose mothers were convicted of criminal offenses. At this home the mothers, who were mostly minors and pregnant at the time of their admission, looked after their children themselves. Spitz (*196*) evaluated the development quotients of the children in the first and the last thirds of their first year. In the first third of the year the development quotient of the children at the foundling hospital was markedly higher than that of the other children, very likely because the parents of the foundling children included those from higher social strata, while the children at the home mostly came from lower social strata. The foundling children were clearly born with a better heredity than the children of the criminal minors.

By the last third of the year, however, the development quotient of the foundling children had fallen dramatically below its initial level, while among the children at the home it had improved, probably as a result of intensive care by the mothers, who directed all their love toward their children, each one wanting to show off her own child at any given moment, somewhat in competition with the other convicted mothers. In the following table, which we have taken from René Spitz (*196*), these comparisons are set down. Above, for comparison, is the

---

* But according to more recent opinions this high mortality is attributable to nutritional deficiencies. The children's home in which Spitz carried out his investigations was in a district in which protein deficiencies were common even in normal families. The other phenomena are the result of hospitalization. They also occur in well-nourished children.

development quotient for a total of thirty-four children from different social classes. Below are the data for the institutional children. These data given are based on surveys of sixty-nine children at the home for mothers and children and sixty-one children at the foundling hospital.

NATURE OF ENVIRONMENT	*CULTURAL AND SOCIAL BACKGROUND*	*DEVELOPMENT QUOTIENTS IN THE FIRST YEAR OF LIFE*	
		AVERAGE FOR FIRST 4 MONTHS	AVERAGE FOR LAST 4 MONTHS
Family	Children of academics	133	131
	Village children	107	108
Institutional	Foundling hospital	124	72
	Children's home	101.5	105

At the foundling hospital the children's development is also dramatically retarded in their second year. The children without mothers cannot eat by themselves and have learned no personal hygiene. Even two- to three-year-old children have not learned to walk. In the ward for children aged between eighteen months and two and one-half years, only two out of twenty-six children could speak a few words. Both children could also walk and a third was just beginning to.

"The picture offered by the eldest children in the home for mothers and children—aged eight to ten months—contrasts sharply with this. The problem here is not whether the children can walk and talk at the end of their first year; with these ten-month-old children the problem is how to keep the curiosity and adventurous spirit of the healthy toddlers in check. They climb up the railings of their cribs like South Sea Islanders climbing palm trees. Special safety precautions have had to be introduced before any of the ten-month-old children succeeded in swinging over the top of his crib railings—which were more than 2 ft. high. They chatter busily to themselves and some of them can already say one or two real words. All of them, however, understand the meaning of simple social gestures. When they are taken from their cribs all can walk with support and a few of them can walk unaided" [Spitz (*196*) p. 84].

The state of health of these children was excellent. During the three and a half years Spitz worked at the home he was able to observe 122 babies, each for a full year. Not a single child died during this time and the examination of the medical records over a period of fourteen years showed that only three children had died. At the foundling hospital, twenty-three out of a total of eighty-eight children died before the age of two and one-half, a truly alarming statistic.

To what extent the damage is really irreversible, as Spitz maintains, remains to be proved. What is certain is that a lack of opportunity to form individual relationships in early childhood produces virtually incurable damage to people's social behavior. This picture fits in well with the findings made by Harlow (*80, 81*) in the case of rhesus monkeys. If females were reared in solitude with inanimate mother-substitutes, they grew up later to be bad mothers. They maltreated their babies and allowed them to be taken away from them without offering any resistance. In their case, too, their social behavior in later life was severely disturbed as a result of their experience in early infancy.

Bowlby observed the consequences of the separation of mother and child in children between the fifteenth and thirtieth months of life. The loss of the mother, according to his investigations, results here in quite similar phenomena, even if the effect on the development of the child is not quite as dramatic as that in the cases described by Spitz. In this situation, too, the child at first protests. He cries, throws himself about, and shakes his crib. Strangers who make friendly approaches are at first rejected. This protest phase can last a week. It is followed by a phase of despair. The active protest tails off into monotonous crying. The child is withdrawn and inactive and makes no demands on the people around him. He appears to be in a state of deep mourning. This relatively calm stage is often mistakenly interpreted as representing a true calm in the child, in the sense of his despair having diminished.

This phase is finally followed by one of detachment: the child no longer rejects the nurses and shows an interest in the world around him. If his mother now comes back she will no longer be greeted as before. Often the child scarcely takes notice of her. If the child's stay in the hospital is prolonged and he experiences a fairly frequent change in his favorite nurses, associated with the shock of parting, then he will finally behave as if neither mothering nor any kind of human contact have meaning for him. The loss of several mother-figures in turn leads to the child's no longer establishing emotional bonds with other people. He becomes self-centered and more interested in material objects. A change of nurses no longer makes any difference to him and equally a visit from his parents does not mean a great deal to the child either: "He will appear cheerful and adapted to his unusual situation and apparently easy and unafraid of anyone. But this sociability is superficial: he appears no longer to care for anyone" [Bowlby (24) p. 28].

Thus is imprinted the attitude of an unstand-offish person, who forms relationships easily, but who never gives them a deep content. These relationships are just as easily abandoned.

There is much in our development that is certainly based on processes of maturation. Certain basic human attitudes, such as attachment, fear, and aggression, always mature in this order and we find this same pattern of maturing in rhesus monkeys reared in isolation [Harlow (80)]. But with human beings, for trust to develop out of this attachment, certain social experiences are necessary, which every child normally has with its mother. They are to some extent events "provided for" in advance, experiences to which the developmental program is open at this point. If the child is not able to evolve the personal relationship with its mother (or mother-substitute) which is anticipated, then a disturbance in its development occurs—the abandonment syndrome. Normally the child learns in the dialogue with its mother that there is always someone there who will look after him in a friendly way and fulfill his social as well as his material needs. He acquires as a fundamental attitude the positive notion that one can rely on one's fellow-men, an attitude that Erikson (57) has described as "basic trust." This basic trust is the foundation of a healthy personality. We give evidence of this fundamental attitude in countless everyday situations, whether we are entrusting ourselves to a means of public transport or asking someone for information in the street. Basically we expect good of our fellow-men, and nothing embitters us more than misplaced trust. This basic trust is the prerequisite for all positive attitudes toward society, for all ability to identify with a group, for all social commitment. The capacity to love people generally is founded upon the capacity for individual friendship. This is a point which in my view has not been clearly perceived by those who, from the best possible motives, seek to achieve the adaptation of human beings to mass society by preventing them forming personal relationships as early in life as possible (see p. 239).

"Children who have grown up without love become adults filled with hate," writes R. Spitz. In place of a "basic trust," the fundamental attitude of these unfortunate people is determined by a "basic mistrust."

11

From Individualized Group to Anonymous Community

The mother-child relationship is undoubtedly the nucleus around which the human community has crystallized. In the course of its development the child considerably increases its circle of acquaintance and forms closer relationships with brothers and sisters, relations and friends. The degrees of trust depend on how well we know a person. Strangers at first release fear in the child, who lives wholly within the individualized group.

Among primitive peoples that live in small groups—and even today in small, remote mountain villages in Europe—adults basically never outgrow this. The inhabitants of a village all know one another. Strangers are rejected, often attacked, or at best tolerated with reserved curiosity.

Within individualized communities, to know and trust people is a condition of life.* But this does not mean that there exists no kind of aggression within the group. What there is,

* There are said to be societies where this is not the case. The inhabitants of Dobu (one of the D'Entrecasteaux Islands) are reputed to be malevolent and treacherous, even within the group. "They are lawless and treacherous. Every man's hand is against every other man," writes Ruth Benedict (*13*) (p. 131). Among the Mundugomur the structure of the society is said to make father and son enemies [Mead (*146*)]. "This enmity between father and son, between brothers and half-brothers, occurs in every Mundugomur family" (p. 466, retranslated from German text). However, the evidence remains very imprecise and generalized, so that I consider the thesis that there are societies without love to be unproven.

however, is to a great extent neutralized through rivalry and striving for dominance. And by being directed toward those outside the group, aggression actually serves to strengthen the bond among members. Since the bond of personal acquaintance has an exceptionally appeasing effect, conflicts within a group very rarely reach dangerous proportions. As we have already mentioned, in the higher mammals conflicts in the battle for dominance are settled in ritualized form (see p. 86).

For the ancient Germans, peace meant "the bond between the individual and his clan and the sense of unity between the clan and each individual" [C. D. Kernig (*109*), p. 722]. The German word for peace, *"Friede,"* is derived from "fridu," the word for a fenced-off territory, and thus expresses the idea of defense against the outside world. Within the clan the bond was so strong that crimes against the family were as unthinkable as murder and hence no legal provision was made for them. Outside the group, however, the clans were in a state of perpetual feud with one another.

As civilizations evolved the individualized groups gave way to anonymous groups in the towns and tribal communities. Ultimately it was no longer possible to know everyone in a town. On the other hand, one could no longer cut oneself off from these strangers in the old way; man now had to learn how to live with strangers. This involved a number of problems.

We know that the bond of personal acquaintance appeases aggressive feelings. In some small human communities, for example, it causes no trouble for all the men to go about daily in warlike apparel. The men may carry weapons and wear ornaments of animals' teeth and feather headdresses or they can show an aggressive display in their bearing. Anyone may demonstrate his strength as a warrior, although if the men were not bound together by friendship this would provoke an aggressive response.* As it is, however, one man does not relate his neighbor's aggressive display to himself, but has a sense, rather, of making a communal threat. They feel themselves united by this: their aggression is directed outward against enemies of

---

* Berkowitz (*15*) has pointed out that the mere sight of a weapon can release aggressive feelings.

the group. In an anonymous group the situation is different. Here every threat display provokes aggressive reactions that may not be appeased through the bond of personal acquaintance. Such aggression could seriously disturb communal social life; we can observe how human beings take account of this and adapt themselves to mass society by toning down male threat display. In all civilizations the process is for the man to become more drab (50). His dress becomes plain, male ornamentation is reduced, his weapons are completely abandoned. Even an ostentatious bearing leads to social ostracism; the more inconspicuous a man appears the better. In this way the areas of friction are smoothed over as much as possible. Only high-ranking people, with whom the group identifies itself, are permitted some outward pomp, but even this is increasingly reduced. Women's display, on the other hand, activates binding mechanisms, and they are therefore exempt from this development.

The social prohibition on the individual's threat display imposes certain frustrations on him, and we can observe how young people in particular rebel against this compulsion to conformity with emphatically individualistic behavior. The "hippie" phenomenon, for example, springs to mind.

The bond between human beings in the anonymous group takes effect through common symbols and concerns. In this process the same group-binding mechanisms are called into play as in the family.

"Be embraced, you millions! This kiss is for the whole world!" wrote Schiller in his "Ode to Joy." In our speeches unknown fellow-men become "brothers," the head of state becomes the "father of his people." Concepts like "little mother Russia" characterize very clearly the type of emotional bond with the anonymous community. National festivals, which are celebrations of brotherhood, are closely modeled on family celebrations. There is, however, more emphasis at public festivals on the unifying force of aggression. Even anonymous communities are exclusive in character, although it is easier to be adopted into them than into an individualized group. But this exclusivity can of course be completely overcome: we have already discussed the possibility of man's ultimately feeling united with the whole of humanity through a community of interests (see p. 101).

This feeling of unity increases as the means of communication increase. Television and radio give us daily accounts of other people and their problems, thus arousing our sympathy across political frontiers. As they have always done in the past, demagogues still try to concoct their dummy enemies and to declare their opponents to be subhuman, in order to divert attention away from difficulties nearer home. But the process of turning one's opponent into a "devil" becomes more and more difficult. The barriers to communication cannot be so easily maintained any more. News techniques and tourism promote world-wide fraternization. Thus technological progress, which is so frequently deplored, can also contribute to the increased humanitarianism of mankind. Heads of state are obliged to take note of world public opinion. This does not, of course, make any immediate difference to the general world situation; wars of aggression have by no means disappeared. But my impression is that the belligerents are increasingly subject to the criticisms of world opinion and will ultimately be checked by these. In this respect Vietnam may well be a test case.

Undoubtedly in the age of atomic missiles fear of a military conflict on the grand scale plays its part. In the face of events which might previously have provoked a war, such as the *Pueblo* affair, the Cuban missile crisis, or the recent incidents on the Russo-Chinese frontier, people attempt to find other solutions. This is certainly also a direct result of the military stalemate. But although the fear associated with nuclear war checks acts of aggression, at the same time it creates a highly explosive situation, which could lead at any time to a critical reaction, especially if we increasingly adopt the strategy of always expecting the worst of our opponents and of treating well-intentioned overtures as "mere maneuvers." This translation of the "enemy schema" into ideology creates deadly mistrust and strengthens the bond within the group only through fear and hostility toward others. Modern communications techniques tend to reduce mistrust, as do increasing personal contacts between peoples of differing ideologies. The growth of ideology, on the other hand, does tend to strengthen aggression.

The growth of ideologies is undoubtedly an expression of our tendency to form exclusive groups (see p. 89) and seems to be a constitutive characteristic of our species. Perhaps in creating an "enemy schema" and clothing it in an ideology we are following certain thought processes quite involuntarily. This could be a question for peace research to investigate. What is clear is that along with this exclusive tendency there exists the readiness to open up the group. There is a genuine functional conflict between this readiness to form a bond and the tendency toward exclusivity. What we must discover is how to give greater weight to the unifying forces; and in this context the elimination of fear is certainly important. In a world whose population is increasing every group will ultimately be afraid of being overrun by the population of an overcrowded country. The defusing of the "biological time bomb" by means of birth control is an essential condition of peaceful coexistence.

A world-wide inclination to outlaw military conflicts seems to be gaining ground increasingly, in opposition to the exclusive tendency of human groups. On the other hand, conflicts within the anonymous group are becoming exacerbated. In this case there are difficulties of adaptation which stem from various causes.

First, within the anonymous group we feel a markedly weaker bond between ourselves and unknown fellow-men than between ourselves and people we know. Toward strangers we are less obliging, conflicts are more bitter. This is particularly evident in the struggle for positions of rank. Politicians do indeed woo the electors by adopting a friendly or "fatherly" manner, but this is often deceptive and one which it is hard to see through in the anonymous group. The one who makes best use of his elbows reaches the front quickest. The unscrupulous and aggressive person who knows how to mask his social deficiencies well enough has a much better chance of rising to the top in the anonymous group than in the individualized community. People of high rank who do not know their subordinates personally are less scrupulous about exploiting them. Since no research findings are available we cannot state whether the tendency to corruption is greater among the ruling classes of anonymous societies than in individualized groups, but my impression is that this is so.

A further factor that exacerbates conflicts within the group

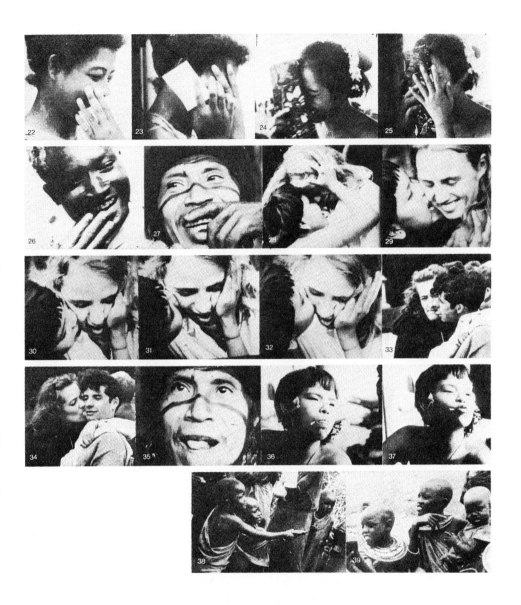

Stills from 16 mm film on which the drawings throughout the text are based. 1–4 for Fig. 1; 5–12 for Figs. 2 and 3; 13–15 for Fig. 17; 16–18 for Fig. 18; 19–21 for Fig. 19; 22–25 for Fig. 20; 26 and 27 for Fig. 21; 28 and 29 for Fig. 36; 30–32 for Fig. 35; 33 and 34 for Fig. 42; 35 for Fig. 45; 36 and 37 for Fig. 44; 38 and 39 for Fig. 50.

has arisen from the eighteenth-century Enlightenment and the rapid growth of knowledge. This has resulted generally in critical attitudes toward the old cultural patterns of order. Customs are no longer inherited uncritically, for we try to base the conduct of our lives upon reason. This means that our own values are regarded as more relative, while other systems of values are regarded with more openness; there is thus a true process of liberalization. Nevertheless, traditions are the basic skeleton of a culture. However they are constituted, they underwrite social order and lend conviction and certainty to the leaders of a culture (p. 168).

The result of modern man's fundamentally sceptical attitude is his lesser inclination to accept traditional values uncritically. But resistance to this transmission process, which may even lead to a complete break with tradition, causes uncertainty. The youthful phase of searching for new values becomes extended and, by the same token, the stabilizing of the personality takes place later. A person ready to recognize other systems of values than his own will voice his own opinions less dogmatically than, say, a religious fanatic whose principles teach him exactly what is right and what is wrong. The demagogue's hypnotic effect is based on his own certainty.

Many people need to be able to adopt a very definite viewpoint, and so we can see how adolescent intellectuals, in particular, make emotional commitments about social and political problems whose existence is undeniable. Interestingly, young people readily take sides on issues that permit an unambiguous identification because what is happening is wrong according to all generally recognized norms; but on the other hand they also often choose events which are physically remote (like apartheid, or the Vietnam war) so that they cannot inform themselves about them directly. In this way these young people do not run the risk of their ideal image becoming tarnished. People want to be able to take sides unequivocally.

A further consequence of the fundamentally sceptical attitude of modern man is his increased unwillingness to recognize authority. And the authorities themselves are no longer so certain of their role. They find their own knowledge often rapidly growing outdated. They have less to offer the young than their own fathers had, and this lack of leadership encourages aggressiveness. Since on the other hand people still feel a need for authorities (and uncertainty increases it— see p. 168), they seek substitute authorities who are, once again, as far away as possible, or already dead, and can therefore easily be idealized like Marx, Che Guevara, Ho Chi Minh.

The attitude of scepticism toward authority widens the "generation gap." Our young people have at their disposal greater specialized knowledge than any generation before them; in addition to this they are learning daily about world problems from television and radio. Is it any wonder that they question whether the traditions which, after two frightful world wars, have led most recently to the Vietnam war, are worth following? They cannot unreservedly identify themselves with the old values and they question their elders' claims to leadership. This is evidence of a healthy social commitment and ought to provoke open discussion. In my view that is not sufficiently cultivated. Then from time to time sharp confrontations occur and groups of young people, made more extreme in their turn, tread just those well-worn paths of violence which it is their ultimate intention to avoid. The conflict between the generations is also heightened, finally, by the fact that people brought up before the Second World War are imprinted with different values from the postwar generations.

The situation is made worse by the fact that the increase in the average age of the population has resulted in a general slowing-up of promotion, especially for the intelligentsia. In Germany and Austria today it is unusual for an academic to reach any position of responsibility before the age of thirty. The best years are lost and the young man who, through no fault of his own, is still only a doctoral candidate at twenty-six cannot start a family and carries less weight in society than a twenty-one-year-old unskilled worker. The mandarins of our ruling class are lacking in a sympathetic understanding of this situation—though they are not short of dogmatic assertions. At a recent conference an academic baldly described student movements as "pubertal" reactions on the part of young people. When I pointed out that most of the students were over twenty-one and that it was scarcely appropriate to speak of puberty—

on the contrary a marked acceleration in the development of young people could be shown—the speaker replied that this acceleration applied only to their physical development; their mental development was much slower. When I asked him for scientific evidence of this, he could offer none.

If the adolescent elites all over the world—and in the case of students this is what we are talking about—are in a state of unrest, then society has done something wrong. And the call for more discipline will not solve the problem.

Discontent, however, extends to much broader strata of society. At another conference—on aggression in our society—a kindly old gentleman observed that people are simply ungrateful. They have never had it so good. In Central Europe there is full employment and the shops offer an abundance of goods: unrest is quite incomprehensive—probably things have become too easy for people. This provoked my observation that one ought at least to examine whether in certain important respects life was not worse for people in a modern industrial society than for previous generations. First of all, our work has to a great extent lost the character of a creative activity. We— or at least most workers—do not reap what we have sown. We do not see the products we create growing beneath our hands. It is hard to feel proud of the tasks performed in the office or at the conveyor belt. Working for wages does not fulfill us; furthermore it rarely demands from us any exceptional physical or intellectual effort. As hunters and farmers we once experienced work quite differently.

What is the truth about our material wealth? Certainly radios, cars, refrigerators, television sets, washing machines, and so on are amenities that make life easier for those who live in the high-rise blocks of our great cities. Cars, in particular, enable city dwellers to escape the city every weekend, to enjoy the sun and the countryside. Yet the vast flight into green pastures at the weekend shows how greatly people suffer in the city. In the past, towns were smaller and most people had a garden to call their own. The poor cottager lived under his own roof, had his few fruit trees, and watched them blossom and bear fruit. Today only a rich minority of city dwellers can afford this luxury. Most of them live cut off from nature. They jostle along sidewalks around which traffic surges, and acquire consumer goods to delude themselves about the fundamental poverty of their lives. They have certainly achieved security and I have no desire to advocate a back-to-nature movement. But I am concerned to indicate those factors which are possible causes of the discontent we feel in spite of all our "prosperity." Thanks to increasing overpopulation we are being crammed together against our will into areas of high population density where we miss freedom of movement, independence, and peace and quiet. It is not that we are antisocial, but too much society is oppressive to the individual.

Experiments on tree shrews and a number of rodents have shown that once a certain population density is exceeded the animals irritate one another so much that hormonal changes are produced which can finally even cause death. This mechanism has been especially carefully studied in tree shrews. The females mark both their young and the entrance to the nest with the secretion of a gland on their chins. This prevents the young being eaten by other conspecifics. With mild overpopulation, first of all the function of this gland atrophies, so the young are no longer protected and get eaten. If the stress becomes greater the function of the mammary glands also atrophies; as the stress increases that of the gonads atrophies as well. The animals lose weight and die (*94*). When we come to human adaptability we have no idea what its limits are. The question is whether we really have to test these to the final degree of tolerance. Is it not sufficient that in our overpopulated metropolises we already get on one another's nerves to a considerable extent and that aggressive feelings are thereby released which clearly disturb our communal life with other human beings?

Changes in our environment particularly affect the family background into which the child is born and inflict a number of deprivations on him in his first years. A. Mitscherlich (*152*) has described the situation very clearly: "The changes in the environment of civilized society as a whole have altered the situation into which the child is born and in which the first years of his life are spent. Birth in a hospital, the mother without the extended family and its traditions to fall back on, the limited radius of activity of a small child in a town dwelling, the loss of stimulation derived from watching people at work outside the home, frequent changes of place, the disappearance of the father to a great extent and increasingly of the mother as well, the intrusion of mechanical toys into the child's world —this total restructuring of experience is to be borne in mind when frustration is mentioned" (p. 58f.). Mitscherlich draws particular attention to the difficulties of identification that arise for the child in this situation. Deficient identification leads to a reduced sense of the bond with one's fellow-men.

We have thus pointed out a number of factors that are responsible for the increased aggression within the group:

1. Evolution from individualized group to anonymous mass society for which emotionally we are insufficiently equipped. We do not feel anything like as great a bond with strangers as we do with acquaintances. They mean less to us and our aggressive feelings toward them are less inhibited. A general reduction in "obliging" behavior is the result and we are more mistrustful toward our fellow-men.

2. As a consequence of the rationalist tradition of the Enlightenment and of modern news-media techniques, our attitude toward cultural traditions and authorities is more sceptical. This leads to a general uncertainty and to the heightening of the generational conflict.

3. Overpopulation, changes in the activities by which we earn our living, and the increase in our life span lead to considerable pressures on the individual. We live in what Russell (*175*) and Morris (*156*) have quite rightly represented as a zoo situation, as prisoners in the cages of our cities. Our alienation from nature is experienced as a deprivation, as shown by the mass exodus from cities on weekends. These frustrations contribute considerably to an increase in human aggressiveness. Even the small child within the family environment which has been changed by civilization is exposed to these pressures.

While the ground seems to be being prepared for some control of aggression between groups, aggression within the group in the anonymous society is on the increase. How to overcome this is one of the most pressing tasks of the present day.

Only with some kind of birth control will it be possible to alleviate the factors creating population pressure and to satisfy the biological needs of the individual for space and quiet. In terms of town planning, our proximity to nature could be restored by means of a new architectonic differentiation of space —one thinks, for example, of the recently developed terraced apartment blocks with gardens for each. The conditions of work could also be redesigned to be more satisfying. Nevertheless we shall always have to live with mass society, and this demands not simply that friction areas be reduced but that a relationship of trust be established corresponding to the one that exists in the individualized group. The search for paths which will lead to this is being made from different directions.

In the Western democracies the power of the state guarantees equality before the law for citizens who are in other respects differently endowed.* Differences in talent, which express themselves in differing achievements, are recognized. The competitive principle is accepted, but this can easily conflict with the principle of equality. Here Marxism intervenes quite logically, arguing that competition causes discord. A harmonious society can therefore thrive only after the abolition of property. And thus ultimately the state can be relieved of its function as the guardian of private property. By the abolition of property a change is to be introduced into our consciousness. The man of good will, without aggressive feelings, for whom work is a joyful obligation, is to be brought into being.

These models for harmonization have undoubtedly been clearly thought out, but they are based in part on assumptions untenable from a scientific point of view. Marxists base all their efforts on the assumption that there is no such thing as human nature, in the sense of innate dispositions, and that man is shaped by his social environment alone. Now there is no doubt that the social environment shapes man to a significant extent —it is in man's malleability that our hope lies—but innate dispositions are equally demonstrable. If only these can be taken into consideration then society might be spared a number of fruitless experiments.

Many Marxists trace the individual's lack of responsibility

---

* The power of the state guarantees the property of the individual and thereby takes over the individual's right to self-help (self-defense, etc.).

toward the collective back to the egoism that evolves within the family. For this reason their attacks are directed first against individualism and against the family—which is regarded as the bulwark of individualism. It is believed that man would be free to develop a bond with the collective if he could release himself from his family ties.

After both the Russian and the Chinese revolutions the revolutionaries directed their attacks against the structure of the family. But people with stronger collective inclinations were not created in this way. Man's natural inclination to form individualized bonds resisted these attempts. This was very quickly recognized in the socialist countries; even in modern China the family is regarded as the nucleus of society. However, Chinese society demands that loyalty to the state should be stronger than loyalty to one's family. On Children's Day in Nanking on June 1, 1951, model children were brought forward to demonstrate this new attitude. Among others, a twelve-year-old boy was shown who had denounced his father as a counterrevolutionary and demanded the death penalty for him [Hsi-en Chen (*100*)]. In evaluating such incidents, nevertheless, we must not forget that in China life was extremely family centered and that the feeling of social responsibility toward those who were not members of one's own clan was scarcely developed.

The personal bond of friendship, too, has on occasion been regarded as an individualistic attitude which was inimical to society. In certain political groups, consistent attempts are made to nip in the bud any bonds of friendship that arise, for example, by means of ritualized accusations on the part of the friend. People are supposed to feel bound to the collective only by identifying with a symbol.

At the present moment new models of social harmonization are being tried out in Europe and the U.S. in various communes. All aggression-eliciting repression is to be eliminated—in particular authoritarian compulsion, sexual restraints, and also the personal fixation on one partner. Once again this movement is especially directed against the family, which is regarded as the fount of all capitalism and of all repression. Living communally, with a shared economy and shared funds,

adult commune members seek to achieve a collective consciousness. They eat out of one dish so that a person's own plate loses
its property function. The marriage partner's monopoly over
the individual's sexuality is abolished so ". . . that women
have an equal opportunity to fulfill collective functions and
therefore—a central factor for the woman herself—to achieve
a high degree of emancipation, a total release from the concept,
so emphatically spelled out in the Bible, of the man as the
woman's master, her possessor in the literal sense . . ." * Free
sexuality should imply not only free intercourse with another
person but also the disappearance of shame. One should admit
openly to "the sexual impulse and its practice"—not merely in
words.

But experience to date shows that such attempts end by
foundering on "bourgeois" behavior structures: "The sexual
tensions overshadowed the life of the commune in an intoler-
able way that made effective political work impossible. The
abolition of allegedly 'repressive' relationships between two
people proved to be a delusion, the supposedly flexible sexual
situation with regard to the exchange of partners foundered on
bourgeois behavior structures, which manifested themselves
within the commune in the form of struggles for status and
power, rivalries and jealousy. . . .

"Thus, for example, even twenty-year-old Liz Söllner, a sec-
retary who lives in an anarchist commune in Munich known as
the 'Südfront,' is of the opinion that at the present moment in
time a complete abolition of the existing pair-relationships is
not possible, because a woman should not merely fulfill the
function of a coitus object: an intellectual relationship must
also exist between the partners" (25).

If the people in question had studied a little ethology they
might have been able to foresee the outcome of the experiment,
for conjugal life is by no means a mark of bourgeois societies.
There is no primitive people unfamiliar with marriage.

There is a current educational ideal that the child should
not turn to its parents by preference but should have a bond
with a number of parent figures. In this way the family is to be

* See M. Braun (25) and P. Brügge (27).

abolished as the bulwark of authority. The members of a commune avoid using the withdrawal and the showing of love as educational means, for they hold the view that this has made man all too easy to manipulate. They do not praise or blame, nor do they allow attachment to material possessions to be established; they swap toys and exchange clothes. No achievement is rewarded because the striving for achievement is seen as a source of frustration and therefore of aggression. No aloofness is permitted. If a child keeps himself to himself he is brought back into the community and if necessary subjected to analysis—since there must be something wrong with him. The fact that small children like wandering off on their own and that a need for peace and quiet is specific to all human beings is not acknowledged. Withdrawal is not tolerated and extreme communards even remove doors from lavatories so as to eliminate every kind of privacy. The aim is to produce collectively bonded and aggression-free, happy human beings: it is believed that this can be achieved through minimum ties with individual people and things as well as an extremely permissive upbringing.

What is overlooked in the process is the fact that this artificial suppression of strong personal bonds is simply creating experiences of deprivation. And this is not because human beings everywhere have been wrongly programmed by their education, but because we come into the world already programmed this way. The studies of babies and small children mentioned before (see p. 217) showed unequivocally that the child seeks a personal bond with a particular human being. If this possibility is denied him, he then suffers accordingly and severe disorders in the further development of the personality can result.* Such people will never enter into strong relationships; they will be withdrawn into themselves—which is just what the communes seek to avoid. We have already referred to the preprogramming for the conjugal partnership and to the fact that there is no

---

* So far, however, the experiment has not been made in the communes of having babies looked after without discrimination by a group of people. All the children have grown up in the care of their own parents who continue to care for them so that they do have a strong relationship with particular individuals.

culture where long-term marriage does not exist. Attachment to objects also occurs in all cultures, and it begins very early in the small child. "Bourgeois" education does not consist in teaching the child possessiveness, but in teaching it early to share with others. But if one refuses a child the right to possessions on principle then one produces experiences of frustration. And apart from this, material culture is based on this love of things. There is no culture whose representatives do not have a few things to call their own, which they look after and adorn. Possession is an incentive to achievement and therefore to cultural development. A society that does entirely without this is robbing itself of a fundamental stimulus. Property becomes suspect only when it gives people the power to exploit others.

In many respects education in the commune is extremely permissive. The belief is that this promotes a sceptical attitude toward authority. But I believe an attitude of this kind can only be founded on a certain resistance. It must be trained in the cut and thrust of dialogue. Furthermore an all-too permissive education leads in early childhood to experiences of deprivation, for a child seeks to find its bearings in the world. It asks questions and makes demands in order to learn the limits of the possible: these must not be set too close together but equally they must not be too far apart. Jean-Jacques Rousseau (1712–1778) was aware of this:

"Do you know the surest means to make a child unhappy? You must accustom him to being given everything. For his demands grow unceasingly. Sooner or later your inability will force you to refuse him something, and this unaccustomed refusal will be a far greater torment to him than the lack of the thing he demands."

Every extreme form of upbringing is fundamentally intolerant and therefore repressive. If the educational theory formulated in the communes were completely logically applied, one would probably arrive—by means of a process of de-individualization—at just what one had most sought to avoid, namely, a person who is easily manipulated, who does not strive for achievement, but who vegetates within the collective.

The family affords a person that love and security which

permits basic trust in his fellow-men to grow. And this trust is the prerequisite for his free development. Certainly an upbringing within the family can also be harmfully authoritarian, but this is by no means the inevitable result of every family upbringing. Only in the family are man's positive social tendencies aroused and with them the capacity for social responsibility and identification. A person who has developed no bond with the family cannot later develop any love for society. But a person who has learned to love parents, brothers, and sisters can later also love a collective. Only he will be capable of seeing his fellow-men as brothers. The human community is based on love and trust: and both are evolved through the family.

12
Prospects

In Chapter 1 I posed the problem of whether humanity is good enough for the requirements of modern social life and whether the commandment to love our neighbors does not place too great a strain on our innate capacities. In other words, can we hope to survive in mass society with our human decency intact?

It is sometimes claimed that we are not adapted to mass society. But in the last analysis no organism is adapted to anything. Adaptation results from particular conditions of selection. On the Kerguelen Islands, wingless insects turn out to have adapted. Mutants that occur in all parts of the world but normally fall victims to selection are at an advantage on these storm-lashed islands. Circumstances are further complicated by the fact that a characteristic can be advantageous to the organism that possesses it in one area of functioning but a disadvantage in another. For fish that orientate themselves visually it is an advantage to be able to recognize their rivals or sexual partners quickly at some distance by means of a few prominent characteristics. But a prominent signal will also be seen by the predator. In such cases the selective pressures working in opposing directions often produce a compromise.

If one measures a species' success by the number of viable offspring it produces, then our species can undoubtedly be said to be adapted to mass society. But the adaptation is by no means complete. Many of our individualistic inclinations are considerably frustrated, and the increase in aggressive feelings leads in mass society to a heightening of conflicts within the group, for strangers initially mean less to us than relatives. This fact has brought forth many people with proposed models for achieving social harmony. Those who derive authority from their own prophetic certainty, and who will therefore even justify force, are dangerous. They aggravate the conflict within the group. Just as medicine developed successfully as an empirical science, so we shall be able to evolve ways to cure the crises of society only from a biological understanding of human behavior.

"A society is sick if its fundamental institutions and relationships (that is to say, its structure) are so designed that they do not permit the employment of the available material and intellectual means for the optimal development of human existence," as Herbert Marcuse says (*145*, p. 11).

By this definition there is no healthy society, but at best societies which are more or less sick. Fear and mistrust formerly dominated man's relations only with members of alien societies. With the formation of anonymous societies we began to mistrust our neighbors as well. Fear aggravates the struggle for positions of power and excludes consideration for others. Trying to get the better of one's neighbor almost becomes good form. Thus superficially the odds would seem in the long run to be against our being a match for the demands of mass society. We are certainly in a social crisis now, but as rational beings we can guide our own future development. If we take thought and make use of the inclinations which are innate in us, the prospects are by no means unfavorable. Our biological investigation of human behavior has first of all shown that the aggressive drive that is innate in us has its own natural antidotes. With their help we are able to establish and maintain the bond with our fellow-men. Indeed we have a strong innate urge for sociability. All these group-uniting mechanisms are phylogenetically very old, and it is in their favor that they have evolved hand in hand with the development of care for the young. With this "invention" both birds and mammals have—quite independently of one another—acquired the capacity for mutual aid and hence for the formation of altruistic groups, which wage the struggle for existence together. Thus mutual aid gains an increasingly significant role in the evolution of the higher organisms. Out of the family groups grew extended families, packs, and finally also the anonymous closed groups of mammals and man. The means of bonding have always remained fundamentally the same and in origin they are essentially derived from the behavior patterns that bind mother and child. The mother-child relationship was historically—and is in the development of the individual—the nucleus of crystallization for all social life. This relationship is already individualized in many higher mammals, probably in order to prevent the danger of babies being exchanged, which might endanger the rearing of the young for a whole number of reasons. Our clear disposition to establish personal bonds has its roots here. It is innate to us. Via the personal mother-child relationship we acquire the "basic trust" from which our fundamental attitude of sociability then evolves, and hence a general capacity for social commitment. For these reasons attempts to prevent the growth of such family ties are highly questionable. What has to be done is to strengthen our trust in fellow-men who are not known to us, and this happens on the family level. Only in this way can we evolve that social responsibility which is a prerequisite for a peaceful communal existence, probably indeed for any further existence at all as a species.

Ruth Benedict (*13*) has described the doctrine of social relativity put forward by environmental theorists as a doctrine of hope rather than despair, because the recognition that cultural values are relative gives rise to a more realistic faith, taking tolerance as its basis. Yet in saying this she is already making the assumption that tolerance and altruism are generally obligatory values. The logic of this escapes me.

For my part, I believe we have grounds for optimism only because we are *by inclination* social beings and can take our bearings, in seeking for ethical norms and in correcting our norms, from our own phylogenetic adaptations. We are not obliged to derive all our ethical norms culturally: many of them are rooted within us and this gives us a degree of certainty.

Good or evil? The disposition toward intolerance and aggression is certainly innate in us, but we carry no mark of Cain upon our brows. The thesis of man's killer nature cannot seriously be upheld; on the contrary investigation shows that by nature we are also extremely friendly beings.

In making this fundamentally optimistic statement I have no desire to minimize our aggressive urges. I am speaking of our potential for good which is by no means always aroused. Not long ago there were some hideous pictures published, showing the extermination of Indians in Brazil.* A loveless upbringing and persecution create the insensitive person and crush his innate disposition to altruism. But if we will stop erecting barriers to communication and making "devils" of our fellow-men —even if they do uphold other systems of values—and instead of this emphasize what unites mankind, then our grandchildren will have a happy future in store for them. The potential for good has been given us biologically just as much as the potential to destroy ourselves. Life has emerged on this planet in a succession of new forms, from the simplest algae to man— man the one being who reflects upon this creation, who seeks to fashion it himself and who, in the process, may end by destroying it. It would indeed be grotesque if the question of the meaning of life were to be solved in this way.

* "Brasilien, Indianer-Mord. Einige Tonnen Schande," *Der Spiegel* (Oct. 27, 1969), 173–186.

Bibliography

1. Aberle, D., and collaborators (1963) "The incest tabu and the mating patterns of animals," *Am. Anthropol.* **65**, 253–265.

2. Adler, A. (1908) "Der Aggressionstrieb im Leben und in der Neurose," *Fortschr. Med.* **26**, 577–584.

3. Andersson, C. J. (1857) *Reisen in Südwestafrika*, Leipzig.

4. Andree, R. (1889) *Ethnographische Parallelen und Vergleiche*, N. F., Leipzig.

5. Andrew, R. J. (1963) "Evolution of facial expression," *Science* **142**, 1034–1041.

6. Anthoney, T. R. (1968) "The ontogeny of greeting, grooming and sexual motor patterns in captive baboons (Superspecies *Papio cynocephalus*)," *Behaviour* **31**, 358–372.

7. Antonius, O. (1947) "Beobachtungen an einem Onagerhengst," *Umwelt* **1**, 299–300.

8. Ardrey, R. (1962) *African Genesis*, New York and London.

9. Azrin, N. H., Hutchinson, R. R., and Hakel, D. F. (1966) "Extinction induces aggression," *J. Exp. Analysis of Behavior* **9**, 191–204.

10. Baker, S. W. (1867) *The Albert Nyanza*, London.

11. Baksay, A. (1891) "Ungarische Volksbräuche," *Die österreichisch-ungarische Monarchie in Wort und Bild, Ungarn II*, Vienna, 69–148.

12. Basedow, H. (1906) "Anthropological notes on the western coastal tribes of the Northern Territory of South Australia," *Trans. Roy. Soc. South Australia* **31**, 1–62.

13. Benedict, R. (1934) *Patterns of Culture*, Boston and London.

14. Berkowitz, L. (1962) *Aggression: A Social Psychological Analysis*, New York and London.

15. Berkowitz, L. (1968) "Seeing a gun can trigger aggression," *Science Journal*, April, 9.

16. Berkowitz, L. (1969) *Roots of Aggression,* New York.

17. Bernatzik, H. (1941) *Die Geister der gelben Blätter,* Leipzig.

18. Bernatzik, H. (1947) *Akha und Meau,* I and II, Innsbruck.

19. Berndt, R., and Berndt, C. H. (1964) *The World of the First Australians,* London and Sydney.

20. Bilz, R. (1943) *Lebensgesetze der Liebe,* Leipzig.

21. Bilz, R. (1948) "Schrittmacherphänomene," *Psyche* **2,** 229–250.

22. Birket-Smith, K. (1956) *Geschichte der Kultur,* 3rd ed. Zurich.

23. Bohannan, P. (1966) "Drumming the scandal among the Tiv," in P. Bohannan (ed.): *Law and Warfare,* New York.

24. Bowlby, J. (1969) *Attachment and Loss. I. Attachment* (The Int. Psychoanal. Library 79), London.

25. Braun, M. (1969) "Ein Kommunarde schreibt uns," *Süddeutsche Zeitung.* **196,** Supp., 16.8.69.

26. Brehm, A. E. (1862) *Reiseskizzen aus Nordafrika,* Jena.

27. Brügge, P. (1969) "Mit sexuellen Normen hart geschlagen," *Der Spiegel,* **23** (51).

28. Buechner, H. K., and Schloeth, R. (1965) "Ceremonial mating behaviour in the Uganda Kob (*Adenota kob*)," *Z. Tierpsychol.* **22,** 209–225.

29. Casal, U. A. (1963) "Der Phalluskult im alten Japan," *Mitt. Deutschen Ges. f. Natur u. Völkerkde Ostasiens* **44** (1), 72–94.

30. Chagnon, N. A. (1968) *Yanomamö the fierce people,* New York.

31. Cook, J. (1784) *A Voyage to the Pacific Ocean (1776–1780),* (C. J. King ed.), London.

32. Coss, R. G. (1968) "The ethological command in art," *Leonardo I,* Oxford, 273–287.

33. Cullen, E. (1960) "Experiments on the effects of social isolation on reproductive behavior in the three-spined stickleback," *Anim. Beh.* **8,** 235.

34. Dart, R. A. (1959) *Adventures with the Missing Link,* New York and London.

35. Darwin, C. (1872) *The Expression of the Emotions in Man and Animals,* London.

36. Darwin, C. (1859) *The Origin of Species,* London.

37. Dennis, W. (1941) "Infant development under conditions of restricted practice and of minimal social stimulation," *Genet. Psychol. Monogr.* **23**, 143.

38. Dollard, J., Doob, L., Miller, N., Mowrer, O. and Sears, P. (1939) *Frustration and Aggression*, New Haven.

39. De Vore, I. (1965) *Primate Behaviour: Field Studies of Monkeys and Apes*, New York and London.

40. Eggan, D. (1943) "The general problem of Hopi adjustment," *Am. Anthropol.* **45**, 372–373.

41. Eibl-Eibesfeldt, I. (1951) "Zur Fortpflanzungsbiologie und Jugendentwicklung des Eichhörnchens," *Z. Tierpsychol.* **8**, 370–400.

42. Eibl-Eibesfeldt, I. (1953) "Zur Ethologie des Hamsters (*Cricetus cricetus* L.)," *Z. Tierpsychol.* **10**, 204–254.

43. Eibl-Eibesfeldt, I. (1955) "Ethologische Studien am Galapagos-Seelöwen (*Zalophus wollebaeki* Sivertsen)," *Z. Tierpsychol.* **12**, 286–303.

44. Eibl-Eibesfeldt, I. (1962) "Freiwasserbeobachtungen zur Deutung des Schwarmverhaltens verschiedener Fische," *Z. Tierpsychol.* **19**, 165–182.

45. Eibl-Eibesfeldt, I. (1963) "Angeborenes und Erworbenes im Verhalten einiger Säuger," *Z. Tierpsychol.* **20**, 705–754.

46. Eibl-Eibesfeldt, I. (1965) *Im Reich des tausend Atolle*, Munich; published in English as *Land of a Thousand Atolls*, New York and London.

47. Eibl-Eibesfeldt, I. (1964) *Galapagos, die Arche Noah im Pazifik*, 3rd ed., Munich; published in English as *Galapagos*, London and New York.

48. Eibl-Eibesfeldt, I. (1968) "Über Desmond Morris' 'Der nackte Affe,'" *Der Spiegel*, **4**, 3.

49. Eibl-Eibesfeldt, I. (1968) "Zur Ethologie des menschlichen Grussverhaltens. I. Beobachtungen an Balinesen, Papuas und Samoanern nebst vergleichenden Bemerkungen," *Z. Tierpsychol.* **25**, 727–744.

50. Eibl-Eibesfeldt, I. (1969) *Grundriss der vergleichenden Verhaltensforschung*, 2nd ed., Munich; published in English as *Ethology: the Biology of Behavior* (1970), New York and London.

51. Eibl-Eibesfeldt, I. (1970) "Männliche und weibliche Schutzamulette im modernen Japan," *Homo* **21**, 175–188.

52. Eibl-Eibesfeldt, I. (1972) "Gruppenbindung und Aggressionskontrolle bei den !Ko-Buschleuten," *Monographien zur Humanethologie* **1**, Piper, Munich.

53. Eibl-Eibesfeldt, I., and E. (1967) "Die Parasitenabwehr der Minima-Arbeiterinnen der Blattschneiderameise *(Atta cephalotes)*," *Z. Tierpsychol.* 24, 278–281.

54. Eibl-Eibesfeldt, I., and Hass, H. (1967) "Neue Wege der Humanethologie," *Homo* 18, 13–23.

55. Eibl-Eibesfeldt, I., and Sielmann, H. (1965) *"Cactospiza pallida* (Fringillidae): Werkzeuggebrauch beim Nahrungserwerb," *Encycl. cinem.* E 597, Inst. wiss. Film, Göttingen.

56. Eibl-Eibesfeldt, I., and Wickler, W. (1968) "Die ethologische Deutung einiger Wächterfiguren auf Bali," *Z. Tierpsychol.* 25, 719–726.

57. Erikson, E. H. (1953) *Wachstum und Krisen der gesunden Persönlichkeit,* Stuttgart.

58. Erikson, E. H. (1966) "Ontogeny of ritualisation in man," *Philos. Trans. Roy. Soc. London* B, 251, 337–349.

59. Ewer, R. F. (1968) *Ethology of Mammals,* London.

60. Fantz, R. L. (1967) "Visual perception and experience in infancy," in H. W. Stevenson, E. H. Hess, and H. L. Rheingold (eds.), *Early Behavior,* New York, 181–224.

61. Feshbach, S. (1961) "The stimulating versus cathartic effects of a vicarious aggressive activity," *J. Abnorm. Soc. Psychol.* 63, 381–385.

62. Frank, F. (1969) *Apo und Establishment aus biologischer Sicht,* Oldenburg.

63. Frank, J. D. (1967) *Muss Krieg sein? Psychologische Aspekte von Krieg und Frieden,* Darmstadt. English original: *Sanity and Survival,* New York.

64. Freedman, D. G. (1964) "Smiling in blind infants and the issue of innate vs. acquired," *J. Child Psychol. Psychiat.* 5, 171–184.

65. Freedman, D. G. (1965) "Hereditary control of early social behaviour," in B. M. Foss (ed.): *Determinants of Infant Behaviour II,* London.

66. Freeman, D. (1964) "Human aggression in anthropological perspective," in Carthy and Ebling (eds.): *The Natural History of Aggression,* New York and London.

67. Freeman, D. (1970) "Aggression, instinct or symptom?" Paper presented at the 7th Congress of the Australian and New Zealand College of Psychiatrists. Melbourne, October.

68. Fremont-Smith, F. (1962) "Saving the children can save us," *Saturday Rev.,* 11 Aug.

69. Freud, S. (1951) *Collected Works,* 24 vols., London.

70. Garcia, J., McGowan, B. K., Ervin, F. R., and Koelling, R. A. (1968) "Cues: their relative effectiveness as a function for the reinforcer," *Science* 160, 794–795.

71. Gardner, R. (n.d.) *Dead Birds,* Cambridge, Mass.

72. Gardner, R., and Heider, K. G. (1968) *Gardens of War,* New York.

73. Gehlen, A. (1969) *Moral und Hypermoral, eine pluralistische Ethik,* Frankfurt.

74. Gibbs, F. A. (1951) "Ictal and non-ictal psychiatric disorders in temporal lobe epilepsy," *J. Nerv. Ment. Dis.* 113, 522–528.

75. Goffman, E. (1963) *Behavior in Public Places,* New York and London.

76. Grzimek, B. (1949) "Die 'Radfahrer-Reaktion,'" *Z. Tierpsychol.* 6, 41–44.

77. Guppenberger, L. (1889) *Volkscharakter, Trachten, Sitten und Bräuche. Die österreichisch-ungarische Monarchie in Wort und Bild. Oberösterreich,* Vienna, 119–175.

78. Güttinger, H. R. (1970) "Zur Evolution von Verhaltensweisen und Lautäusserungen bei Prachtfinken (Estrildidae)," *Z. Tierpsychol.* 27, 1011–1075.

79. Hädecke, W. (1969) *Neue Rundschau* 80 (3), 452.

80. Harlow, H. F., and Harlow, M. K. (1962) "Social deprivation in monkeys," *Sci. Americ.* 207, 137–146.

81. Harlow, H. F., and Harlow, M. K. (1967) "Reifungsfaktoren im sozialen Verhalten," *Psyche* 21, 193–210.

82. Hass, H. (1970) *The Human Animal,* New York.

83. Hass, H. (1970) *Energon,* Vienna and New York.

84. Heinzelmann, F. (1852) *Reise in Afrika,* Leipzig, 228.

85. Helmuth, H. (1967) "Zum Verhalten des Menschen: die Aggression," *Z. Ethnol.* 92, 2, 265–270.

86. Hess, E. H. (1959) "Imprinting, an effect of early experience," *Science* 130, 133–141.

87. Hess, E. H. (1965) "Attitude and pupil size," *Sci. Americ.* 212, 46–54.

88. Hess, E. H., Seltzer, A. L., and Shlien, J. M. (1965) "Pupil response of hetero- and homosexual males to pictures of men and women: a pilot study," *J. Abnorm. Psychol.* 70, 165–168.

89. Hoebel, E. A. (1966) "Song duels among the Eskimo," in P. Bohannan (ed.): *Law and Warfare,* New York, 256–262.

90. Höhnel, L. v. (1891) *Zum Rudolphsee und Stephanie See,* Vienna.

91. Hokanson, J. E., and Burgess, M. (1962) "The effects of three types of aggression on vascular processes," *J. Abnorm. Soc. Psychol.* **64,** 446–449.

92. Hokanson, J. E., and Shetler, S. (1961) "The effect of overt aggression on vascular processes," *J. Abnorm. Soc. Psychol.* **63,** 446–448.

93. Holm, G. (1914) *Ethnological sketch of the Angmagssalik Eskimo: Medelelser on Grønland.* Vol. 39.

94. Holst, D. v. (1969) "Sozialer Stress bei Tupajas *(Tupaia belangeri),*" *Z. vgl. Physiol.* **63,** 1–58.

95. Holst, E. v. (1969) "Probleme der modernen Instinktforschung," reprint in *Zur Verhaltensphysiologie bei Tieren und Menschen,* Munich, Vol. I, 277–289.

96. Holst, E. v., and Saint-Paul, U. v. (1960) "Vom Wirkungsgefüge der Triebe," *Die Naturwiss.* **18,** 409–422.

97. Hörmann, L. v. (1912) "Genuss- und Reizmittel in den Ostalpen; eine volkskundliche Skizze," *Z. Dtsch. Österr. Alpenver.* **43,** 78–100.

98. Howard, H. E. (1920) *Territory in Bird Life,* New York and London.

99. Howitt, A. W. (1904) *The Native Tribes of Southeast Australia,* New York and London.

100. Hsi-en Chen, T. (1953) "The Marxist remolding of Chinese society," *Am. J. Sociol.* **58,** 340–346.

101. Huxley, T. (1888) *The Struggle for Existence and Its Bearing Upon Man,* London.

102. Immelmann, K. (1966) "Zur Irreversibilität der Prägung," *Die Naturwiss.* **53,** 209.

103. Itani, J. (1958) "On the acquisition and propagation of a new food habit in the troop of Japanese monkeys at Takasakiyana," *Primates* I, 84–98.

104. Itani, J. (1963) "Paternal care in the wild Japanese monkey *(Macaca fuscata),*" in C. Southwick (ed.): *Primate Social Behavior,* New York, 91–97.

105. Jerusalem, W. (1890) *Laura Brigsman: Erziehung einer Taubstumm-Blinden,* Vienna.

106. Jolly, A. (1966) "Lemur social behaviour and primate intelligence," *Science* 153, 501–506.

107. Kawai, M. (1965) "Newly acquired pre-cultural behaviour of the natural troop of Japanese monkeys on Koshima Island," *Primates* 6, 1–30.

108. Kawamura, S. (1963) "The process of sub-culture propagation among Japanese macaques," in C. Southwick (ed.): *Primate Social Behavior*, New York, 82–90.

109. Kernig, C. D. (1969) *Frieden, Sowjetsystem und demokratische Gesellschaft, eine vergleichende Enzyklopedie*, Freiburg.

110. Kinsey, A. (1949) *Sexual Behavior in the Human Male*, Philadelphia and London.

111. Koenig, O. (1969) Verhaltensforschung und Kultur. *Kreatur Mensch*, Munich.

112. König, H. (1927) "Das Recht der Polarvölker," *Anthropos* 22, 689–746.

113. Kolbe, P. (1719) *Gegenwärtiger Zustand des Vorgebirges der Guten Hoffnung*, Nuremberg.

114. Kortlandt, A. (1967) "Handgebrauch bei freilebenden Schimpansen," in B. Rensch (ed.): *Handgebrauch und Verständigung bei Affen und Frühmenschen*, Bern, 59–102.

115. Kortmulder, K. (1968) "An ethological theory of the incest taboo and exogamy," *Current Anthropol.* 9, 437–449.

116. Kosinski, J. (1966) *The Painted Bird*, New York.

117. Kotz, E. (1922) *Im Banne der Furcht. Sitten und Gebräuche der Wapare in Ostafrika*, Hamburg.

118. Kotzebue, O. v. (1825) *Entdeckungsreise in die Südsee und nach der Beringstrasse zur Erforschung einer nordöstlichen Durchfahrt*, 2 vols., Vienna.

119. Kramer, G. (1949) "Macht die Natur Konstruktionsfehler?" *Wilhelmshavener Vorträge, Schriftenreihe d. Nordwestdeutschen Univ. Ges.* 1, 1–19.

120. Krämer, A. (1968) "Soziale Organisation und Sozialverhalten einer Gemspopulation der Alpen." Diss. Univ. Zürich.

121. Krauss, F. (1965) *Das Geschlechtsleben des japanischen Volkes*, Hanau.

122. Kropotkin, P. (1903) *Mutual Aid: A Factor of Evolution*, London.

123. Kruijt, J. (1964) "Ontogeny of social behaviour in Burmese Red Jungle Fowl (*Gallus gallus spadiceus*)," *Behaviour Suppl.* 12.

124. Kühme, W. D. (1965) "Freilandstudien zur Soziologie des Hyänenhundes," *Z. Tierpsychol.* 22, 495–541.

125. Kummer, H. (1968) "Social organization in Hamadryas baboons—a field study." *Bibl. Primat.*, Basle.

126. Kummer, H., and Kurt, F. (1965) "A comparison of social behavior in captive and wild Hamadryas baboons," in H. Vogtberg (ed.): *The Baboon in Medical Research*, Univ. Texas Press, 1–16.

127. Kuo, Y. Z. (1960/61) "Studies on the basic factors in animal fighting," *J. Gen. Psychol.* 96, 101–239 and 97, 181–295.

128. Lack, D. (1943) *The Life of the Robin*, Cambridge.

129. Lack, D. (1947) *Darwin's Finches*, Cambridge.

130. Lagerspetz, K. (1964) "Studies on the aggressive behaviour of mice." Suomalaisen Tiedeakatemian Toimituksia. *Ann. Acad. Sci. Fennice*, ser. B., 131. Helsinki.

131. Lang, K. (1926, 1928/29) *Die Grusssitten*. Völkerkde, Vienna. 4, 43–45, 108–110, 190–192, 252–259; 5, 27–32, 103–106, 169–175, 230–233; 6, 23–27, 106–110, 178–180, 243–247.

132. Lawick-Goodall, J. van (1967) *My Friends the Wild Chimpanzees*, Washington.

133. Lawick-Goodall, J. van (1968) "The behaviour of freeliving chimpanzees in the Gombe Stream Reserve," *Anim. Beh. Monogr.* 1 (3), 161–311.

134. LeMagnen, J. (1952) "Les Phénomenes olfacto-sexuels chez l'homme," *Arch. Sci. Physiol.* 6, 125–160.

135. Leyhausen, P. (1969) "Experimentelle Untersuchung eines angeborenen Auslösemechanismus," 11th Ethological Conf., Rennes (France), 2–10 Sept.

136. Lorenz, K. (1937) "Über die Bildung des Instinktbegriffes," *Die Naturwiss.* 25, 289–300, 307–318, 325–331.

137. Lorenz, K. (1943) "Die angeborenen Formen möglicher Erfahrung," *Z. Tierpsychol.* 5, 235–409.

138. Lorenz, K. (1954) *Man Meets Dog*, New York and London.

139. Lorenz, K. (1952) "Die Entwicklung der vergleichenden Verhaltenforschung in den letzten 12 Jahren," *Verh. Dt. Zool. Ges.*, 36–58.

140. Lorenz, K. (1961) "Phylogenetische Anpassung und adaptive Modifikation des Verhaltens," Z. Tierpsychol. 18, 139–187.

141. Lorenz, K. (1966) On Aggression, New York and London.

142. Lorenz, K. (1965) Darwin hat doch recht gesehen, Pfullingen.

143. Mao Tse-tung (1952) Reden an die Schriftsteller und Kunstler in neuen China, E. Berlin, 59.

144. Marcuse, H. (1967) Das Ende der Utopie, Berlin.

145. Marcuse, H., et al. (1968) Aggression und Anpassung in der Industriegesellschaft, Frankfurt.

146. Mead, M. (1930) Growing Up in New Guinea, New York and London.

147. Mead, M. (1968) "Die Persönlichkeitsbildung bei den Arapesh," in G. Bittner and E. Schmid-Cords (eds.): Erziehung in früher Kindheit, Erziehung in Wiss. u. Praxis, Munich.

148. Megitt, M. J. (1962) Desert People, London and Sydney.

149. Milgram, S. (1963) "Behavioural study of obedience," J. Abnorm. Soc. Psychol. 67, 372–378.

150. Milgram, S. (1965) "Liberating effects of group pressure," J. Personality & Social Psychol. 1, 127–134.

151. Milgram, S. (1966) "Einige Bedingungen von Autoritätsgehorsam und seiner Verweigerung," Z. exp. u. angew. Psychol. 13, 433–463.

152. Mitscherlich, A. (1969) Die Idee des Friedens und die menschliche Aggressivität, Frankfurt.

153. Mohr, J. W., Turner, R. E., and Jerry, M. B. (1964) Pedophilia and exhibitionism, Toronto.

154. Montagu, M. F. A. (1968) Man and Aggression, New York and Oxford.

155. Morris, Desmond (1967) The Naked Ape, New York and London.

156. Morris, Desmond (1970) The Human Zoo, New York and London.

157. Moyer, K. E. (1969) "Internal impulses to aggression." Trans. N. Y. Academy Sci. Ser. II, 31, 105.

158. Murphy, R. F. (1957) "Intergroup hostility and social cohesion," Am. Anthropol. 59, 1028.

159. Musil, A. (1928) "The manners and customs of the Rwala Bedouins," Am. Geogr. Soc., Oriental Expl. & Studies 6, 455.

160. Nevermann, H. (1941)   *Ein Besuch bei Steinzeitmenschen, Kosmosbändchen*, Stuttgart.

161. Nicolai, J. (1964) "Der Brutparasitismus der Viduinae als ethologisches Problem. Prägungsphänomene als Faktoren der Rassen- und Artbildung," *Z. Tierpsychol.* 21, 129–204.

162. Packard, V. (1963)   *The Pyramid Climbers*, New York and London.

163. Plack, A. (1968)   *Die Gesellschaft und das Böse*, 2nd ed., Munich.

164. Popitz, H. (1968)   *Prozesse der Machtbildung. Recht und Staat*, Tübingen, 362–363.

165. Prévost, J. (1961) "Ecologie du Manchot empereur: *Aptenodytes forsteri* Gray," *Exped. polaires Françaises*, Miss P.-E. Victor. Publ. No. 222, *Actual. Scient. et Industr.*, No. 1291, Paris.

166. Prévost, L'Abbé (1746)   *L'Histoire Generale dés Voyages*.

167. Rasa, O. A. E. (1971) "The effect of pair isolation reproductive success in *Etroplus maculatus* (Cichlidae)," *Z. Tierpsychol.* 26, 846–852.

168. Rasmussen, K. (1908)   *People of the Polar North*, London.

169. Robson, K. S. (1967) "The role of eye-to-eye contact in maternal-infant attachment," *J. Child Psychol. Psychiat.* 8, 13–25.

170. Roper, M. K. (1969) "A survey of evidence for intrahuman killing in the Pleistocene," *Current Anthropol.* 10, 427–459.

171. Rosenkötter, L. (1966) "Auf Exkursion in die Menschenkunde," *Frankfurter Hefte* 21 (8).

172. Rothmann, M., and Teuber, E. (1915) "Einzelausgabe aus der Anthropoidenstation auf Teneriffa. I. Ziele und Aufgaben der Station, sowie erste Beobachtungen an den auf ihr gehaltenen Schimpansen," *Abh. Preuss. Akad. Wiss. Berlin*, 1–20.

173. Rudolph, W. (1968)   *Der Kulturelle Relativismus, Forschungen zur Ethnologie und Sozialpsychologie*, Vol. 6.

174. Rüppell, E. (1829)   *Reisen in Nubien, Kordufa und dem peträischen Arabien*, Frankfurt.

175. Russell, C., and Russell, W. M. S. (1968)   *Violence, Monkeys and Man*, London.

176. Sackett, G. P. (1966) "Monkeys reared in isolation with pictures as visual input: evidence for an innate releasing mechanism," *Science* 154, 1468–1473.

177. Sauer, F. (1954) "Die Entwicklung der Lautäusserungen vom Ei ab schalldicht gehaltener Dorngrasmücken (*Sylvia c. communis*)," *Z. Tierpsychol.* 11, 1–93.

178. Schein, W. M. (1963) "On the irreversibility of imprinting," *Z. Tierpsychol.* 20, 462–467.

179. Schenkel, R. (1956) "Zur Deutung der Phasianidenbalz," *Ornith. Beob.* 53, 182–201.

180. Schenkel, R. (1967) "Submission, its features and function in the wolf and dog," *Am. Zool.* 7, 319–329.

181. Schleidt, W., Schleidt, M., and Magg, M. (1960) "Störungen der Mutter-Kind-Beziehung bei Truthühnern durch Gehörverlust," *Behaviour* 16, 254–260.

182. Schrader-Klebert (1969) Die Kulturelle Revolution der Frau. *Kursbuch* 17, 1–46.

183. Schultze-Westrum, T. (1968) "Ergebnisse einer zoologisch-völkerkundlichen Expedition zu den Papuas," *Umschau* 68, 295–300.

184. Schuster, M. (1959) "Waika-Südamerika, Palmfruchtfest," *Encycl. cinem.* E 178, Göttingen.

185. Schutz, F. (1965) "Homosexualität und Prägung bei Enten," *Psychol. Forschung* 28, 439–463.

186. Scott, J. P. (1960) *Aggression,* Chicago.

187. Selenka, E. and L. (1925) *Sonnige Welten,* Berlin, 39 and 328.

188. Shaw, C. E. (1948) "The male combat 'dance' of some Crotalid snakes," *Herpetologica* 4, 137–145.

189. Sielmann, H. (1958) *Das Jahr mit den Spechten,* Berlin.

190. Simpson, C. (1963) *Plumes and Arrows, Inside New Guinea,* London and Sydney.

191. Sommer, R. (1966) "Man's proximate environment," *J. Social Issues* 22, 59–70.

192. Sorenson, E. R., and Gajdusek, D. C. (1966) "The study of child behaviour and development in primitive cultures," *Pediatrics* (Suppl.) 37, 149–243.

193. Spamer, A. (1935) *Die Deutsche Volkskunde,* 2 Vols., Leipzig.

194. Spencer, B., and Gillen, F. J. (1904) *The northern tribes of Central Australia,* New York and London.

195. Spitz, R. A. (1965) *The First Year of Life,* New York.

196. Spitz, R. A. (1968) "Die anaklitische Depression," in G. Bittner and E. Schmid-Cords (eds.): *Erziehung in früher Kindheit*, Munich.

197. Staehelin, B. (1953) "Gesetzmässigkeiten im Gemeinschaftsleben schwer Geisteskranker," *Schweiz. Arch. Neurol. Psychiat.* 72, 277–298.

198. Staehelin, B. (1954) "Gesetzmässigkeiten im Gemeinschaftsleben Geisteskranker, verglichen mit tierpsychologischen Ergebnissen," *Homo* 5, 113–116.

199. Steinvorth de Goetz, I. (1969) *Uriji jami! Life and Belief of the Forest Waika in the Upper Orinoco*, Caracas.

200. Sugiyama, Y. (1965) "Behavioural development and sound structure in the two troops of Hanuman Langurs (*Presbytis entellus*)," *Primates* 6, 213–247.

201. Szondi, L. (1969) *Gestalten des Bösen*, Bern.

202. Tauern, O. D. (1918) *Patasiwa und Patalima: vom Molukkeneiland Seran und seinen Bewohnern*, Leipzig.

203. Tiger, L. (1969) *Men in Groups*, New York.

204. *Time*, Jan. 17, 1969, 34.

205. Tinbergen, N. (1951) *The Study of Instinct*, Oxford.

206. Tinbergen, N. (1963) *The Herring-gull's World*, London.

207. Treppert, D. A. (1964) "The psychiatric patient with an EEG temporal lobe focus," *Am. J. Psychiat.* 120, 765–771.

208. Ulrich, R. E., and Azrin, N. H. (1962) "Reflexive fighting in response to aversive stimulation," *J. Exp. Analysis of Behaviour* 5, 511–520.

209. Waelder, R. (1962) "Demoralisation and reeducation," *World Politics* 14; quoted from A. and M. Mitscherlich: *Die Unfähigkeit zu trauern*, Munich.

210. Wagner, H. O. (1954) "Massenansammlungen von Weberknechten," *Z. Tierpsychol.* 11, 348–352.

211. Washburn, S. L., and De Vore, I. (1961) "The social life of baboons," *Sci. Americ.* 204, 62–71.

212. Wheeler, W. M. (1928) *Social Life among the Insects*, New York.

213. Wickler, W. (1961) "Über die Stammesgeschichte und den ökologischen Wert einiger Verhaltensweisen der Vögel," *Z. Tierpsychol.* 18, 320–342.

214. Wickler, W. (1966) "Ursprung und biologische Deutung des Genitalpräsentierens männlicher Primaten," *Z. Tierpsychol.* 23, 422–437.

215. Wickler, W. (1967) "Vergleichende Verhaltensforschung und Phylo-genetik," in G. Heberer: *Die Evolution der Organismen.* 3rd ed., Stuttgart, Vol. 1, 420–508.

216. Wickler, W. (1967) "Vergleich des Ablaichverhaltens einiger paarbildender sowie nicht paarbildender Pomacentriden und Cichliden," *Z. Tierpsychol.* 24, 457–470.

217. Wickler, W. (1969) *Sind wir Sünder? Naturgesetze der Ehe,* Munich.

218. Wickler, W., and Uhrig, D. (1969) "Bettelrufe, Antwortszeit und Rassenunterschiede im Begrüssungsduett des Schmuckbartvogels *Trachyphonus d'arnaudii,*" *Z. Tierpsychol.* 26, 651–661.

219. Wied, M. Prince zu (1825) *Die Reise nach Brasilien,* Vols. I and II, Vienna.

220. Weidkuhn, P. (1968/69) "Aggressivität und Normativität," *Anthropos,* 63–64.

221. Wilkes, C. (1849) *Narrative of the U. S. Exploring Expedition during the Years 1838–1842,* 2 Vols.

222. Wilson, A. P. (1968) "Social behaviour of free-ranging Rhesus monkeys with an emphasis on aggression." Diss. Univ. Calif. Berkeley, Dept. Anthrop.

223. Wynne-Edwards, V. C. (1962) *Animal Dispersion in Relation to Social Behaviour,* London.

224. Zerries, O. (1964) *Waika,* Munich.

INDEX OF NAMES

INDEX OF SUBJECTS

Aldine de Gruyter

HUMAN ETHOLOGY

Irenäus Eibl-Eibesfeldt

*(Director of the Research Institute for Human Ethology
at the Max Planck Institute, Andechs, Germany)*

**1989. xvi + 848 pages. References, index.
ISBN 0-202-02030-4. Cloth**

Here, for the first time, Professor Eibl-Eibesfeldt's masterful work on ethology is available to the English-speaking audience. Based on the original German edition, **Human Ethology** has been expanded and revised. Findings from vast numbers of studies from different disciplines within the human and biological sciences are integrated into an encompassing theoretical framework to further our understanding of the most complex species of all, Man.

The text is profusely illustrated with photographs and drawings from the author's massive ethnological field research.

"Human Ethology *is one of the most significant books published in the behavioral sciences in recent years. This monumental 848-page interdisciplinary tour de force draws upon virtually all of the sciences and arts to present a coherent view of human behavior from an ethological perspective. It is a remarkable achievement. The book can be read either as an encyclopedic exposition of the ethological approach to Homo sapiens, or, because of its immense scope and cross-cultural perspective, as a fascinating handbook of human behavior to be read piecemeal or used as a reference."* —Contemporary Psychology

CONTENTS (Main Headings)
1. Objectives and Theoretical Bases of Human Ethology • 2. Basic Concepts of Ethology • 3. Methodology • 4. Social Behavior • 5. Intraspecific Aggression: Conflict and War • 6. Communication • 7. Behavior Development (Ontogeny) • 8. Man and His Habitat: Ecological Considerations • 9. The Beautiful and True: The Ethological Contribution to Aesthetics • 10. Biology's Contribution to Ethics • Bibliography

Aldine de Gruyter *(a division of Walter de Gruyter, Inc.)*
200 Saw Mill River Road • Hawthorne, New York 10532

Aldine de Gruyter

FATHER-CHILD RELATIONS

CULTURAL AND BIOSOCIAL CONTEXTS

Barry S. Hewlett, *editor*

1992. xxii + 376 pages. References, index.
ISBN 0-202-01188-7. Cloth

D ue to the greater involvement of American fathers in the direct care of their children in recent years, interest in the impact and nature of the father's role in nurturing children has increased. While studies about fathers in the industrialized, literate West have proliferated, little is known about the role of fathers in the preliterate, non-Western world. This collection examines the diversity of paternal roles found in human cultures among various types of societies: hunting and gathering, horticultural, and pastoral; polygynous, polyandrous, and monogamous; and both societies that are very peaceful and those that actively engage in warfare as a mode of existence.

The book recognizes the importance of understanding both the biological and the cultural aspects of the father's role. Some of the contributors utilize evolutionary or biosocial models, including those of developmental psychology, to examine the father's role, while others rely upon the symbolic analysis of cultural and social anthropology. One chapter is devoted to male-infant relationships in nonhuman primates, a further comparative perspective.

The anthropologists who have contributed to this collection are field workers who have lived intimately over significant periods of time with the people about whom they are writing. These research reports from the field have been edited to make them wholly accessible to the non-specialist.

Aldine de Gruyter *(a division of Walter de Gruyter, Inc.)*
200 Saw Mill River Road • Hawthorne, New York 10532

Aldine de Gruyter

Breastfeeding

Biocultural Perspectives

EDITORS
Patricia Stuart-Macadam
Katherine A. Dettwyler

1995. xiv + 430 pages. References, index.
0-202-01191-7. Cloth   0-202-01192-5. Paper

Breastfeeding is a biocultural phenomenon: not only is it a biological process, but it is also a culturally determined behavior. As such, it has important implications for understanding the past, present, and future condition of our species. In general, scholars have emphasized either the biological or the cultural aspects of breastfeeding, but not both. As biological anthropologists the editors of this volume feel that an evolutionary approach combining both aspects is essential. One of the goals of their book is to incorporate data from diverse fields to present a more holistic view of breastfeeding, through the inclusion of research from a number of different disciplines, including biological and social/cultural anthropology, nutrition, and medicine. The resulting book, presenting the complexity of the issues surrounding very basic decisions about infant nutrition, fills a void in the existing literature on breastfeeding.

 Aldine de Gruyter *(a division of Walter de Gruyter, Inc.)*
200 Saw Mill River Road · Hawthorne, NY 10532 · Tel: (914) 747-0110

Aldine de Gruyter

FOUNDATIONS OF HUMAN BEHAVIOR
An Aldine de Gruyter Series of Texts and Monographs

SERIES EDITORS
Sarah Blaffer Hrdy, *University of California, Davis*
Monique Borgerhoff Mulder, *University of California, Davis*